Incorrigible

Incorrigible

Ron and Diane Enfield

Blue Northern Press

For information about this title or to order other books and/or electronic media, contact the publisher:
Blue Norther Press
ronenfield@bluenortherpress.com

Library of Congress Control Number: 2021907677
ISBN: 978-1-7370767-0-4

Printed in the United States of America
Cover and Interior design: Blue Norther Press

Publisher's Cataloging-In-Publication Data
(Prepared by The Donohue Group, Inc.)

Names: Enfield, Ron, author.
Title: Incorrigible / Ron and Diane Enfield.
Description: [Cherry Hill, New Jersey] : Blue Norther Press, [2021]
Identifiers: ISBN 9781737076704
Subjects: LCSH: Enfield, Diane, 1939-2018. | Enfield, Ron--Marriage. | Spouses--United States--Biography. | Adult child abuse victims--United States--Biography. | Dementia--Patients--United States--Biography. | Wives--Death--Psychological aspects. | LCGFT: Autobiographies. | Biographies.
Classification: LCC HQ734 .E54 2021 | DDC 306.872092--dc23

FIRST EDITION

To the memory of

Jennifer Jay Palmer and
Diane Lee Christopher,

and the forgotten girls of the
Minnesota Home School for Girls

Preface

I personally cared for Diane as illness and dementia incapacitated and overwhelmed her. I lived 50 years with the love of my life, and—before the end arrived—the woman I met became someone she never wanted to be. Grief is my burden now, but I accept it because it has brought me the gift of understanding others who grieve. I wrote this memoir for those who suffer from seeing their loved ones crumble under the onslaught of dementia, and also to keep alive the memory of who my wife once was. She spent years sorting out and writing down her childhood memories, and I promised her I would tell her story to the world.

The events and people in this story are real. The names of some people have been changed. In some past events the dialog has been reconstructed based on the writer's best recollection of what was spoken.

This book was written by two authors: myself, and my late wife Diane. She wrote the early chapters to tell about her life before we met. Reflections taken from her journals appear throughout the later chapters.

Note *Throughout this book, Diane's writings appear in this italic typeface, to distinguish them from mine.*

Contents

INCORRIGIBLE

This is the story I want to tell my daughters about love and lying, when love and need get confused in a young girl's mind and she makes wrong decisions for her life—decisions which affect her entire life and the time can never be recovered. I want to tell my daughters because they need to know how "making the wrong decision" is based on lying to yourself and "staying in the relationship" is the result of rationalizations and female enculturation rather than realizing "what is best for me. And that "Love conquers all . . ." "Tis a woman's whole existence. . .," "till death do we part, in sickness and in health . . ." are big parts of the mythology of women's oppression and subjugation.

— DIANE ENFIELD

Incorrigible—it's an ugly word, don't you think? At the age of fourteen, I added incorrigible to my vocabulary when I heard it used to describe me. Then and for the rest of my life I felt branded, like Hester Prynne in The Scarlet Letter who was forced for the rest of her life to wear the embroidered letter "A" on her chest. Years later that story enlightened me about my own character. I was this thing that all could recognize and shun self-righteously.

My family moved so often I couldn't keep any friends or outside contacts. I was lonely and desperate for contact with kids my age. I met a group of teenaged boys and girls, outsiders, who accepted me. I began hanging out with them and breaking curfew. That year I got involved with the juvenile court and was placed on probation for truancy, failing grades, and finally for stealing.

The stealing wasn't an act of defiance on my part. Although it was wrong, I was motivated by compassion for one of the girls who befriended me.

Joanne was very poor. She lived in an unheated house with two young brothers under the age of ten and her father, an alcoholic. Joanne's mother hung herself the year before we met. Before school in the mornings, I'd meet her at her house, and wait while she made breakfast for her brothers and saw them off to school. Her father was usually passed out on the couch in the living room, covered with coats and stinking of alcohol. Minnesota winters are very cold. The tiny kitchen was the only room in the house that was warm, heated by the gas burners on the stove. The air in the room would be hot from the waist up and freezing from the waist down.

One day, Joanne and I decided to attend a local Settlement House dance Saturday night. The dance was an escape — with music and movement and feeling like grownups. It was January, deep snow covered the ground and the temperature was ten degrees below zero. As we walked to school — discussing what we would wear, who we'd see there, which boys from school might attend — the heel of Joanne's shoe broke off. When we stopped to try and repair it, I saw that both soles had large holes in them, through to her feet. She cried about not having another pair of shoes to wear to the dance. She didn't even have any snow boots.

"I have an idea," I told Joanne. "You know Mrs. Barlow puts all of her money from her sales in a cigar box underneath the counter. We can borrow ten dollars from her. We won't tell her though. You distract her and I'll get the money. She might miss it, but she'll just think that she made the wrong change for somebody."

Joanne was horrified. "Diane, that's stealing. I can't steal money from anyone. My daddy would beat me within an inch of my life."

I threw my hands up in the air. "You're not stealing anything. I am. Nobody will know, trust me. You distract her and I'll get the money. You can't go the rest of the winter without decent shoes. We don't have any choice. You'll get frostbite and lose a toe or worse. You don't want to lose a toe, do you? If it bothers you that much, you can save up money and pay her back. When you can get it together just put it in an envelope and slide it under the door of the shop."

We entered the store and Joanne distracted Mrs. Barlow by showing her the holes in her shoes and asking if there was anything she could buy to repair them, while I reached into the box and took out a ten-dollar bill from the larger pile of bills. It would be enough to buy Joanne a pair of shoes for the dance. I looked at the folded ten- and twenty-dollar bills and thought of what I could do with that money. The temptation was strong, but I wasn't a thief. I just wanted to get Joanne to the dance.

Once outside, I realized that we would have to walk to town. We didn't have enough money for a bus and the shoes. We set out walking to downtown Minneapolis, but between Joanne's broken heel and the snow getting through the holes in her shoes, it was slow going. By the time we got downtown the stores were closed for the day. We didn't go to the dance.

The following Monday at school, I was called out of class in the first hour. I didn't think it had anything to do with the money and I was nervous, trying to figure out what I had done to be called out. In the principal's office I was questioned about my whereabouts Friday afternoon. Not knowing that they knew about the theft, I lied and said I went straight home. A juvenile officer was brought in and I was confronted with the theft and my lies. It was my first offense of any kind, so I was put on probation. My father returned from California, and my parents rented an apartment in a totally different section of the city, hoping to separate me from the hoodlums I was seeing.

By the middle of the summer I was again desperate for friends and activity. I began taking a city bus to the old neighborhood and returning home after curfew at night. Of course, my parents complained to the probation officer and forbade me from going out at night and from seeing my old friends. One night, later than usual, fearing the confrontation I knew would happen when I got home, I decided I would just not go home. I stayed with one of the girls. I didn't understand why my parents thought I was doing something wrong. I missed Joanne and my friends, and I just wanted to be with them a few times a week.

Within a few days, I got a job at a Five and Ten store in downtown Minneapolis working as a clerk behind the cosmetic counter. I was thirteen years old and passing for sixteen, the earliest age you could work at a job. After several days, my mother found me at work and told me to come home, and I did. The probation department was contacted, and I was scheduled to appear in Juvenile Court with my father. At court, my father told the authorities that he and my mother had done everything they could to "keep me in line" and couldn't—that I was refusing to stay home, sneaking out after bedtime, violating curfew, and now staying out all night. He made it sound worse than it really was, and I was starting to get scared. The stern-looking judge labeled me "incorrigible" and declared me a ward of the state. I was shaking with a mixture of anger and fear. I couldn't believe what I was hearing. I couldn't believe that my mother would let my father do this to me. That day, I was put in a dirty jail cell with a hard, thin mattress and a pillow that reeked of urine. I was held overnight to be transported to a juvenile facility 125 miles north of the city near Sauk Centre, Minnesota, made famous for its small-town mentality by Sinclair Lewis in his novel "Main Street."

A plain metal sign with black letters on a white background announced my future to me: The Minnesota Home School for Girls. The car I was riding in turned down a dirt road, lined with tall old trees, their leaves now dying in a blazing show of colors—red, gold, and brown. Behind them, plowed brown earth fields stretched to the horizon against bright blue skies. To the west, the setting sun covered the marshes with a burnished copper blanket, broken by tall spears of dark brown cattails and blackbirds with bright red-tipped wings. I opened the car window and felt the edge of winter's cold on the north wind. The wind would alternate with warm breezes from the southwest, promising a full two weeks of Indian Summer, soon to come.

It was September 1954. I was fourteen, my birthday was the next month and I was beginning the tenth grade in high school. The records, from the Probation Department, said I was "Incorrigible — a juvenile delinquent." Years later I looked up incorrigible in a dictionary: "incapable of being corrected, or amended, not reformable, depraved" and at the very last, it read, "unalterable, determined."

Now then, I thought, that's more like it: determined. The best definition of who I was in that last word. Determined to go on living in spite of whatever life might hit me with, determined to taste every sweetness and puke out all the bitterness, determined to see every leaf turn from green to gold or red, to feel the wind and rain in my face, the heat and cold, to understand my friend's life as if it were my own, its pain and burden, its loss. It seemed to me this was what life was about.

I don't understand why — the reason was never clear to me — all I knew was there was this crazy thing inside of me, driving me to feel, to suck it all in, deeply taste the sour, smell the stench and retch violently, sob in great waves of sorrow, scream in anguish, burn with desire and laugh when I wasn't crying. This thing inside me, soaring to the music in my head, the beat pounding in my veins, when I danced or ran. Life seemed to be color and sound, feelings of joy and deepest sorrow, long hours of deep reflection and questions I couldn't articulate, demanding answers that never came.

I suppose you want to know what this place looked like. You might imagine iron bars on the windows, and high, gray cement walls with guards walking on top of them. No, the drama cannot be seen so easily. You are more likely to see what I did when I returned many years later, "Why it looks like a college campus — a beautiful setting."

It was located perhaps a mile off the main highway, in the middle of long stretching dirt fields, marshes, several old white barns and sheds, surrounded mostly by water. "The easier to catch you Dearie. . . no need for fences or high walls." Somewhat like a peninsula, water surrounded the institution on three of its sides, marshes to the east and west and the fast, running Sauk River to the north. The river was hidden by a stretch of thick woods and lay at the bottom of a hill. The two and three-story massive gray stucco houses were called cottages, trimmed in white wood and dominated by large white pillars topped with curls and leaves and ornate decorations, looking much like the homes rich people and their servants would live in, with gables, tall brick chimneys, leaded glass windows and massive, solid wooden doors with brass handles and knockers. They had porches on the side and in front, shaded by tall, spreading old trees in the yards. The cottages, seven or eight of them, were separated from one another by wide lawns and surrounded a long, grassy oval mall encircled by cement sidewalks.

At one end of the mall stood the largest house, red brick with white wood trim and dark green shutters, with a half circle driveway in front. To the south of the large house was another group of one-story gray buildings: the administration office, where the infirmary was located, and one with a sign reading "Reception Center." The word reception meant warmth, fun and parties to me until that day. There was nothing warm or friendly about that building or its purposes. I can't recall what was said to me when I first arrived, I can only remember what they did.

I felt so frightened, and yet the trees — that tall one with the maroon-red leaves — it was so beautiful, strong, not like me.

I wondered, why won't someone tell me what's going to happen, how am I supposed to act, what if they don't believe I'm really a virgin, is that important? How can they tell if you are, what kinds of girls are here? How long will I have to stay? Why didn't Mother come to see me before they took me away? My little sisters will be coming home from school by now, what will they tell them about me? Will they miss me? I wonder how far I am from home. I never thought to look at the highway mileage signs — why not? It's so cold up here, I guess it's from being farther North. That terrible cell with the bare light bulb on all night, well now I've seen what jail is like . . .

"Diane? Diane? Diane!" a voice sharp, strangely distant called my name.

"Hmmm?" I responded, fighting to bring myself back to reality.

A thin woman in a sagging grey dress of a uniform was glaring at me. "Take off your necklace, you can't keep that. Do you have any cigarettes, matches, lighters or medication?"

"Yes, uh, cigarettes in my purse."

"I mean have you hidden any in your clothes or on your body?"

"Hidden, on my body?" What? Why would I? Bewildered I started to answer but she interrupted me.

"You're not allowed to have those things here."

"You mean I can't smoke? My mother knows I do, it's OK, I mean she doesn't take them away from me anymore."

"The State Law says it's illegal for anyone under eighteen to smoke, and that's what this place is about. Laws."

She was cold, her eyes hardly looked back at me except when necessary.

Why couldn't she see that I'm not like the others . . . or am I?

"Mrs. Jackson is the housemother here at the Infirmary and she will tell you what to do next."

We stood in front of a thick metal door with a small window at eye level, a thin mesh of wire between the glass panels. The door was locked. I heard a buzz and it swung open to a long hall with highly polished wooden floors. Halfway down the hall was wood-

en desk with a woman seated behind it. Greeting the woman beside me, she opened the folder she had been handed.

"Diane!" Not really a question but I politely tried to answer her...

"Yes, well it's Diane. . ." She ignored me.

I glanced down the long hallways. Heads were sticking out of doorways, looking me over, checking me out and disappearing in silence. Always, the silence hung like a shroud over the long halls with their gray walls and polished floors.

"Come on Diane, you'll take a bath and get disinfected."

I took a step back, "What, I . . . I don't need a bath. I took one yesterday at home, before. I'm clean, I mean I really am."

"Standard procedure here, all new girls take baths, no telling where they have been."

She led me into a large white tiled room with five bathtubs standing in a row. Everything was white, like a hospital. The long afternoon shadows fell across the square tiled floor. A cold wind whistled softly through the tall, narrow, curtainless windows. She laid a clean white towel and wash cloth along with a new bar of yellow laundry soap down on the painted white enamel stool that stood near the tub.

"Hurry up, Diane! Get your clothes off and get in that tub!"

Oh, my god, I thought, I can't undress here in this strange bathroom in front of this strange woman with the tight lips and narrows eyes. Please God, don't make me do this, it feels, it feels wrong.

She obviously wasn't going to leave the room so what could I do?

Slowly I began to unbutton the new white blouse my mother had bought me the week before I went to court. I had so few new clothes, I wanted to take good care of it. Her hand reached out and grabbed the blouse.

"Hurry up Diane, let's go. I don't have all day for this."

My navy-blue skirt was new too. I stepped out of it carefully.

Her eyes never left my body. I felt like a slide specimen under a microscope. Her lips seemed to curl in disgust. Those eyes always staring. I slipped the straps of my bra off my shoulders and shivered, a feeling of sickness swept over me. I slipped my thumbs under the elastic waistband of my underpants hoping they would be clean. Did girls who slept with boys have clean underwear?

Surely this woman with the hard, narrow eyes would be able to see that I was a good girl, a virgin. I mean if one could see such things.

"Any tattoos or unusual marks on you? Turn around so I can see."

Tattoos? Did girls have tattoos? I'd never seen such things. Tattoos, like sailors and truck drivers? Girls, girls like me, young and . . .

Wanting to please and soften this woman's attitude toward me, I held out my left hand to show her the small, dime-sized tan birthmark on my wrist.

"My mother used to say . . ." but she cut me off.

I am angry, very angry, raging inside about this. How could my mother have let this happen to me? I was just a kid, a child, a young girl. I knew nothing about the world, about tattoos, about sex, about signs of a girl's lost virginity.

She left, taking all my clothing with her. All the clues that told me who I was and where I had come from and was going back to were gone.

I slipped into the warm water and felt the fear melt into the soft comfort surrounding me.

Then she was back in the room, snapping orders again.

"Here, pour this over your head and body when you finish bathing and shampooing your hair."

"What do I use for shampoo?" I asked.

"Why the bar of soap, of course."

"Soap, a bar of soap, laundry soap? I can't wash my hair with a bar of yellow laundry soap. My mother told me never to use bar soap on my hair, besides, I can't pour that green stuff over my hair, I'll never be able to comb it out." She was losing patience with me. I could see the irritation on her face.

"OK, OK," I said, feeling trapped. She left the room again and I stood up in the big old-fashioned tub, the sickly-looking liquid smelled like the bathroom in the Greyhound bus station. The sound of keys clanking together announced her re-entry. Now she was carrying a bundle of white.

"Here is your gown and slippers — put them on after you use this!'

"I can't use that stuff in the pitcher, what is it?"

"It's disinfectant. We disinfect all new admissions for lice!"

"LICE?" I couldn't believe it! Tattoos, new admissions and now lice. My stomach tightened, my throat felt as if I was being choked. I couldn't talk and tears welled up, spilling hot on my face.

Gone, everything was gone. My clothes, my purse, the few belongings I had, my body stripped of my own smell and shrouded in this shapeless white bag. My world was gone, there was no more world for me, only cold strange women with blue veined legs and black oxfords.

I followed her down the long hall, rounded the corner into the adjoining hall to the open doorway of a small narrow room. It was quite bare, the walls were white with no curtains, rug or pictures on the walls. The room was devoid of color. A single metal bed stood against the wall with white sheets and a blue wool blanket. On the opposite wall was a tall wooden bureau and a single black book lay on top — the Bible.

CLICK! The door shut and a key turned in the lock. A wild instant of fear passed over me. I can't get out! What if there is a fire or . . .

Something inside me burst into a ball of flaming red. I shut my eyes tightly, my fists curled into balls, pounded the mattress. Inside I was screaming, gagging, retching and eventually breaking into tears. For hours, I lay sobbing, slowly emptying myself. The day had turned to evening, all lay black outside my window. I heard the wind blow dry leaves against the window. Mercifully, gratefully I slipped into sleep in the blackness.

The following three days were the longest of my life, as my senses registered the changes in my life and I tried to make connections between past and present. Failing to do so, I moved in and out of reality at lightning speed. Early in the morning of the first day, I woke to the sound of a key turning in the lock of my door. I heard shoes stepping quickly across the floor into the room, then returning, and again a key in the lock. Reluctantly, I opened my eyes and sat up. I wasn't to be let out. My eyes hurt, swollen from the hours of crying. I opened, then closed them, revolting against the harsh light flooding the room. I took an inventory of my body. Everything seemed to be in its normal place, though I felt stiff and out of sorts. Panic began to rise in me again as I stared at the locked door. Locked! Locked for how long? I asked myself, as if there could be an answer inside my head.

I got up from the bed, stood in front of the window and in the pale dawn light saw the heavy, thick steel bars stretched across the window. I felt anger rising in my throat. I turned toward the door, ready to beat it with my fist, when I noticed that my early morning visitor had left a tray with food on top of the bureau. Breakfast I thought, naming something familiar. But there was no comfort in that meal set before me: a cup of black coffee (something I'd never tasted, and was told by my mother wasn't good for children), a dish of oatmeal floating in thin blue milk and a piece of burnt toast with a very small pat of butter and a half an orange. Disgusted, I turned away and crawled back into bed, covered my head with the blanket and attempted to shut out the world.

"I'll starve myself to death." Yes, that's what I'd do. I began to fantasize my funeral, with my parents standing over my casket, viewing my carefully composed, innocent body. They'd be sorry for what happened to me. It was all their fault, I thought, as I drifted back into sleep.

I drifted in and out of sleep throughout the long second day, the hours interrupted only by meal trays for lunch and dinner. I did not eat. The next day I stayed awake, constantly reviewing the events that had brought me to this place. I sought to blame each familiar face from my past. I interviewed and questioned those witnesses from my life as to my innocence. My confusion grew, the loneliness of the small bare room deepened, and my fear of being held there interminably brought me to panic. Hysterically, I pleaded with my mother, begging for her understanding and forgiveness, but always faltering when asked to confess my sins, my part in bringing about this situation. I could not see where I was wrong — not wrong enough to deserve this kind punishment.

Toward the end of the day, as the light left the sky outside my window and the little room grew darker, I began to make deals, with my parents, with the juvenile authorities, with God. "OK," I said to myself, "Maybe you don't think you did anything wrong, but you're going to be punished anyway." I wanted out now, out of this room, out of this nightmare. I began to think that it would only happen if I agreed that it was all my fault. I was bad, ugly. I'd thought only of myself and now I had to confess my sins. Isn't that what I had been taught in Sunday School — that God will forgive you for your sins? It must be true that I had committed sins and needed to own up to them so I could be forgiven and released from this misery. Someplace in my head I heard my own voice telling me to accept the blame, "Say it! Say you're sorry and you can get out of this place." So I did. I agreed that my parents, the court, and now the cold, thin-lipped women that held the keys to my door. They were right and I was bad, a bad girl.

Several examinations were done, including a gynecological exam, which I had never experienced before, and which further traumatized me. The hours passed slowly in that lonely room and when I was awake, I cried continuously until exhaustion forced me back into sleep. I was transferred from the Reception Center to a cottage for new girls who were awaiting sentencing by the Youth Commission. We'd meet with a board of people who would decide if we were to be sent back home on probation or held at the school for an indeterminate time before being released on parole. I didn't understand any of this procedure and had no control over its outcome. The strangeness was frightening to me and many of the girls I met were bullies and very disturbed. Talk between the girls was about getting out, their boyfriends on the outside and whether they had had sex. I was a virgin and this fact seemed to be particularly objectionable to my housemates. The girls, often very agitated by my answer, stated that I was plainly lying. Many would ostracize me for this. The month I spent in this cottage was filled with anxiety, bitterness, resentment, and shame. I thought only of getting out, going home and of running away from this place.

The opportunity came sooner than I expected and the decision was made on the spur of the moment. I ran because the rumor mill spread the word that I'd be held over and not receive probation and home release. In the dark of a cold frosty October night, as the cottage group returned from seeing a movie, a short walk from the school auditorium to the cottage, I sprinted away from the group of twenty-five girls strung out along the sidewalk. I ran stumbling over the frozen ground to the side of the school, then across several fields of roughly plowed frozen earth until I reached the school's dairy farm, a hundred yards away. A barbed wire fence blocked me from the road. I caught my coat on the fence and cut the side of my leg open on one of the sharp barbs. Blood ran down my leg, but I never felt the pain then. The fence was a chicken yard or a pigpen or something and I had to exit the same barbed wire on the other side. I could see the headlights of a car heading up the road and I knew it was the men who worked the grounds and farm of the school. They were sent out to search for the girls who ran away. I was about twenty-five feet from a ditch that lay parallel to the road. I ran and fell into it, pressing myself flat against the earth. My coat was dark, and they didn't see me. When they had passed, I ran across the road into the woods. Suddenly I realized I was not alone — three other girls had followed me around the side of the school. I barely knew them. Two were reservation Indian girls and the third a skinny Black girl. All had been in the same cottage with me.

The terrain was dangerous, with marshland, deep rivers, and sand pits belonging to a gravel company on the edge of town. We started to run across a railroad trestle bridge, not knowing how it was constructed. Joan went first and fell, straddling the timber slats and slamming her crotch onto the thick rough wooden railroad tie, screaming in pain. Jeanette and I pulled her out while fearing for our own lives. The drop from the sides of the tracks was fifteen feet to the river. Next, we ran into the gravel yard, and came to the edge of a sand pit. I thought I should climb down into the pit and up the other side because it would be easier than trying to find a path around the perimeter in the pitch black. I knew nothing about the dangers of sand pits and began sliding towards the bottom. There was nothing to grab onto and I clawed the sand with my hands and feet, attempting to stop the slide. Sand fell into my face, covering my eyes and into my open screaming mouth. Someone threw me the edge of a coat and after several tries, I caught it. The damn thing ripped in half but held at the collar, reinforced with extra stitching and strengthened by the lining. Slowly they pulled me out. At the top I was hysterical, screaming and trying to catch my breath. I could have died, smothered by the sand.

When we entered the edge of the town, we hid in an open church yard, then tried to cross an adjacent yard where a tall pole held a yard light. The men from the farm saw us as we rounded the brightly-lit end of a machinery shed, and were waiting to grab us at the road's edge, shoving us into the back seats of their cars.

Back at the home school, we were taken to Pioneer, the discipline cottage. This cottage stood apart from the others and had greater security measures in place. The girls who lived there were tougher, older and had more severe problems including breaking parole and major escapes (runs).

There was Millie, who was in Sauk Centre for murder and she had also assaulted one of the housemothers, inflicting serious physical damage. Millie was a very tall (probably about six feet), a thin Black girl, nearing the age limit when a girl had to leave this facility. The next stop for her would be the women's prison at Shakopee, Minnesota. One of the oldest girls, Dianne, had been a prostitute and lived in a neighborhood of the Black community where crime was rampant. She had a Black pimp and was doing drugs at a time when few others did. She hung out on the streets and in the bars that white people in Minneapolis avoided. She was as fat as Millie was skinny and she had bad skin, an acne that never cleared while she was at the school. She hung only with the Black girls on the campus and was thought to be the coolest and the toughest.

Gloria was full-figured, with standout breasts which she used to her advantage as a prostitute on the outside. Her bleached blonde hair was the color of new straw and nearly as brittle. She painted her lips like Joan Crawford — bright red and squaring the natural arching lip lines and curves. She wore her skirts and sweaters tight and walked the perimeter of the school gym at assembly times with a younger girl on each side of her. Gloria's arms hung over each of the girls' shoulders. These girls were her newest "girlfriends," and were protected by Gloria in exchange for passing notes to others and handling contraband items like cigarettes and letters mailed to outside boyfriends. Somehow, she had connections. She was rumored to be a lesbian.

To a fourteen-year-old girl like me, a tough eighteen-year old was a fearsome thing. She could beat the hell out of me and who knew what else. These girls were self-acknowledged alcoholics, runaways and parole breakers who hung on the meanest streets of the Twin Cities, Minneapolis-St. Paul. A few were Indians from reservation towns in the northern part of the state. All would eventually be on their way to the women's prison.

The rooms and hallways at Pioneer lacked the graciousness and gentility of the other cottages. They were bare, shabby and downright dirty. I was put into a room with a bare metal bed, covered with a thin, stained mattress of blue and white ticking. It had a nearly flat pillow without a case, no sheets and a dark blue scratchy wool blanket for covering. They took my clothes away and gave me a cotton flour sack nightgown and no shoes. The only other items in the room were a white enamel portable pot with a lid, to be used as a toilet and emptied once a day, and a roll of toilet paper. The windows were heavily barred and would only open three inches. The door was always locked. It had a seven- or eight-inch square window where the housemother could look in to check on me. The walls were painted white but scratched with stories. Girls had taken bobby pins and safety pins, whatever they managed to get hold of and written out their histories. The tragic, bare facts of their lives of incarceration and love.

jailed in the cities

sentenced to 18 mos SC

on run to Chicago

arrested and brought back to SC

love James Dawson

out spring of 50

back to jail fall

back to SC

on run two wks

my heart belongs to Jimmy he's my true love

Breakfast came on a tray when the door was unlocked by the housemother — black coffee and dry toast with gray slop they called oatmeal — every two to three days. Lunch was more watery black coffee with two slices of bread and one piece of baloney. Dinner wasn't much different. By the third day, I was given a few very tattered magazines which I scoured for pictures of food. I hadn't eaten the stuff they were calling meals and I was getting very hungry. I licked the pictures of Jell-O and turkey and made lists of menus in my head, slowly going over each bite I took in my mind. It would be ten long days before I had a real meal again. The deprivation of those days would affect me the rest of my life.

I read every story and advertisement in those torn magazines several times, then I took to reading the histories scratched in the wall. When sleeping the hours away no longer worked, I found a button on the floor in the corner of the room. I devised a game for myself. Closing my eyes, I'd throw the button up in the air and listen carefully as it dropped. I'd reach out in the direction of the sound the button made when it hit the floor. If I could find it on the first try, I'd reward myself with a simple sensory experience. For instance, a long smell of the fresh air through the three-inch opening of the window. Cupping my ear against the wooden door, listening for people talking or for their footsteps, counting them until they stopped, guessing what they were doing. Licking the paint on the wall and then the window frame, tasting the difference and describing it with words. I examined every finger, nail, toe and scar or mark on my body, in minute detail. Then it would be back to the button toss for the next experience.

The bare bulb that lit the room was left on all night, and eventually I stopped noticing it. But in the years after that, I could not stand any ceiling light fixture to be on when I was in the room. Even passing houses at night, if I saw such a light burning it seized my attention, and I felt feel annoyed at the people who used such ugly lighting.

I have a bitter-sweet memory of a night in June, before I left Sauk Centre months later to return home, filled with confusion, longing and excitement. An old phonograph played songs that pulled all of us deep into recent memories of boyfriends, home, and family. Tall windows opened to the soft evening twilight and a gentle breeze filled the room with the earthy smell of growing crops. I glanced around the room, taking each fellow inmate in, one at a time. They were an interesting bunch of girls: Black, American Indian, and white teen-agers, mostly children of the working poor, some still quite innocent, others with recent memories of an unwed pregnancy or neglect and abuse by their families. They were too rebellious and too independent for society and their young ages.

They were fighters, struggling to survive. Almost none of them had committed any violent crimes, though they may have shoplifted. Some of the Indian girls had histories of heavy drinking.

One or two of the older girls may have been involved in prostitution. Mostly what they did was to run away from home, refuse to go to school, smoke cigarettes, break the curfew by hanging out and acting "boy crazy." Now, on the edge of summer, their thoughts were on hometown streets and old boyfriends, yearning to be touched and loved. They were walking wounded, and their emotions surfaced easily, evoked by the music.

Family, Interrupted

Adults who were hurt as children inevitably exhibit a peculiar strength, a profound inner wisdom, and a remarkable creativity and insight. Deep within them - just beneath the wound - lies a profound spiritual vitality, a quiet knowing, a way of perceiving what is beautiful, right, and true. Since their early experiences were so dark and painful, they have spent much of their lives in search of the gentleness, love, and peace they have only imagined in the privacy of their own hearts.
— *Wayne Muller*

As a small girl, I was adventurous and independent. I explored the neighborhood around our basement apartment at 1310 East 22nd Street, a block south of Lake Street in South Minneapolis. I found a Baptist Church several blocks away and I loved to go to Sunday School there, sing songs, and hear the stories they told. I took my little sister Pat with me under protest. I was so eager to attend that once we arrived early and sat outside for an hour waiting for the church to open. In school I loved reading, and the teacher scolded me for reading ahead in the book. Arithmetic gave me trouble, especially long division. I was jealous of a boy named Philip in my class. He had skipped grades and the teacher favored him. I stole his milk money and got in trouble for that.

Before I was ten years old, when my family was still living in Minneapolis, our life was stable. We observed the usual traditional holidays, Christmas, Easter, and Thanksgiving. There were picnics in the summer, and wiener roasts in the fall. Sunday drives and dinners in Wisconsin. Most of those activities were planned and initiated by my grandmother, my uncle Barney, and my parents' friends. Often my mother did not attend these events. As I got older, I recall that my parents often argued before we went out for the day or evening. Sometimes, my mother was upset by not having the right clothes to wear, or that she didn't want to be in the company of someone else who was going. She didn't like our Sunday outings to Wisconsin because often they involved stopping in a tavern to drink beer and she didn't want her daughters in those places.

But by the age of ten I knew what authority was — everybody's rights but mine. My Sunday school, my parents, other adults, my sisters, my school mates were always right — I was wrong. In any dispute between myself and another, I'd blame myself. I had internalized this belief firmly in my mind. Yet, some other part of me resisted this blame and warred against it. This conflict drove me to a sobbing, raging loneliness, and eventually years of depression. I would seek those secret places to be alone where I could cry and talk out loud, repeating the incident over and over. The corner of the school yard where no one else played, lagging behind the group on the walk home, in some secret spot in the neighborhood where the bushes shielded me from the world, in a dark corner of our basement, and in my bed at night. The way an animal seeks its den when it has been physically wounded. When it was possible, I would hold the pain inside until I could find that place to be alone in and cry. When it was not possible and the pain was overwhelming, I would cover my face and shield my head, but then exposure brought the double whammy of shame and humiliation.

The beginning of school in the fall was an exciting time. There were new notebooks, school shoes, pencils, some clothes, and other small supplies to be bought and cached and fondled until the first Monday following Labor Day. In Minnesota, the morning temperatures would have cooled, and the days were still bright and sunny. I walked to school through several blocks of a residential neighborhood to the commercial shopping district where the streetcar tracks turned in their course to the center of the city. Sometimes I walked with my younger sister but often alone. It was a safe walk and I usually followed the route laid out by my mother when I first started school in kindergarten. I looked forward to school and the new day. I wasn't a shy child, nor did I wish to stay at home.

In the first days of September, the class would be occupied with the new curriculum and special projects scheduled for the school year. Fourth grade, or as I remember it, fifth grade with

Ms. Ryan was a mix of good and bad memories. Her classroom was on the west side of the building in the southernmost corner, and the late afternoon sunlight was golden as it flooded the room.

I remember making vocabulary books. We were to write in these books at school and keep them in our desks. Each week the teacher would give us a list of ten to fifteen words we must learn for the spelling test at end of the week. We had to use a dictionary to break each word down phonetically and write the definition after it. I never seemed to get through the list, as each time I got the list, I'd write all the words down at once and never leave enough space for the longer definitions. Then when I began to fill in the definitions, I'd run out of room and mess up the page. The messiness of my book drove me wild and I was constantly starting over, though I did learn the importance of words.

We also learned how to write letters and address envelopes. This task involved using real ink and pens, for the first time. There were no ballpoint pens in those days. The format for the letter and the addressing of the envelope was no problem for me, but I never could finish the work because I couldn't manage the medium. The cheap newsprint paper soaked up the ink, and allowing the pen to sit on the paper resulted in huge blots of ink. The point never flowed across the paper smoothly and often tore holes in it. Starting over was something I did at every lesson. For years I have been fascinated with pens, notebooks, and paper. I wonder if this is why?

Occasionally Ms. Ryan would reward us with a sort of game, a contest similar to a spelling bee, but using birds, flowers, and state capitals. Each time we could name one, we'd get a Wheat Thin cracker. I loved this game, but never really won.

Kids would bring in apples and cards for the teacher, but I never had anything to give her. I remember wanting to get her attention like the others. My need to be like everyone else was a strong motivation. I found a way. In my wanderings around the neighborhood stores I found one that sold packages of colored clay. I think I took the money from my mother, but I don't recall that part of the story—only that I bought the colored clay and made a tiny yellow coiled clay basket and filled it with tiny pieces of fruit. I made a yellow banana, some blue grapes with green leaves, a red apple. I brought it to school for Ms. Ryan. She placed it on the front of her desk. No special attention was given to me for this gift, but for years I remembered it.

When we had Social Studies, we were given U.S. maps to fill in with the names and products of each state. I did an especially good job on California, as I knew from hearing family discussions that it had oil wells and oranges trees. My artwork was very detailed.

In the early fall the school had a dental campaign to get the children's teeth in shape. A large poster board with each child's name on it was hung at the front of the classroom facing us. We were given printed handouts requesting the parents have dental examinations and dental work done on their children. We were supposed to get a blue star for every dental appointment we had, and a gold star if the dentist signed the slip that the work was all done. I tried to get the stars because the real reward was a picnic and wiener roast at Theodore Wirth Park. It meant a day off from school and a bus ride to the edge of the city where the park was located. I didn't get the work done, and I didn't get the gold star. About five or six of us had to stay behind that afternoon. My parents didn't take me to the dentist, and I was punished for what they didn't do. It wasn't my fault. I remember how the weather was beautiful, the sun was shining, and it was warm outside. The leaves had begun to fall, red and gold upon the ground. I could hear them rattling in the wind through the open windows. This was a grave injustice and I could never forget it. I put my head down on the desk and wept bitterly.

Yet, this was the year of my schooling that I would always recall as the best year and the year I learned the most in school.

Later that fall, my Uncle Chuck who had been living with us got married and left for California. Sometime after the new year, my parents began to talk of moving to California to follow Chuck. I began to talk about it to my class for Current Events reports, describing California as if I had already been there. This got me a lot of attention for a while and I reveled in it. In February, my Aunt had returned to Minnesota to take care of some personal business, and it was decided then that I would accompany her back to California on the train. This was going to be a really big thing for me, and I spent weeks getting ready for it. I remember staring out the window of the coach as we crossed the desert, expecting to see bleached cattle skulls like in a Western movie, and disappointed when there were none.

CALIFORNIA

Los Angeles was the kind of place where everybody was from somewhere else and nobody really dropped anchor. It was a transient place. People drawn by the dream, people running from the nightmare. Twelve million people and all of them ready to make a break for it if necessary. Figuratively, literally, metaphorically -- any way you want to look at it -- everybody in L.A. keeps a bag packed. Just in case.
— *MICHAEL CONNELLY*

In school, I could read well and enjoyed it. I loved English and spelling but got lost in diagramming of sentences and the grammar. Math became a mystery to me in the third grade and I was stuck in long division for many years after. I don't remember what my grades were, and my parents never seemed to pay much attention to them. They never punished me for bad grades. It was just not important when their life had so many other problems. There were so many schools in the years following our family's move to California (and back and forth to Minnesota) that I have no real memories of what I was taught. Most of all I was concerned with fitting in, getting accepted and making friends. I had none and was usually moved to a new school before I found out if I was acceptable to anyone.

Physically I was strong, and I lifted and moved furniture with my father many times as we moved. I was by their definition a tomboy and was not acceptable. I came to believe this was what my classmates thought of me also. I was somehow different, and that difference made me unworthy of their interest or friendship. I understood none of this except in contrast to my younger sister Pat, who was thin, frail-looking, shy, and quiet. Pat, though just two years younger than me, never seemed to venture out into the world. She became the favorite of the entire extended family, re-

ceiving praise and small gifts from other family members and friends. I couldn't take on the same behavior as my sister. It was just not possible for me. I couldn't slow down or conform to the desires of the adults surrounding me. Because I couldn't change myself, I felt incompetent and unacceptable. I spent the rest of my life in conflict and self-repression.

I suppose my feelings of incompetence were mainly out of confusion. My father was usually tired and was never physically affectionate with me. Largely, no one touched me or gave me much physical affection. Although they talked and argued with each other, they never engaged me in a conversation unless it was a reprimand for something I had done wrong, or not done. Words I often heard as describing myself were" rambunctious, self-willed, wild, rough and not lady-like, boisterous and dramatic.

My father was an angry man, and my sisters and I knew it from our earliest memories. He was hardest on me, whipping me with his belt when I had misbehaved for something I can't even recall now. It wasn't too many times. I guess my mother put a stop to that. My sisters were younger by two and four years and escaped that punishment. I felt it was particularly humiliating because I'd never heard of girls being whipped, especially on their bare bottoms.

Dinnertime was an ordeal for me as Dad watched me like a hawk, waiting for me to make a mistake and give him the opportunity to unleash his temper. I remember I drank my glass of milk before I ate my meal, and when I looked up at him to ask for more, he would explode. If I didn't like something on my plate it was easier to find a way to hide it. When I was forced to eat the offending substance, like asparagus or cooked carrots, I would gag and choke. Partially it was my fear of him, and I took to trickery by hiding cooked vegetables in my pockets, or on the ledge underneath the kitchen table. Sometimes I asked to be excused from the table to go to the bathroom, where I could flush them down the toilet. Nothing worked for very long, but it didn't stop me from trying to find new ways to get around his scrutiny.

I find my way to places on my own using my memory. I walked all over every new neighborhood we moved into, mapping out the northern and southern highway routes between California and Minnesota, memorizing each major city one would pass through. I began to read maps and plan my own fantasy trips. I could use public transportation and read the city bus and trolley schedules. I could apply for a library card and had a general understanding of the library set up. When we lived near a library, I rented armloads of books but invariably returned them way overdue, stacking up huge fines, most of which were never paid. I memorized the routes to all of my relative's homes and could have walked or driven to them alone.

The Golden State didn't work out as my father expected, and after living with my aunt and uncle for a few weeks, we returned to Minneapolis. Mother, Dad, Pat, Cheryl and I stayed with Gram at the house she rented from Albert Erickson, a longtime friend. My grandmother used the downstairs part of the house and a bedroom upstairs was my Uncle Barney's bedroom. The room was larger than most bedrooms I'd ever seen, with a watermelon-green linoleum floor and three or four loom-woven, multicolored cotton rag rugs covering it. There was an old wind-up Victrola and a stack of large, platter-sized black 78 rpm records with Jimmy Durante, Rudy Vallee, and Bing Crosby. I played them over and over. On the dresser top was a model airplane made from silver plastic. I slept on a sofa with a black-painted wooden frame, a caned back, and a velvet-cushioned seat.

Mother discovered she had tuberculosis, TB, and Grandma responded by scrubbing the house down. That upset Mother. There was an argument between Mother and Gram, and Gram called Albert to intervene. Mother was on the phone trying to call Irene and George, and Albert struggled with Mother over the phone. Mother was crying and hysterical. Later, in the early evening Dad, Mom, my sisters, and I went to Elliot Park. We girls played in the shallow wading pool while Mother and Dad sat on park bench talking. Mother was crying. We returned to Grandma's and Mother slept on the porch bed. Grandma was in the kitchen, ironing a white shirt for Uncle Barney. She was crying and wouldn't talk to me. She said something to me about my mother. I felt torn between my love for my mother and for my grandmother.

Minnesota law required people with TB to be sent to Glen Lake Sanitorium. My mother was adamant about not going there. Her brother, my Uncle Red, had been previously hospitalized there. It is where he met Aunt Beth, who was working as a young nurse. They were married and moved to California several years earlier. Mother told me about her girlfriends who died from TB in the sanitorium. The next thing I remember is that Mother and Cheryl returned to California.

My father, Pat, and I continued to stay with Gram. We went to Washington Grammar School. I remember threading my way to school and home again by a route of my own devising. Sometimes, it meant stopping at the window of the Annex of the St. Barnabas Hospital, where I would talk through the window to an old lady, who was a patient. This later became part of a children's story I tried to write, "The Deep Blue Morning Glory." One day, I stopped to see the old lady, but her bed was empty. I sneaked into the hospital to see why she wasn't at the window. Her bed was made up. One of the nurses found me and told me that she was "gone." I never really knew what happened to her.

Sometimes, we'd go through other people's back yards, lifting a loose fence board and squeezing our bodies through the narrow space. I used to tell Pat stories about witches living in these houses. We'd run up and down the outside stair wells in various buildings, and occasionally through Elliot Park, which was against the rules my mother had laid down for us.

From the upstairs kitchen window in Albert's apartment, I could look out over the black silhouetted treetops and see the lights in downtown Minneapolis. The Weather ball atop the Foshay Tower was the one thing we always looked for. It would be white if the weather was going to be colder, red for warmer, and green meant the temperature was going to stay the same. If the ball was blinking, rain or snow was predicted.

My Aunt Charlotte and Uncle Gus lived in Springfield, Illinois. Gus was mother's older brother. They offered to take care of me to help put my parents and Gram, who was struggling to care for Pat and me. Pat stayed with Gram, and my father left for California. I spent the next year with them in Springfield, in their small house across the street from the Pillsbury mill where Gus worked. I loved the quiet, orderly way Charlotte ran her household. There was talk of adopting me, but my parents backed out, and the next summer Uncle Barney and Gram drove me to California where Uncle Chuck and Aunt Ginny lived.

There wasn't enough room for Chuck to house our whole family of five. He suggested Dad buy a house on his GI Bill. Housing tracts were being built fast and furiously in Southern Calif. It was natural for my father to buy his a few miles away from Chuck and George's places. He bought a small two-bedroom rancher in

Pico Rivera, planted a lawn and got taken by a patio salesman who told him the referrals he brought to the company would pay for that "beautiful, brick patio-barbeque." Soon after, he bought another dog — a dark Brindle Purebred female boxer, which he named Duchess.

The barbeque never got used and Duchess never got her vaccinations. My sisters and I started school at South Ranchito Grammar. I was in the sixth grade, my sister Pat was in the fourth grade, and Cheryl was in second. The school held social dances, and while I was thrilled by the prospect, I was the new kid and shy. To the Tennessee Waltz, I dreamed of a boyfriend. Trying to be a normal young girl living in the margin between childhood and emerging womanhood, I played like a tomboy and dreamed of the romantic future.

Accidents happen and they happen to children most frequently. It was my job to feed the dog but one evening I wasn't at home when its dinnertime arrived, so Mother told my sister Pat to give Duchess her food dish. Pat and the dog were on the brick patio and she was teasing the dog with her food. She slipped and fell, gashing her leg deeply on the barbeque spit hardware. My father was home and Pat was taken to the neighborhood emergency center for stitches. Of course, I was blamed for not being there to do my job.

In autumn, the dog died of distemper while I sat on the cold porch cement floor, holding her head in my lap, her eyes and nose pouring, her soft brown body heaving in labored breaths. I sobbed and I cried, begging God to help Duchess and me. My mother called me to come into the house, it was too cold out there. I couldn't leave that helpless creature to face this thing alone.

The orange grove that stood between our housing tract and the school's playing fields was torn down to make room for more houses. The trees were uprooted and piled in great mountains, an invitation to adventure as several neighborhood boys and I tunneled through the "jungle" pretending to be Great White Hunters. I dragged my sister along and the two of us emerged at home, way late for lunch, our newly dry-cleaned coats covered with the black smudge that had covered the orange trees, our faces coated with the stuff, and our hair a tangled mess. Mother kept us home from school that afternoon, scouring us in the bathtub and cutting our hair into very short bobs. My sister wore a head scarf to school for weeks afterwards.

I was tormented by constant earaches and toothaches but remained healthy otherwise. Active, physical things were my form of play and whenever I could, I climbed and ran and most often with the boys. One day after school, a group of us discovered the old house that had once been part of the orchard. Now it had been torn down and lay in rubble, a heap of siding and boards with jagged ends and protruding rusted nails. A few citrus trees of lemon, grapefruit, and tangerine stood where a pleasant yard had once been. In the midst grew a very old, tall tree with a kind of fruit I had never seen before. Green oval forms hung in the tree, nearly matching the leaves. I grabbed one of the old boards and threw it up into the tree hoping to knock one down to the ground. Again, I tossed the board and missed. On the third attempt, I grabbed the board and found my ring finger impaled on a long rusty nail, still attached to the board. My screams soon brought adults to the scene who helped me home. My father and I made the trip to the local emergency facility my sister had been too most recently. My father treated me very harshly, showing me no sympathy. I tried to tell him it was an accident, but he thought only of the money this was going to cost.

I was sent to stay with Chuck and Ginny and enrolled in Passons Blvd. School. After I got there, I had no friends to play with, tell secrets to, eat my bag lunches with. I had no activities to occupy myself. I was alone but I can't tell you now if I was lonely. Something was happening to me, but I didn't have a name for it then.

I can remember the feeling. I tried to find things to do as my Aunt and Uncle were at work all day. Sometimes I walked down to the dry riverbed, the Rio Hondo, but there were bums and vagrants living in thrown together wooded sheds down in the reeds. Somehow, I knew to stay away from there. My aunt and uncle found out I went down there, and gave me a harsh scolding.

Another school was just too painful to stay in, and one day I just didn't go. Instead I walked around the neighborhood streets until I found some older kids who were also skipping school. They seemed to have been doing it for some time, and knew the ropes. Their parents worked and the house was theirs for the day. They must have realized quickly that I was too young to be around, as I was asked to leave. I never went back. I found a tiny dull green lizard in the back yard and put it in a shoebox. A pet! I named her Lizzie (not too original) and kept the shoe box on the top bunk of the bedroom I slept in. One night was enough, as I dreamt that Lizzie got loose from the box and was crawling around in my bed. The next morning I let her go in the grass. My aunt and uncle found out about my skipping school and they told my father I was "too difficult to take care of."

My memories get confused here as I can't remember the sequence of moves but I remember living in a small white house in Montebello when my father worked for Standard Coffee Company and later Pellissier Dairy driving a milk delivery truck. My sisters were at this house and the front yard was full of ivy instead of grass. I also lived alone with my parents in an upstairs apartment near Olympic Blvd., in Montebello and we had another Boxer dog. I learned to make hamburger patties with ice in them. Mother was sick then and stayed in her "house coat" all day. This was in the summer because I didn't go to school.

Later that night, after everyone had gone to bed and was asleep, my mother called to me from her bedroom, as she did frequently. She didn't attempt to wake my father, as he was very difficult to rouse and became quite nasty when his sleep was disturbed for any reason. In later years, my mother would send me in to wake him and usually I got out of his way fast. Once I didn't and got hit in the face pretty hard. I was afraid of his temper until I was about 18. When I was in the early years of grade school he used his belt on my bare skin if I had done something wrong. I hated him then and my sisters feared him even more.

Usually Mother's request was for chopped ice to eat. If she felt that her lungs were making her cough, she could eat the ice and stop the cough. This time was different because there was blood in the tissue she had used. The furnace was off, there were no rugs on the floors, and the house was very cold. Barefooted, I went into the kitchen, pulled out an ice cube tray and emptied it into a clean dish towel. Holding the towel closed, I used a hammer to crack the cubes into tiny pieces which filled a small bowl.

When I went back to bed, I was shivering from the cold house and handling the ice. Within a few minutes she called me again. She was clearly more anxious, and I began to get really frightened. "Diane, you'll have to get the doctor who lives across the street, NOW! I am coughing up blood. Tell him I am hemorrhaging." By the time I returned with the doctor, my father was awake and civil. My sister Pat was also awake and the two of us cow-

ered and shivered in our bedroom. I was on my knees next to the bed praying to God, begging him to save my mother from dying.

The next morning the ambulance came and took my mother away. My sisters and I were very upset since we couldn't understand what was happening. Perhaps this was the beginning of my abandonment. After that I was expected to take care of myself and any errors in my judgment, any mistakes I made, filled me with shame and were only mine to correct. I took to hiding my needs and my mistakes, for it seemed there was no one to help me, and no one who cared. Was my mother dying? Would we ever see her again? The following weeks, life was a blur for me.

My mother was taken to LA County Hospital where because of the crowded conditions she lay for hours on a gurney in the hallway. People were dying all around her, as she told us later. I remember going with our father to visit her there once, but since children were not allowed into the building, we had to stand on a busy street corner next to a drugstore and wait. It was hot that afternoon, and the people who passed us were poor, mostly Mexican, and badly dressed. The street was busy with traffic, and the sidewalk was littered with trash and blackened splotches of chewing gum. A Black man stopped to talk to us, drunk and badly in need of a bath, his breath saturated with alcohol. I knew better than to let my little sisters pay him any attention, pulling them away into a boarded doorway several steps away. We stood for what seemed hours, watching the tall, dark-stained red brick hospital building across the street, hoping for a glance of my mother at one of the windows, until the late afternoon sun's slanting rays pierced the dust covered leaves of the carob trees that lined the sidewalk.

My mother was diagnosed with active tuberculosis and spent the next two years in the Olive View Sanatorium in Sylmar. In the meantime, my grandmother arrived on the train from Minnesota. No one else could take care of us while my father worked.

By the end of October, my grandmother was ready to return to her home in Minnesota. When she stayed with us, she pressured my mother into having us baptized. On Halloween, a Lutheran minister came to the house and it was done. It seemed strange to me. None of us went to church, and we never discussed religion in our house. I thought Halloween was the wrong time for a religious ritual. The minister dabbed water on our foreheads as we stood, dressed in ghostly costumes and eager to begin one of childhood's special annual events. Nothing our family did seemed normal and it was always painful for me to feel that I didn't fit in.

Grandma had to get back to her house and her job. She took my sisters on the train with her back to Minnesota. She had to pay her own train fare and she made less money than my Dad. Cheryl went to stay with Aunt Charlotte in Illinois. She had suffered from all the family disruption and had to be held back in school. On top of that she had infected tonsils that had to be removed. She was only seven years old and being away from her mother and the rest of us must have been terribly hard for her. For reasons I never learned, Aunt Charlotte was not kind to Cheryl. She and my sister Pat told me years later that she spanked Cheryl and yanked her by the hair when she was angry. Cheryl was at Charlotte's for about three years.

Grandma lived on Colfax Avenue North and Pat attended school there until she graduated from sixth grade. She enjoyed those years with Grandma. She went up to the lake in the summer, on downtown excursions, visited Albert's house (Grandma's long time old male friend), picnics with Barney and family friends of my parents. It was a quiet, stable time for her, and she was well liked by my grandmother and my uncle. Pat was a shy, quiet child, and never made any trouble.

Then I was living alone with my father. I remember spending time in several different juvenile facilities for neglected children after getting in trouble while my father was away from home driving Greyhound buses. Next door to our house our neighbor had a garden with raspberry bushes. I wanted to eat some of her beautiful, red berries. I was playing with a couple of kids from around the block and we got the idea we could pick some and she would never notice—there were so many. We started picking a few, then a few more. We couldn't reach the ones at the top, so we pulled the vines down where we could reach them. By the time the neighbor came out of her house and saw us, we had broken and ruined several of the vines.

She called the juvenile authorities, who found that I was inadequately supervised, what with my father being away long hours driving buses, and I was taken into custody. They considered placing me in a foster home, and even gave me a choice between two strikingly different ones. The one I wanted to go to in La Canada was highly structured and organized. Another, a Luther-

an Home for Children, was too noisy and disorganized for my liking. For reasons I was never told, I couldn't go to either one. I was sent to Julia Lathrop Cottages instead. I stayed for several weeks and went to court while I was there. I had an EEG exam with electrodes pasted to my head. I didn't go to school until I reached MacLaren Hall in El Monte, a home for neglected and abused children.

After attending five different elementary schools in sixth grade while my parents were moving around, I went to seventh grade in Alhambra. One afternoon, the school held a dance for seventh graders in the gymnasium. I had no clothes for an event like that, but I knew my mother did. She was still away, held in the sanatorium, so I couldn't ask her. Even though I was forbidden to go into her things, I believed she would have given permission, and that was enough for me. I wanted so badly to fit in with the class, even to look pretty, that I ignored the rules and slipped into her room. I opened her dresser drawer. My hands rummaged through the soft, silky garments, folding and replacing them neatly in the drawer. I held a soft lavender nightie up to my face and breathed in deeply, sensing my mother's presence in the lingering scent of her perfume. A feeling of longing and loss passed through me. I found a sheer blouse and skirt that fit — sort of — with help from a safety pin. In the bathroom, I applied her bright red lipstick, and patted beige-colored powder over my cheeks and forehead. Then I carefully drew a dark brown line on each eyebrow. Finally, I brushed black mascara over my pale, blonde eyelashes.

So confident of the impression I made, I never noticed the glances and stares from the other kids, even from the crossing guard and the teacher as I made my way to school and into my classroom. I thought it was all in appreciation of my appearance.

The dance was a disaster. The last item I took from my mother's drawer was a pair of falsies, foam rubber with nipples that were meant to be worn underneath a brassiere, the one thing I didn't take. Everyone could see them and laugh at me, and they did. I was humiliated beyond my worst imagination and ran home, crying in shame. On top of that, Lady, our dog, needed to go out in the morning, and I used so much time preening for the dance that I didn't have time to take her out. She couldn't help relieving herself inside her pen, and when my father got home, he raged at me for using my mother's things, and for the mess inside the house. I'll never forget how ashamed I was.

I always thought I was the different one, different from other people I knew my own age. The truth is I didn't know much about their daily lives, or what their parents thought about their behavior. The only interaction I had with any teenagers was short lived — months, if that long. I had no idea where I stood in comparison to any other kid my age. My hair was a dirty dishwater blond. I was tall for my age, people said, though I was only 5'7." I weighed 125 lbs. and thought of myself as having a nondescript figure and only slightly budding breasts. While other girls had hair styles with names, mine hung in strange half curls, a clumsy attempt to imitate the others. The bright California sun washed the color out of everything, including me. I faded like the weed-infested lawns and adobe-dusted hills. All the connectedness I'd once felt was gone. I wanted to belong to a place, yet I could do very little about finding one. In a vague sort of way, I didn't exist.

My father had rented a small, two-bedroom apartment on the second floor of a Spanish styled four-plex. The roof was covered with paprika red tiles and the building itself had white stucco walls with arched windows. On top of each window were twisted, hammered black wrought-iron spears hung with canvas curtains that were tied to the sides of each window. Once the curtains served the purpose of shutting out the blinding sun, now they stayed in their tied-back positions. A cement driveway lead to garages at the rear of the building. Alongside it, a strip of earth was planted with rose bushes.

For years I hated roses. They grew easily in California and everyone had roses in their yards. The faded brown petals littered the ground and the thorns torn at my fingers when I tried to pick them. The ground wasn't real dirt as far as I was concerned but more like dusty and full of clods. It sucked water into itself with a gluttony of thirst.

The apartment was typical early California style, built in the thirties or forties to resemble Spanish Colonial buildings. Our rooms faced the south side of the building but always seemed dim and gloomy. The long dark hallway leading to the bath and bedrooms had fake candle holders that were electrified with orange glowing bulbs that gave little light. That is about all I can remember of this apartment, as I didn't care much for it. Yet, it had two redeeming features: In the back yard was a three-sided wooden grape arbor overgrown with dark twining leaves. In the shaded coolness were two metal-framed, old fashioned porch swings with plump padded cushions. The perfect place for hiding and dreaming.

The other special thing was our landlady, Mrs. Page. She was a widow about 50 years old, short, round and very cheerful. A kind, generous soul, she allowed my father to move in without paying the customary security deposit and last month's rent. My grandmother was staying with us to help my mother, who had just returned from the Sanatorium. Our family was finally back together again.

We moved to the apartment shortly before the school year began and in those last weeks of summer, we discovered the nearby park and public swimming pool. As often as I could, I spent my days in the park and the pool, loving the freedom but usually alone. My sisters were too young to roam with me, even though it was quite safe. My only other pastime was one of the joys about our new living arrangement — Mrs. Page. She belonged to the ladies' auxiliary of the Cootie Lodge. On the night of her regular weekly meeting, she would emerge wearing her Cootie finery, a burgundy velvet hat and vest adorned with hundreds of tiny jeweled pins. In a variety of sizes and shapes, the small pins spread out over her ample chest in an eye-catching array. The Cooties played Canasta, all the rage in the Fifties. Mrs. Page loved the card game. She was eager to teach me, my sister Pat, and Ruth Anne, a girl who lived across the hall from me. Rushing to finish our dinner each night, we met under the grape arbor, taking our places on the swings and setting up the card table between us. Until near midnight we "melded' and "went out" with laughter and constant challenging comments.

School began in September. I walked through the wet early morning grass in the park, then through the adobe dust of the school's baseball field. I looked forward to school at the beginning of each new year, but always found it difficult to make new friends. My problems with math and focusing attention on my work soon showed up again. No one noticed and gave me any help. Around this time a girl's looks, hair style, and clothing become very important, to attract attention from boys. I was very distressed as I became aware of this and knew my parents didn't have the money to spend on me. So, I kept silent and simply day-

dreamed about having those things and being one of the popular girls.

The telephone didn't ring at my house after school or evenings. I don't think we had a phone at all, so I couldn't sit talking on it for hours. I lived on the wrong side of town, away from wherever it was that everyone else lived. None of my classmates lived in my neighborhood. Whatever was "in" was a big secret to me. The clever sayings that kids considered cool were never part of my vocabulary, but I spoke very clear, polite English. What I thought about was of no interest to anyone as I had no friends, my sisters were too young to care, and my parents too besieged with their own personal problems. I lived inside my own head a lot, imagining that I had girlfriends to do things with, beautiful clothes, a real hair style and a boyfriend who took me to parties.

My mother was in and out of the hospital. When she was home, she stayed in bed most of the day, her room darkened by shades pulled to block the bright California sun. She washed her own dishes, sterilizing them with water boiled in a teakettle. She didn't hug me or kiss my cheeks, and when I forgot and came to close to her, she pushed me away.

The girls in my class were dizzy about one boy in particular. Tom Allard had a short, stocky build, dark brown hair, and green eyes with long fringing lashes. He was the best student in the class, with straight A's on his report card. The other top students constantly competed with him. He was the teacher's favorite, sat in the front row, and answered all the questions first. We must have thought the teacher was teaching Tom exclusively. He dressed perfectly in style, with just the right type of crease, roll, and color for every occasion. He acted self-confident, almost cocky. He seemed to have it all, then.

There is a clique in every school, that group of kids who are the best looking, get the best grades or play sports and get lots of attention. They hang out with each other and exclude the guys and girls who don't meet their ideas of specialness. Tom began Park School in kindergarten and grew up with most of the other kids in the class. They all lived near the school and Tom lived right across the street. His mother was actively involved in the PTA, his father was a member of the Masons and owned a roofing company. To top it all off, Tom was the rich kid in class, with a basketball court and a swimming pool in his yard. The house was a Spanish Colonial design with a manicured lawn and a rose garden kept in perfect shape by a Japanese gardener. An American flag flew prominently from a flagpole on their perfect lawn. Several expensive new cars were parked behind the gate that closed off the driveway. To everyone in the neighborhood as well as his school mates, he was a privileged kid on the top of the heap.

My mother came home from Olive View on a visit, and did not return, against medical advice. Her TB was still active, and she spent much of the day resting in bed, hoping to heal the disease. Although Streptomycin was being used successfully to treat her TB, I think she probably didn't know this and I later learned that she was afraid of hospitals and doctors, a fear she got from her mother, Ellen, who died of the disease one year before I was born.

When I was in ninth grade, Dad bought furniture for the house. He also bought a backyard patio from one of the many salesmen who roamed the newly built housing tracts, selling everything from fencing, landscaping, water conditioners, and patios. Dad couldn't pay for that either. He was driving a bus for the city and that wasn't a high-paying job.

Within a few months, the finance company was knocking at our door and upsetting my mother, because they were threatening to repossess our furniture. That was the first time I heard that ugly word – repossess. My mother was humiliated and became hysterical. Her crying brought me to the door. With roles reversed, I stood up to the man, like a mama lion protecting her cub, ordering him out of our house and yelling at him for threatening my sick mother. I was very frightened, but I was just as angry. My mother cried and it made me sick to my stomach and angry in my head. I wanted to kill that man for hurting my mother.

My father filed bankruptcy and our house was lost. Grandma brought my sisters back from Minneapolis and stayed long enough to help him pack up the house. My sisters went to stay with our Aunt Bernice, who was now separated from my Uncle George. Their life had turned downward when George was fired for stealing suits from the men's store where he worked. Bernice was living with Kathy in North Hollywood. My sisters were put into school there for a while.

New Normal

Seems school was OK for me until California—it was all new—walking across open, dusty fields—carrying a lunch bag, gone all day. Then it began, all the moving—a new school every year, new friends to be made and never were, living on the edge of the school district, never near enough to other classmates, new teachers, worries about things like the bills my parents always fought over, fights with relatives...

— *Diane Enfield*

Starting high school in California was the same as starting any new school, and there had been quite a few by that time. I was always the new kid in class, in the neighborhood, the one who sat alone at lunch, walked to school by myself, and had no friends. I never accepted the loneliness. I made friendly gestures to any girl or boy who sat next to me in class, stood in front of me in the cafeteria line, or took the same route home after school. The ones who responded were usually the outcasts of the group. I couldn't identify them that way then. I didn't know there were such people — outcasts. I thought of myself as "the new kid" in school. In my family I thought of myself as "different" in a bad way, not as "accepted" like my two sisters. They seemed to do the right things, to behave the way they were supposed to. Not that they became part of any school clique or popular set—they remained among the invisible, the marginal girls — those not distinguished by great beauty, rich husbands, professional careers, exceptional talent, or doting parents and perfect childhoods.

One day I was riding the bus to my freshman year at Covina High School, struggling with Algebra, and no one to help me with it. I was watching the girl down the block get accepted immediately by the cheer leader-football crowd. I was making fiber flower corsages at the art supply store in town and trying to find a friend ... and the next day I was on the train with my mother en route to Minnesota.

I was thirteen when my mother and I went back to Minneapolis to live with my grandmother and my uncle. It was the fall of 1952. I had already started the school year at Covina High School in Southern California, and Mom and I were still living in the two-story tract house in West Covina. We had only been there since the last part of May. I think we took the train in November.

It was cold, gray, and rainy when we arrived. The leaves were off the trees and lay slick on the wet pavement. Snow followed quickly, calf high, reddening and numbing my legs and feet. No money to buy boots. No money for anything I needed, and probably not anything my mother needed either. My father stayed in California, the house was lost in bankruptcy or some other sad financial snag. The dog, our third, sucked into some whirlpool of darkness that always seemed part of my life. I didn't say goodbye to any of my friends because I didn't have any.

It was like the Wild Mouse Ride at some amusement park in the past. You'd be riding along on a straight path when suddenly you'd be violently jerked off it, and on to a totally different direction. About the time you adjusted to the new path, the jerk and change of direction would hit you again. The difference between that ride and my life was who controlled the decision to ride. I don't recall ever crying about leaving; I just saw it as another new adventure, at least I did for many years.

Abrupt change was the constant in my life. A new school, a new neighborhood, a new house. One day my sisters were living with us and the next they were gone. Mother was sick and then she was home. I got disciplined by any adult who happened to be in the same place as I was. Sometimes it was one of my parents, my grandmother, or one of several aunts and uncles who randomly appeared to be in charge of me. Now at my grandmother's house, there were three people telling me what I did wrong but no one telling me what to do for myself.

I walked to school in the cold, in clothes not suited to the changing weather. Once I found my way around the school and my classes, finding friends was uppermost on my mind. I drew attention to myself in class by ignoring the subject matter and making smart comments. At Christmas, my uncle gave me a pair of ice skates. I went every day after school and stayed till the last minute before running home to dinner. The skating became a focus for my life. I loved the feeling of the wind rushing past my face, the cold no longer bothered me. I returned to the warming house, face flushed and body steaming, to relieve the pressure on my tightly laced feet, and see if anyone my age was there. Mostly it was boys who played ice hockey and clowned around in the warming hut. The smell of wet, woolen hats and mittens offended my nose. I got good on those skates. I was fast and could even skate backward and in circles. One night, near the end of the season, an older guy showed up at the ice rink. Without ice skates.

Art Paulson was sixteen. He had quit high school and worked at a gas station in a neighborhood I was forbidden to enter. He was about my height, which was short for a guy (5'7"), with black hair greased into a pompadour (style of the times), wore a black leather jacket and jeans. Art was the epitome of "cool' for the times. Looking more like a hood than he ever was, he was attractive to me and focused his attentions on me.

The outcasts began to gravitate to me, at my locker and in the hallways. The favorite area for hanging out was in the vestibule (a small area forming an airlock between the increasingly bitter outdoor temperature and the school hallways). Here the gang of fringe people stood and smoked illegally.

There was Eve Crane, a dark-haired, smart beauty whose short, stocky frame overwhelmed her self-esteem. I met her later in Sauk Centre but never knew what status offense she had committed to be sent there. I knew only that she was living with her divorced mother.

So was Diane Anderson: medium-height, thin build, dirty blonde hair, with blue eyes and an overly large mouth that smiled a lot, showing even, white teeth. She would break the worst of societal rules by hanging out with blacks, eventually becoming pregnant. Years later I would seek her out and find her living in a Minneapolis suburb, with several children, married to a policeman and trying hard to be a regular wife and mom. Then another twenty years passed by and I called her. She was surprised. She talked to me, her voice full of cool, street language, as if no time had passed. She was working in a factory, divorced, and living with her daughter who was, according to her, "a smart dancer, who socked away all her money and owned property."

I never called her when I got into town, as I promised. I made that mistake once before, when we were both on a home visit from Sauk Centre at Christmas time. Then she took me into the Black ghettos of Minneapolis and St. Paul, into the bars and after-hours clubs that flashed blue neon beer signs and white spotlights that lit up the eyes and toothy smiles of an all-Black clientele. My age didn't seem to matter to the men. I was barely fifteen and the husky voiced middle-aged Black man that propositioned me was on the far side of 40. Those people were too cool for me. I sounded way too straight and way too young and I knew it. From an after-hours jazz joint I followed a couple of people Diane seemed vaguely familiar with to a dilapidated, second floor apartment, that was nearly bare and barely lit. A bare bulb hanging from the ceiling shone a light on her unwholesome sphere of interests. We had nothing in common except surviving the years in Sauk Centre.

Several other girls also hung out with the smokers in the school, girls I tried to befriend, but who seemed to share inside jokes that often made me the butt. Jenny and her twin sister Gerry Jenson, Diane Lawson. Never very attractive girls, they all had some noticeable flaw. Diane's nose was permanently snubbed and sat atop two huge front teeth. Jenny was nearly six feet tall, rail-thin with stooped posture. Spit was always forming at the sides of her mouth, with long threads of it strung from lip to lip when she spoke. She was bony and angular, awkward from having grown tall too fast. Her sister Gerry was a fraternal twin and nearly as short as Jenny was tall. She had a pug nose and freckles, and her hair hung around her face in clumps.

We formed a club with red jackets, and a name I've now forgotten embroidered on the back. I never had one. Walking down the avenue, strutting our belonginess with me bringing up the rear, one bitterly cold winter night. None of us in clothing warm enough for the weather. Broadway Street Northeast was the cruising street, not that many of us had cars for cruising; we mostly walked. We walked a circuit of small cafes, from a tiny six-stool diner called Mickies to the Chinese Café and on to a bar with a pool hall. Sometimes we haunted the roller rink, though we now considered ourselves too old for that crowd. The boys we were after didn't hang around roller rinks. Mostly they were high school dropouts, reform school guys, "hoods." We drank bad coffee in heavy mugs, Cokes with a paper straw from green bottles, and smoked Lucky Strikes, Camels, and Pall Malls. No one ever seemed to have the money for anything more. Usually I was home by eleven, which was way too late for a thirteen-year-old girl on a school night, according to my mother. I am sure she was right. I never did any homework — I'd given up.

In the month or so before Christmas, the excitement at school revolved around a dance that was scheduled and the class Christmas party. The party was to be held on the Friday before the school holiday closing and the dance the same evening. I wanted to go to that dance desperately and I needed a new outfit so I could fit in. I asked my parents to give me clothes for my Christmas gift and allow me to get them early for the dance and party. My father took me downtown and I selected a powder blue pullover sweater and a smoky brown "pencil line" skirt. The skirt hugged my figure, it was the latest in style. I was very excited with my new outfit and felt as if I measured up, at last. Mother was annoyed with the skirt telling me that she thought it was too grown up for me. Yet, all the girls in my class dressed in them and I couldn't understand her objection. The afternoon of the class party, I received a lot of attention about my new clothes and I felt attractive and accepted. It was a new and glorious feeling for me. As the day wore on I was even more exhilarated, thinking about the dance that evening. Knowing that my father would refuse to drive me to any event, I made arrangements to go with one of the other girls. Something happened to the arrangements, I never got to the dance. Within the next few days we moved again.

I had moved with my parents quite a bit by the time Mother and I returned to Minneapolis to live while we waited for my father, who was still in California, to make the next plan for reuniting our family. I am not sure where my sisters were at this time, Pat may have been with us at my grandma's and Cheryl was either in Springfield, Ill or both may have been with my Aunt Bernice in California. My home and family life were in a deep state of confusion, and consequently so was I.

School was boring. I couldn't concentrate or focus on the learning I had to do there. I was too busy trying to figure out answers to my loneliness and my own personal needs. Again, I had no friends to pal around with, talk to, do the things that normal teenagers were doing. In fact, I had no idea what a normal teenager should be doing with their life.

I suppose Bob Richardson, whom I met when I was about fourteen, should be named as my first love. From the fall of the ninth grade at Jordan Junior High School until I met Bob in the late spring of the school year, I'd met a few of my classmates. I hung out at the local roller rink with Art and Anna Mae, hung out on Broadway Avenue with an assortment of teenagers (all from other dysfunctional families) and eventually met Bob. He had just been released from the Red Wing State School for Boys. He was older than me, I think he had just turned seventeen in May of that spring, and I was fourteen the previous fall. I guess he had either graduated from high school or quit, I never did find out which it was. He was one of the richer teenagers on the street, though his family wasn't really that well off. Both his parents worked, and they owned their own house, which was meticulously clean and orderly. His parent bought Bob a fairly new, flashy bright red Ford convertible in which he cruised the avenue and the local root beer stand drive-in. No one else that hung out owned a car. I lost my virginity to him one summer evening, after I had spent the previous nine months—a school year—in Sauk Centre.

Most of these kids came from divorced families who were on welfare. They lived in substandard, multiple-family housing, the interiors of which were disorderly and often dirty. Their mothers worked at low-level jobs in factories, restaurants, and bars. I don't remember anyone besides Bob and Anna Mae having a father, and only Bob's father worked. The guys were often several years older than the girls they "dated." I suppose this was because the girls their own ages had moved beyond the avenue into marriages, pregnancies, prison, or bar nightlife where the" real men" were. I don't recall hearing any success stories where a girl returned to school, went to college, made a good marriage, or got a career job. Mostly these kids were truants, jobless, recently released from the state juvenile system homes, or barely hanging onto the edge of a normal life.

For reasons I will never understand, Bob and I picked each other, and remained something beyond friends for another five to seven years. Most of the time we were away from each other — Bob in the St. Cloud Reformatory on several separate sentences, myself in Sauk Centre on two different occasions before I left Minneapolis to return to California with my mother. Within four months I quit school and ran away from home, back to Minneapolis. I was seventeen. I stayed in Minneapolis for a year, visiting Bob at St. Cloud, waiting for him to get released.

The following autumn he finally got out on parole, and within a few days I saw him with another girl, Josie. I learned he had been writing to her during the same time he was writing to me. Josie was a welfare mother and lived with her baby at home with her mother. The way that I thought then put Josie into the slut category. I found it disgusting and mortifying to know that somehow, we were classed together as "his girlfriends." I was overwhelmed by this knowledge and left town a few days later, returning home to my parents most current house in California. My father was not glad to see me.

At home, I spent hours listening to popular love songs on the radio, crying and brooding over my feelings and loss. I thought all my dreams of being loved and getting married were gone.

What was I going to do with myself and my life now? I had no idea. I hadn't graduated from high school and my job skills were nil. I had no idea that I was smart, and no one who could help me understand this. I signed up for adult high school in Alhambra but couldn't discipline myself to get to class, or to believe it would lead to anything. Then I got a job as a trainee nurse's aide at the Alhambra Community Hospital, working the 11pm to 7am night shift in the Ob-Gyn Department of that small hospital. At first it was interesting, and I learned a lot. I spent time reading the medical textbooks that were available at the nursing station and was fascinated by all the things that could go wrong with women and babies and their bodies. It opened a new world to me, the world of medicine, and it has engaged my attention ever since.

I thought about what I might do in the medicine field. I could not see any way of becoming a doctor. I doubted my intelligence and ability. There was no past school record to indicate otherwise. Furthermore, I didn't know about colleges and medical schools and the educational process for that exalted profession. I considered nursing, often wearing the nurses hats that were left on the coat room shelves by the off-duty staff. I'd simply pin them on to my head after I had walked a few blocks away from the hospital, stopping at the local cafe for morning coffee, watching for admiring glances.

This satisfaction soon paled, and I stopped the charade. I began to get bored and unhappy with a job I knew could not get me anywhere. The money was paltry, even in those years, and the work was tedious and unchallenging.

True love

True love, like any other strong and addicting drug, is boring — once the tale of encounter and discovery is told, kisses quickly grow stale and caresses tiresome... except, of course, to those who share the kisses, who give and take the caresses while every sound and color of the world seems to deepen and brighten around them.
As with any other strong drug, true first love is really only interesting to those who have become its prisoners. And, as is true of any other strong and addicting drug, true first love is dangerous.
— *Stephen King*

About nine-thirty one summer Friday evening, my sister Cheryl and I were walking home from shopping in Alhambra. Alhambra was a small, neat, clean, and safe suburb of Los Angeles. The stores were closed, and we were walking slowly, taking our time getting home. I saw a guy driving past us in a brand-new, white Ford Fairlane with a gold stripe on its side. I recognized him immediately when I saw his face, even though it had been five and a half years since we were in the same eighth grade class at Park School.

I yelled out his name, "Tom Allard! Hi!"

He swung his car around, blocking our path as we came to the next cross street. I was excited — he was still as good looking as I remembered. He asked us where we were going, and offered us a ride home. I accepted because I knew him. He said he remembered me from grade school, though I felt sure he was lying—remember, I felt like I was invisible then. I was turning cartwheels in my mind, and my stomach was full of butterflies as we talked about ourselves. When we reached our apartment, Cheryl got out of the car and walked inside. My family had moved about ten times since I met Tom in the eighth grade. The next thing I knew, he asked me to go to the drive-in movie with him. "Oh, my

God," I thought, "This is a real date with someone I am really attracted to." He was the guy every girl in that eighth-grade class wanted, and he was asking me out.

I still lived at home with my parents, and although I was 18, I knew they would put up a fuss if I asked to go. I told him I had to be home early, so we went to a popular local drive-in restaurant, ordered cokes and fries, and talked. Then he drove me home, and we sat I front of the apartment talking for many hours.

Tom told me he graduated from Alhambra High School, and he was on summer vacation from his first year at USC. He was transferring to UCLA in the fall. He'd be back in school after Labor Day, a few weeks away. He was majoring in English and pre-law and had joined the Beta Theta Pi fraternity. He was tanned and good looking. He had green eyes and perfect teeth. His appearance was meticulous.

I know I didn't tell him that I had quit school, or much of anything about my past five years. There was nothing to be proud of. My parents had moved many times, and I had spent nearly two years in the Minnesota State Home School for Girls, under court order as a ward of the state. Mostly, my life was lonely and confused. I had no friends except my sisters. I slept on the living room couch in the small two-bedroom apartment my parents rented near the start of the summer. From the ninth grade until shortly before meeting Tom again, I was involved with Bob Richardson, who spent most of his teenage years on probation or parole for car theft and other offenses. After quitting high school, I ran away from home in California to be with Bob in Minnesota, while he was in the State Reformatory. I had attempted suicide once. I was not employed.

The only good thing about my life was the apartment building's swimming pool—I loved the water and used it every day. Tom asked if he could see me the next day, and asked for my phone number. I was in heaven. It seemed like the first break in my life. What a break it turned out to be! Tom was my knight on a white horse, my big chance—a miracle.

Part of the in-group in high school, Tom was captain of the basketball team, senior class vice-president, a National Merit Scholarship recipient and always on the honor roll with nearly straight A's. He competed with his best friend Eddie from grade school on. Eddie grew past six feet tall and became the captain of the football team and senior class president. Tom stopped growing at about five feet ten, not large enough for the football team. Yet both boys were the most desirable males in their peer group:

Tom with brown hair and beautiful, heavy lashed green eyes and Eddie, a tall blonde, blue-eyed, and always tan Golden Boy. To his family and schoolmates, Tom seemed normal and blessed with good looks, athletic ability, and intelligence. He was admired and envied. At graduation he had Honors at Entrance to three major California universities, choosing USC for its prestige. He planned to be a lawyer.

At USC, something happened between Tom and another friend, Arnie. He would sometimes refer to the "screwing he got from Arnie," but refused to discuss the details. Tom also began taking Dexedrine to study for exams. The pills came from an ex-high school buddy whose father was a well-known physician in Alhambra. At the end of his freshman year at USC, Tom decided to transfer to UCLA, where he joined the national fraternity Beta Theta Pi.

I made careful preparations for his picking me up the next day, showering and dressing with special care. I borrowed a book about the life of Sigmund Freud from our bachelor neighbor next door, Bob. Wearing a pair of tortoiseshell reading glasses (with almost no lens correction) I sat with my open book, waiting for him to arrive. Sending my sister to the door, I affected my sexiest pose. After we were sitting in the car, he told me he was really impressed with my choice of literature and asked me if I was interested in psychology. I assured him I was. That must have been the perfect bait for him. He was likely experiencing the early symptoms of his schizophrenia and starting to feel desperate about what was happening to him.

Several days passed and I didn't hear from Tom. I began thinking of a way to see him in case he didn't call again. I called him up and told him I had some record albums he might like to hear — would he like it if my sister and I came over? His parents and sister were away at a local resort on vacation, and his house was empty. He agreed, and so did Cheryl, reluctantly. Tom and I made pretenses of interest in the records, as we played them and the three of us talked, though my sister was four years younger than us and shy. Tom drove Cheryl home about ten p.m., and we returned to his house. He took me out to the pool and suggested we go for a swim, as I had brought my bathing suit. We splashed water at each other, wrestled and I got dunked under and then he finally kissed me. We were so physically attracted to each other, it just never ended. The next thing I knew I was in his small twin bed and we were attempting to make love. I can hardly recall what it was like, but we were both relatively inexperienced. I had been with Bob Richardson twice, and it was Tom's first time. We fell in love.

We tried to elope to Las Vegas, but we were only nineteen years old, and the groom had to be twenty-one. We returned home to face our parents. Tom was due to start class at UCLA in two weeks.

I was certainly not the kind of girl Tom's parents had in mind for him. I was a far cry from his old high school sweetheart, Barbara. However, they agreed to help us out. They would give us the same amount of money for an apartment of our own that they would have paid for Tom's fraternity room and board. We looked at places, but every one was too expensive, too far from school, or a dump. We gave up. Tom's semester was about to begin, so he had to move into the Beta Theta Pi fraternity house as planned previously. I would continue to stay at my parents' apartment.

When he invited me to the first frat party of the year, I was filled with a mixture of emotions. Of course, I wanted very much to go, as it would mean getting a look at the life I was never able to be part of before. It was planned as a dressy cocktail party, and I shopped for several days before I found what I thought was the perfect outfit. Who paid for the outfit I can't recall, but I purchased a confection of a dress, a perfect combination of sweet and sexy. The skirt of the black dress was made with several layers of sheer fabric overlaying a taffeta underskirt. It floated at knee length. The midriff was made of the same shirred fabric from the fitted waist to the bodice. My shoulders were barely covered with a single layer of the fabric tucked into the shirring, underneath a layer of flesh-colored taffeta overlaid with black Chantilly lace. I bought black satin pumps and clutch bag, and completed the outfit with white satin elbow-length gloves, that buttoned at the wrist with tiny white pearls. It was the most beautiful dress I had ever worn, and I felt elegant in it.

The September weather normally would have been perfect for the dress, as it was usually cool in the evenings. However, it changed that day and stayed in the 80s into the evening. I had so few clothes over the years that I knew little about appropriate clothing styles. I knew the gloves would be best left off. They were hot, but they were an absolute necessity because they covered large psoriasis plaques on my elbows, and my nylon stockings did the same for my knees. Despite the heat, I could not remove them for comfort's sake.

When we arrived at the fraternity house, I could see several girls sitting on the stone railings of the outside deck. My heart fell into my stomach when I saw they were wearing tank tops, Bermuda shorts, and white tennis shoes. In a panic, I turned to Tom, but he was already shaking hands and greeting his fraternity brothers as we climbed the stairs. I was instantly surrounded by a circle of guys, shaking my hands and introducing themselves. Their last names were a list of well-known celebrities. Off and on Tom filled me in, "Dan's father is the owner of the Yankees. He was married to Sonya Heine."

Then I was smiling, saying hello, fielding questions flying at me from every direction—questions like:

"Do you go to school here?"

"What's your major?"

"Where'd you meet Tom?"

"What's your father do, again?"

"Why haven't I seen you around before?"

Tom's frat brothers and their girls were looking me over, eyes going up and down my body and my dress, their hands drawn up to cover whispering mouths—it undid me. The heat from the night and the crowd became unbearable. I had to get away, immediately. Tom had disappeared into the crowd. I mumbled some excuse to the son of Ray Miland and headed down the stairs to the street. I began to cry hysterically. I was a nothing. My beautiful dress was in bad taste, my father was a bus driver, I had no major, I hadn't even graduated from high school—they knew it, I knew they knew it. They were laughing at me.

At the corner I was out of sight. I wiped the tears and snot on my gloves, and began to run through the streets of Westwood, having no idea where I was. I found a phone booth and called Gladys, Tom's mother, sobbing and blubbering into the phone as I tried to explain. She was mad at me for leaving!

"How do you think it made Tom look to his fraternity brothers?! What were you being such a baby for?"

I was flabbergasted and speechless.

"You go right back to that party," she ordered, "We can't come all the way out to UCLA to pick you up!"

Then Tom drove up in his car alongside the phone booth. I got in and sat crying harder, choking on my words, saying nothing comprehensible. I guess he took me home then.

We needed to be together. I knew I was desperately lonely, but I didn't know then how badly he needed me, too. We planned that I would find a job and an apartment near the university, so we could see each other when he had time between studies. It was too far to go back to Alhambra with the course load he had. I moved to Westwood and talked my way into a job in the Industrial Relations Department at UCLA. They hired me as a secretary for Professor Tannenbaum. The apartment was about three blocks from the school. One wet, gray weekend, Tom, my sisters, and the neighbor, Bob Ford, helped move me into the new apartment. We celebrated with pizza, and later took a drive down to a gloomy, stormy beach. Tom began to stay away from the fraternity house where he lived, spending more time at my apartment. He began to avoid the fraternity functions. We went out less and less, and when we did go out, it was just the two of us, alone.

Slowly Tom moved more and more of his stuff into the apartment: a desk and study lamp, some clothes, his books. I was trying to learn my job at the University, but I was totally unskilled and my typing was slow and full of mistakes. The notes I took in shorthand could not be translated, so I made up the messages. I was worried about the job for good reasons. One beautiful fall afternoon, Tom took me out for pizza at Michelle's on La Cienega Blvd. It was one of the college kids' "in" places. The shield-shaped gold emblem with the onyx facing, embedded with a tiny diamond, was a pre-engagement ritual, he told me. The pin was physical evidence that I needed, to believe that Tom meant it when he told me he loved me, promising me we'd get married when he graduated. It meant I was acceptable, and not just a girl from the wrong side of the tracks that he could lay and leave.

Meanwhile, those fall evenings found Tom studying in my apartment, taking "breaks" to make love. Sex was like a drug to us. I'd be in bed asleep only to wake and find him on top of me, kissing my thighs, or he'd be seated at the desk wrapped up in English Lit, and I would unbutton his pants and fondle him until he gave up, and back in bed we'd fall. Saturday and Sunday mornings in bed stretched on to mid-afternoons or early evenings. Tom was getting flak from his fraternity brothers, for not participating in the house functions. Nothing else got done. Tom and I didn't keep a regular schedule. He was taking Dexedrine to stay awake and study and had taken it since high school. Within a few weeks, I took some of the drug on several occasions, and found I could stay awake for several days and get my apartment cleaned, and I began writing long, long diary entries about my feelings. I knew almost nothing about the drug, except it was used for losing weight. Even Tom's mother took them for dieting. Com-

ing down from those pills was really bad. I got so depressed I could do nothing, including showing up for work. I was fired, of course. I lost my job and couldn't pay the rent. I had to move out. But where?

By this time, Tom felt that my moving back with my parents would not be a good idea. He talked to his parents and asked them to let me stay there. They decided I should go back and finish high school, and then go on to college. I was smart, Tom told them. They agreed. Tom went back to UCLA to finish out the semester, returning home on weekends whenever he could. Tom decided to quit school when the Spring semester was over and move back home himself. Things were apparently getting worse for him, though he never tried to explain the strange things happening to him.

Getting me back into school was a problem. I quit high school in the beginning of my senior year. I knew my school record was a mess. I needed to do my junior year over, because of the inadequate tenth and eleventh grade classes at Sauk Centre. So, there I was, back in the real world in California, enrolling in a new school and trying again, taking the eleventh grade over in another attempt to clean up my life and create the path I really wanted. But by the first weeks of biology and algebra, I was back in a mess.

When I moved into the Allard's house, I got some of the help I needed. They took me to a dentist and my teeth were capped, cavities filled, and a set of bridges for top and bottom inserted. I had a few bills, which Tom's Dad paid. They sent me to Pasadena City College, a junior college which accepted people without high school diplomas into classes. I liked the classes, Anatomy and Physiology, Marriage and Family, and some others I can't remember. I joined the Chi Delta Sorority, and as far as the Avards were concerned I was on my way. I shared a room with Tom's sister Cindi, who was in eighth grade at the same elementary school where I first met Tom, six years earlier. I used their swimming pool and took all my meals with them. At nineteen, I still didn't have a driver's license, and was walking or taking a bus wherever I went. I found a ride to and from school, so that problem was solved.

Tom quit school at the end of the fall semester and took a job working for his father at the roofing company as a laborer. At the end of each day he was filthy and exhausted. He began to argue and criticize his parents, and fight with everyone. He took a job as a mail carrier and moved out to his own apartment to try and sever ties with his family. He signed up for evening college classes at California State College, Los Angeles, and began a routine that included psychotherapy at a small psychiatric hospital near his apartment. The therapist was involved with Timothy Leary's ideas about LSD therapy, and talked Tom into taking LSD at another small psychiatric hospital, Capistrano by the Sea. At the time, Tom was reading the Tibetan Book of the Dead, the Bhagavad Gita, and a mixture of other books I had never heard of. He was trying to build himself up by lifting weights, and taking mega-doses of vitamin C and niacin.

He came over to his parents' house to use the washing machine, check out the contents of the refrigerator, and see me. He began to get more hostile to his family. He refused all offers from his mother except food and laundry. He made nasty remarks to everyone, zeroing in on their weaknesses with the fierce accuracy of a sniper. He called his father Dick "a tyrant, a little man with a nasty, violent temper," his sister Cindi, "a spoiled brat," took to calling his mother Gladys, "Glad Ass." He told me she was, a two-faced hypocrite and a liar. He called his older brother Richard Allard, Jr., "Dickie Boy," emphasizing Dick's continued financial dependence on his parents. They all continued to put up with his verbal abuse. Any attempt to make ordinary conversation with him was met with searing insults. He was convinced his parents were the source of his need for therapy, and that they had "screwed him up." He said I needed to move back to my parents, or I too would be infected, so I did that.

My family moved again, but stayed in Alhambra. My sister Pat graduated from high school and worked as a clerk in a local finance company. My sister Cheryl was still in high school in the same town. The place was a small two-bedroom apartment, and again I slept on the couch. The house was always full of tension. My father continued to use sleep to deal with his depression and fatigue, causing arguments at the dinner table and upsetting everyone. I still had my ride to school for a few weeks, and then it was gone. Not having a car was a major problem, especially in California. I couldn't connect with a bus line to the college, couldn't make the sorority meetings or parties, and I didn't have any money for anything. Getting a job seemed the only way now. I quit school, but never told Tom's parents. What good would it have done? I couldn't ask for more help, and why would anyone give me a car, which was what I needed?

I was only a block from the public bus to downtown Los Angeles, so I applied for a job at the Psychiatric Department of the LA

County Hospital. The secretarial job was paid partially by LA County and part by the USC Department of Psychology and located in the Psychiatric Unit of the hospital. My boss, Dr. Edward Stainbrook, was the hospital's Chief Psychiatrist and a professor at USC. Again, my lack of secretarial skills worked against me. After several embarrassing incidents, I was let go.

Tom broke up with me. He refused to see me or talk to me about the break-up. Feeling rejected, angry and desperate about Tom leaving me, I bought a pellet gun that looked like a real revolver, found Tom at his parents' house, and confronted him in the doorway, pulling the gun on him. Tom's father rushed out and struggled with me to get the gun. In the end, I talked to Tom, but he was adamant about ending the relationship.

Nothing fell into place for me, and I attempted suicide by swallowing pills. My brother-in-law took me to the hospital, where my stomach was pumped. Shortly after that, I left California and returned to Minneapolis, where my parents had moved once again. I wasn't welcome when I arrived at my parents' apartment in Minneapolis, so I stayed with my grandmother a few blocks away. I looked up old friends, but they either had moved, or were living lives of equal desperation. I got a job as a cocktail waitress, wearing a skimpy costume and putting up with continual assaults by the men in the bar. I did everything I could to stop thinking about Tom. I dated a football coach at the University of Minnesota and my friend Anna's ex-husband, and finally met Bill, a car salesman whom I found very attractive.

Then the bombshell hit: I was pregnant. With instructions from a friend who worked at a hospital, I attempted a self-administered abortion. I succeeded in aborting the fetus, but it caused me to hemorrhage badly. Holding pressure with a towel to try to control the bleeding, I rode the bus to General Hospital and was admitted. After I returned home, my mother handed me the aborted fetus that she retrieved from the toilet, and told me to take care of it. It was one of the cruelest things she ever did to me. Bill dumped me. Soon I returned to California to stay at my sister's apartment.

Within a few days, Tom was at my front door. He missed me. He told me he was still in love with me, but I must not see his family—they weren't good for him. Tom was still working for the post office. He moved to another apartment and gave up his plan to continue college at night school, but he was still seeing a therapist as an outpatient. He refused to discuss his therapy with me. Tom relented on the issue of my association with his family but main-

tained his own distance. Seeking a solution to what seemed inevitable, Tom's parents offered to pay my bills and tuition at Pasadena City College if I would go to school. I agreed to go, but still couldn't discipline myself, and quit.

Tom broke up with me again.

On the Rebound

"The current girlfriend, boyfriend, wife, or husband is often an utterly unsuccessful attempt to stop missing or loving the previous one."
— Mokokoma Mokhonoana

I met Dave Palmer in August 1963 at a small bar in Pasadena. That summer I was living down at the beach, taking care of two young adult women who were polio invalids. The job was not the greatest, but it gave me a chance to stay at the beach for a couple of weeks and get away from the memories of my breakup with Tom. While I was down at the beach, I met quite a few different guys and for a while I was making two dates a night. I was at my most attractive stage of life, thin and tanned, my skin was clear of the psoriasis due to the tan, and the sun streaked my hair nicely. For some reason I quit that job and moved back home with my parents. They were living in a small apartment in Alhambra and were not happy to have me back. Maybe I could have gotten myself together then but being back in Alhambra with all the old memories of Tom and me were blocking my thinking.

One evening I made arrangements to go out with my girlfriend, Dorothy. She and I had worked together at the Star News Paper in Pasadena, handling the classified ads. Dorothy was still working there. She wanted to meet a man and we decided to meet at a bar called Barnacle Bill's on Foothill Blvd. It was a small bar, filled with people when we went in. We sat at the bar and ordered our drinks. I reached to get a cigarette and when I went to light it, someone behind me flicked a lighter on and held it up to light my cigarette. I turned around to see who it was. Yes, I thought he was handsome, tall, sandy blonde hair and well built. He sat down next to me and we began talking. Dorothy was off talking to someone else by this time. We talked and flirted until nearly closing time. He asked to take me home and I agreed though it was totally out of character for me. I guess I was very attracted to him and he seemed to have enough safe, local credentials. The night was warm, and I was feeling very free. My mind told me not to think, just act, forget Tom, and get on with life. I wasn't ready to end the evening, and neither was he. Though our reasons were probably entirely different. I suggested we go for a ride to a place I knew in the nearby San Gabriel Mountains. Camp Williams was a familiar favorite of mine and every chance I got I found my way there. I loved the tree shaded stream and the restaurant's outdoor patio with its colored lanterns.

By the time we got there, the lights were out and the small cafe was closed, but the wind rustled through the canyon oaks and the sound of the creek drew me down the dirt road to it. We sat on a grassy bank and he put his arms around me, drawing me down and kissing me with passion. At first, I enjoyed the feeling of this stranger. He was new and exciting. Of course he was interested in more than kissing, and his hands began to cup my breast. Suddenly electrified by the position I'd put myself in, I sat up and shoved him away.

"I'm sorry, but I didn't mean for this to go so far."

"What did you expect when you brought me here?"

I realized he was right, but I was able to explain myself. He behaved like a gentleman and I was impressed with his behavior. We left and he drove me home. It was nearly 5:30 am when we finally parked in front of my place. He asked me to go out again with him that evening and I agreed.

Dave was staying with some old high school friends in Rosemead, just off Valley Blvd. It was Memorial Day weekend and they were planning a trip to the Colorado River as well as a reunion party with other friends. That night we went together to the home of his married friends. There were fifteen to twenty people at the party. My mood was decidedly upbeat and the part of me that can be very provocative and on parade was out. Thinking that he and I were just a temporary twosome, I poured on the personality. I am ashamed to admit now that I told one lie after another. The more attention I got from Dave and his friends, the bigger the lies got. I told them I had graduated from UCLA with a major in Psychology, and then I proceeded to hand out advice and free analysis. They really seemed to like me and gathered in a circle around me asking questions. By the time we left, Dave was smashed. I can still recall helping him down the three low steps to the sidewalk. I can't recall who drove from there, and it makes me think about the many times I've warned my daughters about riding with people who drink.

We went to an all-night cafe on Rosemead Boulevard. across from the high school where he graduated. We drank coffee and talked for several hours. By that time, he was sober and told me he was enrolled at San Jose State College as a major in Electrical Engineering. He joined the Army after high school, becoming a paratrooper in the 82nd Airborne. When his stint was over, he returned to his parents' home in Citrus Heights, California and attended American River Junior College. He was using his GI funds and a small scholarship for school. I don't remember what I told him about myself. It began to seem there was magic between us. Now I think it must have been strong sexual attraction, but then I just felt like I was being pulled along by fate. He talked about the way he felt about me, something he couldn't explain and had never felt before.

"Maybe you're in love with me," I said.

Oh, to be sure I was glib. The idea came to me like a flash and the words flowed out of my mouth like golden honey. He took the hook and I was so surprised that I couldn't stop. I felt like I had some superpower over him.

"Why don't you ask me to marry you?" I asked.

He hesitated for a moment and then he asked, "Will you marry me?"

"Yes, when?" I answered.

He seemed puzzled, but I continued, "How about now, right now?"

"Do you mean it"? he asked.

It was wild, a game I thought. This was a very exciting game we were playing, and I wasn't ready to let it end yet.

We left the cafe and drove to the house of the friend he was staying with. Several guys were sleeping when we walked in. Dave woke them up and began introductions. His best friend Bill made some attempt to reason with us, but Dave didn't hear him.

We were both incredibly high on this adventure and left for my apartment to get my things. I packed a few necessary items, making sure to include my white negligee (I finally found a real use for it). My mother and father woke up and my mother confronted me sternly. My father stayed in bed, advising my mother that it was useless to try to reason with me. It upsets me now when I try to reason with my own daughter and remember how I couldn't hear what my mother was telling me. I thought it was my life, my own adventure and no one else was going to live it for me. I couldn't foresee the consequences that might ensue from that impetuous decision.

We set off on the San Bernardino Freeway to the Mojave Desert and Las Vegas. It was only a few hours before dawn when we left LA. Near Barstow we stopped for breakfast. I only drank coffee. The bright morning sun had dawned and the glare from the desert floor hurt my eyes. I put on my dark glasses, knowing I was hiding from more than the stark desert light. By now I felt a gritty unwashed film on my body and clothing irritating me. I became aware of doubt popping up among my thoughts and quickly put it aside. To turn back was to face my parents and give an explanation for my actions. Nothing in my life would have changed. At least I had made a drastic change in the direction of my life. I wanted to get married and have a family of my own, I wanted someone to love. I was so unsure of my power to attract a mate that I thought this might be the only way someone would be interested in me. After all, nothing that happened in my life so far led me to believe that anything else was true. Tom left me, and my first love Bob Richardson preferred the company of a girl even further down on the social ladder, an unmarried mother from a family of welfare recipients and alcoholics. A brassy bleached blond named Josie, with a loud coarse voice. Her very name was an insult to me. I knew too little about the world and what was possible for me. Women were expected to marry and raise a family unless they couldn't get a husband. The few women I knew that worked were old maids or post-menopausal married women in dreary jobs as department store clerks. College was not an option for me and if there were any others, I wasn't aware of them. Society dictated few options for women. My family's financial position narrowed the choices even further. I can't say I went over all those ramifications during that long drive to Vegas. Most of my understanding of what life had to offer came to me through the process of acculturation during my years growing up. Opportunities to take other paths always seemed to require risks. This was another one of my attempts to find a better life.

Dave sensed my discomfort and attempted to make conversation. He wanted to talk about our future. I was too afraid if I talked I might change my mind, so I made an excuse about being too tired. He seemed cheerful enough and if he had any doubts himself, he never voiced them. By the time we got to Vegas and bought a wedding ring, a plain narrow gold band for me, it was noon. The License bureau was closed for lunch hour and we were told to come back at 1:00 p.m., Back at City Hall later, we filled out the applications for a marriage license. I was so nervous I had to start over twice. I recall thinking that I had used up my three chances to change my mind. First, at the breakfast stop, then again when the license office was closed and finally with the mistakes as I filled out the application. I could have turned back, and now I wonder at the meaning of that foreshadowing.

Shortly after we completed filling out the license applications, we entered the judge's chambers and took the standard wedding vows. I felt giddy and faint as we walked, holding hands, out into the hot, bright desert day. The balance of the daylight hours we spent in one casino or another playing the slot machines and drinking Gin and Tonics. I was never much of a drinker. Even through my teenage years, drinking was something I rarely did. By the time I met Dave, my limit was two beers in a bar a few times a year, at most. This was not the case for Dave as I understood years later. I couldn't tell you how much he drank that day. Dave had some money with him; however, I didn't ask him about it, and I recall only that it wasn't a lot. When we won several jackpots in a row it was a big surprise, and we talked about it as an omen of good fortune for our union. At some point in the day, Dave called his mother and father in California. His father answered the phone, then told Helen that Dave was in Las Vegas and was married. I believe there was some comment about whether he married a show girl. Apparently, his mother almost fainted during the conversation. Dave told them we would be in Sacramento to see them as soon as we could after getting settled in college at San Jose State.

By late afternoon, we had been up over 48 hours. The combined effect of the excitement, desert heat, liquor, and success at the slot machines began to wear on Dave. He suggested we get a room and some rest. The alarm bells went off in my head. I was going to have to sleep with this man I hardly knew — take off all my clothes and have sex! The thought of such intimacy with this virtual stranger scared the hell out of me and I said I would like to get my hair done at the hotel's beauty salon while he took a shower and a short nap in the room. My brain was working overtime as I sat under the hair dryer, feeling sheer panic.

Back in the room, I suggested we go out for a special wedding dinner, which we did. As we were dressing for dinner and drinking champagne, I glanced out the hotel window. We were on the tenth floor and dusk was falling over the desert. The sky was pink with blue and deep purple hills and mountains in the distance. As the sky above shaded to a deeper blue the stars were just begin-

ning to twinkle, and within moments the heavens were full of the tiny white lights. It was magic to me. I felt a joy that I rarely experienced — an excitement that made me tremble. All too quickly, the moment passed and panic resumed its hold on my imagination. Dinner, I thought — we haven't had dinner. Dave reluctantly agreed to go out to dinner. A photograph of the two of us at the Stardust Hotel Restaurant shows how very young and beautiful we were then. We toasted our marriage with Pearl Divers — mine had a real pearl in the bottom of the glass. Dinner ended and I could deny Dave no longer. He was tired, though I was filled with fearful nervous energy.

Back at the hotel, I insisted on making phone calls to my grandmother and parents to tell them I was a married woman. I didn't hear much enthusiasm from their end, which was probably notable. Finally, exhausted and exasperated with my delay tactics, in a determined voice Dave told me it was time to go to bed. I insisted I needed a shower. I couldn't figure out any other way to take off my clothes in private. I showered and put on the white negligee. As I left the bathroom, the light from the bathroom illuminated my body. I reached for the light switch and heard Dave let out a long deep sigh. I slipped into the bed and his arms went around me, and as he bent his head to kiss me, I let go of my fear and melted into his body.

The following morning we returned to LA, stopping to pick up my belongings and Dave's friend, Jim. I can't recall my parents' reaction to our marriage. I am sure they were upset and bewildered but when I think about it, I just cannot remember any words between us. I do remember that I wrote a note to Tom. I drove over to the post office where he worked and left it under the windshield wiper. It was short and to the point. I told of the regret and pain I felt about the end of our relationship. I'm sure he never expected such a rash act from me.

We headed for San Jose and Dave's apartment for the fall semester. His roommates were there already. I recall a small celebration. Later we discovered someone had strung a bell under the bed springs. That twin bed was too cozy for two people our size. Within a few days we found our own house, a white frame, one-bedroom at the edge of town. Dave set up a study area in one corner of the living room and we painted the old kitchen and bedroom furniture white. The day we did the painting Dave and I had a water fight in the yard. We were full of excitement and tension as we chased each other around the house and yard with the hose and buckets of water. Sex between us was good, and I enticed him into making love often, whenever the mood struck.

We drove to Santa Cruz to wander on the beach, quiet after the end of the season. We walked along the boardwalk and through the deserted amusement park. Dave, Jim, and I went to a fair in San Jose and spent all our money on some silly game, finally winning a pink and white teddy bear. I saved it for Jennifer. Dave joined a club for veterans returning to college and I joined the wives club. I opened my big mouth and they elected me President. The club made a float for the homecoming parade honoring the vets and held a spaghetti dinner for the football team. Dave and I planned I would get a job to help pay our living expenses, but I hadn't leveled with him about my lies and I started to get nervous. I landed a receptionist job in a physician's office which didn't pay much.

Shortly after getting settled in San Jose, we visited Dave's parents in Sacramento. They had scheduled a company party for the night we arrived, and Dave helped ready the garage for the shindig, rigging a parachute to cover the ceiling like a tent.

I felt very strange being there. At one point in the evening I left the house and walked down the block crying. The next morning the Palmers held a Bloody Mary brunch. I was surprised at all the alcohol being consumed. My family rarely drank or socialized in that fashion.

Sometime in October I found out I was pregnant. I begged a ride to LA with Dave's friend, Jim, who had to make the trip. When we reached LA it was past midnight, and since I hadn't told my parents to expect me, I couldn't go to their house. I asked Jim to drop me at my sister Cheryl's house in Alhambra. She was married and had a baby son. I knocked on the door quite a few times before she opened it. I expected to be let in, but she stood in the barely opened doorway and whispered that I couldn't stay there.

I stumbled down the steps before I began to cry. It was late and I didn't know what else to do, so I walked a couple of miles to Tom's apartment. He let me in. We hardly talked, he just kept telling me I was a married woman now and didn't belong there. We slept in the same bed because there was nowhere else for me to sleep. He wouldn't have anything to do with me, though I was crying and upset. After seeing my parents in the morning, I left and returned to San Jose.

Dave and I made another trip to Los Angeles, but I can't place the exact date or purpose. My memory is vague. I argued with him while he was driving, and I hit him with my hairbrush. It may have been Christmas time, as I have a small photo of Dave at Chuck and Ginny's house in Whittier. He and I spent Thanksgiving with his parents in Sacramento.

Dave fell behind in his studies because I was demanding he spend time with me. I couldn't figure out what else to do with myself. Near Christmas, Dave took me to stay with his parents while he finished withdrawing from school. We stayed with them for a few weeks until he found a job driving a laundry truck and rented an apartment. About this time, I began to call Tom and talk about us. Tom convinced me I made a mistake in getting married and that we would have gotten together if I just waited. He told me that he still loved me, and I thought I still loved him. I think I had some screwed-up ideas about romance and high drama. My actions were guided by ideas I read about in true confession magazines, and I was drifting, letting the current sweep me wherever it went. I wanted what other girls seemed to want, boyfriends and marriage. There were other things as well, like clothes and dates, but I couldn't seem to get any of that either. In my father's eyes, which never seemed to look directly at me, I saw and felt shame. I knew it was better not to be in their house. I was not wanted and whatever I was, I was not valued. I wanted my own someone to love me and think I was wonderful. Both Dave and Tom said they loved me and wanted me — so I wanted both of them. However, I didn't know that Tom was in the beginning stage of schizophrenia.

My phone calls to Tom became more frequent. I'd leave the apartment and call from a pay phone. Finally, I convinced myself that I had to leave Dave. When we went to bed in the evening, I'd pretend to be asleep and ignore his hands. He never made demands, and I think someone told him my lack of desire was due to being pregnant.

In February of 1964, I left. Perhaps if I simply took my clothes and left it might not have been such a shock to him. That's not what I did. I knew I might have to live alone with the baby, and that desperation drove me to take nearly everything. We didn't have much. I called a moving van and when Dave returned home from work that night I was gone, and the apartment was bare. When I think of what I did to him, I feel sick and ashamed. On the other hand, I realize that I began to make decisions based on the baby I was carrying. I know they were not always the best choices, but I wasn't capable of looking ahead or considering the consequences of my actions. That came later, gradually.

As I look back, I understand that my concerns were only focused on my own feelings. I guess you could call that selfish, a self-centered awareness that typifies childhood and adolescence. Becoming an adult means developing empathy, feelings for others. I think the chaos of my childhood kept me from thinking about others. I felt sad for my grandmother and my mother when there were arguments or events that hurt them, and I felt deep sorrow—pity for people who were handicapped or obviously poor, but I didn't see a connection between my actions and their lives. Today, my sense of empathy is quite well-developed and one of my greatest strengths. Yet I found myself extremely unwilling to imagine what Dave felt when he walked into our dark, empty apartment that evening. At one point he bought me a puppy to keep me from being lonely. I guess I left it alone in that apartment.

My insensitivity sickens me.

Turning Point

"The tapestry of my life was a ruin of unravelling threads. The brightest parts were a nonsensical madman's weaving. And now every day was a grey stitch, laid down with an outpatient's patience, one following the next following the next, a story in lines, like a railway track to nowhere, telling absolutely nothing."
— *Alexis Hall*

I flew back to LA and turned up at my parents' apartment. I told them I didn't expect to be there long. I knew my father wouldn't want me there. I found out about ADC (Aid to Dependent Children—welfare) and applied for it. Dave and I spoke on the phone. He wrote letters telling me that he was lonely for me and that he still loved me. He came to visit me once and bought me some shoes. Tom refused to see me because I was still married, but I began to visit his family. When I moved into a furnished apartment, he came over once to check things out, and Gladys bought me a crib. Things I needed for the baby I bought myself from the meager monthly welfare check. I had no car and had to walk or take the bus, but I didn't go anywhere except to visit Tom's family or my own. I found a doctor for my prenatal care and planned to have my baby at the same hospital where I worked several years earlier.

My uncle Chuck always bought fireworks to shoot off on the Fourth of July. That day I rode with my family to his house for a barbecue and fireworks display. Some time in the afternoon I began labor and went to the Alhambra Community Hospital. Jennifer Jay Palmer was born around 7:00 am the following morning. As soon as I could get out of bed afterwards, I called Dave to tell him we had a daughter. I don't recall his reaction. He said he'd be down as soon as possible.

Before Dave came to see us, I did a lot of thinking. I began to think I'd made a big mistake. I loved Jennifer with an intensity I couldn't have imagined, and her future was in my hands. How could I deny her the opportunity to have her real father in a real family? I hardly saw Tom, a couple of times at his parents' home but only once alone and I didn't feel the same toward him. Jennifer was all-absorbing, and her needs became the central focus of my daily life and thoughts.

I began an encounter with myself, with my soul, facing the lies I told Dave, my unfairness to him and the possibilities that lay ahead if I didn't face the truth and the reality of my life. I had to change, for her sake. I realized that I hadn't given my marriage and Dave the honesty and maturity they deserved. I would ask him to take me back to Sacramento with him, I would start over. There would be no more lies in my life. As hard as it was to face the truth about myself and my life, I would do so because anything less would be an injustice to my sweet, innocent baby daughter. I didn't know if I loved Dave. I wasn't sure any more about whatever it was I felt for Tom, but perhaps living the truth would make it all clear. I made a resolution, the first real commitment ever in my life: I would not lie to Dave, no matter what.

Within a day or two of that promise Dave came to see us. When I asked him to take me back to Sacramento with him, he asked me if I loved him. There was my first opportunity to start a new life. I couldn't lie to him. I told him I wasn't sure whether I did or not.

That was it! It was all or nothing with him and I failed to give the right answer. A thousand times since then I have wished I lied — said yes, I love you. Perhaps, I did — perhaps, love can only be said to exist when it has been tried by adversity, when the flames are fanned by years of building and shared moments of joy. Whatever love was — at that moment I was only beginning to know it. He left but returned with his mother, a case of baby formula and $20 or so. I spent the rest of the afternoon crying hysterically.

The following day I began to panic, what was I going to do now? I believed that he would never reconsider taking me back. I began to think that they might try to take Jenny away from me. The terror of that grew each hour. Several days passed with the worry of that possibility nagging my every action. Tom's mother suggested I see an attorney, his father told me I could prevent that from happening by getting a restraining order. I saw the attorney and discussed the restraining order. He told me that I had to have cause for such a legal proceeding. We spoke for a while until we decided that we could use the drinking I'd seen

Dave and his mother indulge in as a reason. I was distressed by the idea that I hadn't seen much excessive drinking. He told me it was probably the only thing we could use. So, it was done. For years I felt guilty about that restraining order, but no matter what, I couldn't afford to lose Jenny. She was my reason for living now.

Months later the divorce was scheduled in court. That day, we met in the corridor outside the court room. I was standing with my attorney and he was alone a few feet away. Our eyes met, we both smiled, and I realized the intensity of our sexual attraction to each other. In an instant, the flame returned and flared. I wanted to run to him, to cry, to beg him to forgive me, to sleep again in his arms and make love. My attorney held my arm and Dave turned and walked away. For years I wondered if things could have changed at that moment.

During the next year security investigators came to my apartment and asked questions about Dave. He left for Viet Nam and Air America. The court-ordered child support began to be late and finally months behind. The welfare payments of $138.00 per month only just covered our rent, utilities and food. Tom's parents bought Jenny clothes and I made do with the clothes I still had. Visiting my family and Tom's family were my only recreation. Tom began to come over and bring us food. Sometimes, rarely, we went for day trips to the desert or mountains. Tom's illness began to get progressively worse.

I still didn't know that his rudeness was due to his developing schizophrenia, and his behavior grew more bizarre. He was seeing a psychologist weekly and one day he told me he was going into a hospital near San Juan Capistrano. Shortly after he returned from a week-long stay at that hospital, he showed up at my apartment in a state of agitation. One of his eyes appeared to be injured. The entire white of the eye was bright red. Hours of conversation later, he said he was poisoned at the fast food restaurant where he ate at every day. Apparently convinced of the poisoning, he returned home and made strenuous attempts to vomit. In the process, he caused a hemorrhage in his eye. He was totally convinced, and when I tried to reason against him it only infuriated him further.

In the months that followed, Tom's behavior became worse, affecting his family and me in crazy making ways. I began to accompany him to see different psychiatrists. He desperately needed help but never told his parents or me just how bad things really were. His paranoia kept him from following advice anyone *gave him. He eventually allowed his parents to pay his bills and to support him, and even demanded that they give him $10,000 to make up for the college degree he was never going to get. His tireless harassment was too much for his parents and they gave him the money. Although this seemed to give him a certain amount of security, he continued to badger and blame everyone else for his state of mind. Nothing gave him any peace and he allowed none to anyone else.*

Tom decided we were going to get married in Tijuana. He talked me into the idea, and we drove to Mexico. We reached San Diego by dark and took a motel room. The next morning I was awakened by a knock on the door. Tom was in the room, standing stark naked. I thought he must have just come out of the shower. I answered the door and the desk clerk was standing there. He told me he called the police, and they were on their way. I was able to learn that Tom had left the room and wandered around outside in full view of other guests, totally naked and uttering obscenities at them. The clerk left and Tom dressed making some excuse about getting out of there. The police met us at the checkout desk and questioned Tom about the incident. He convinced them that he was fine and that the clerk was mistaken, so they let us leave. By now I was becoming alarmed and frightened by his behavior, but totally confused about what to do.

Tom drove across the border into Tijuana, stopping to ask a man on the street where he could find someone to marry us. The man led us to the office of a lawyer or justice of the peace — I don't know which now. He read us a short ceremony and we signed some papers. Once we left the office, Tom was intent on returning to Los Angeles immediately. The drive back to LA got even more bizarre. I convinced him to let me drive. He stared out the window at the passengers in other cars, making strange signals with his fingers and hands at them. He was constantly muttering under his breath. By this time, I was really scared and thought only of reaching his parents' house.

Within a few blocks of his parents' house, he demanded I park in front of a large Catholic church. He bolted from the car and ran into the church. He lay down in front of the alter, face flat to the floor, arms outstretched in the shape of a cross. Nearly hysterical, I pleaded and cried, trying to get him on his feet and out of the church. A priest approached Tom where he was lying on the floor and began asking him what was the matter. I asked the priest to keep Tom occupied while I went to get his father. Dick

Senior came back to the church with me and after several hours managed to get Tom up and back to the house.

At the house, Tom suddenly seemed to remember he just was married and wanted to perform his conjugal duties, pulling me into the spare bedroom onto the bed. With the door open and in full view he began to tear his and my clothes off. His mother and sister tried to reason with him, but he was reaching the point where we were both naked and it was obvious he was not going to stop. I struggled against him, but it was no use. I cried out to Gladys to please just shut the door. Within seconds he was up and off me and out the front door, stark naked into the front yard, attempting to get into his car.

Later that night, somehow, he managed to get himself admitted to the hospital in San Gabriel where he was going to weekly therapy sessions. We were told that he'd had a complete psychotic break, whatever that was! All I knew about madness was from a book. His family and I visited him over the next few days. Most of the conversation with him was strange and illogical, with intermittent moments of absolute clarity and lucidity. He continuously quoted and read from the Bible, stopping to demand that his mother get him some other edition. We brought him some clothing article and the 8x10 photograph of myself he kept at his apartment. He was on several psychoactive drugs, among them Thorazine. He began to complain about their effects on him and we could see he was slurring his words and dragging his feet as he moved ever more slowly each day.

About two a.m. the phone rang in the darkness of the small apartment. A voice told me there was an emergency at the hospital and to come immediately. I dressed myself and bundled Jenny up in a blanket, stopped to call Tom's parents and then waited by the street for them to pick me up. Cindi and Gladys picked me up and we drove to the San Gabriel Hospital emergency room entrance. I gave Jenny to Cindi and they waited in the car while Gladys and I ran into the hospital. She stopped in the waiting room while I (familiar with hospitals) pushed through the swinging doors into the care unit.

Tom lay on a gurney covered with green surgical sheets. His face was white, and the sheets were covered with blood. So much blood! I screamed and the nurses grabbed me, pulling me into the outside hallway. Tom had saved his Thorazine pills for several days, then took them all at once in a suicide attempt. Apparently, he then grabbed my photograph, broke the glass, and slit his throat. He cut wide and deep, narrowly missing his vocal cords but severing the neck arteries. Another emergency at the hospital that evening had just completed when the call about Tom came through. The team of surgeons managed to save Tom's life by a narrow margin. If they hadn't still been at the hospital, he would have died. Perhaps it would have been best for everyone. Things only got worse after that.

In the days after the surgery, at times Tom seemed to be more in touch with reality. The doctor told us that trauma often produces a clearing of the minds' faculties. His grasp on reality began to fade as he demanded his mother bring him the Bible. He attempted to read verses from it to whoever would listen. I refused to indulge him and suffered the wrath of his mother, who felt it was a harmless activity. After all, she insisted, it makes Tommy feel good and religion is good for people. I wanted Tom to stay in the here and now as much as that was possible for him. I would not be a party to his delusions. When he healed sufficiently, he was transferred to a private care facility, Las Encinitas. That expensive convalescent sanitarium once housed Mario Lanza when he was suffering from the effects of alcoholism.

The grounds were beautiful, carefully maintained lawns and gardens of tall palm trees among old spreading Live Oak trees, flowering oleander, camellia and rose bushes. The one-story buildings with their red Spanish tiled roofs were spread over a spacious property. A six-foot-tall hurricane fence enclosed its perimeter. Because Tom had attempted suicide he was placed in the special, high-security locked unit in the center of the complex. An even higher hurricane fence surrounded it, and its entrance gate was controlled by an electronic locking system.

The male attendant sat at a desk just inside the doorway to the unit. The bare, stripped-down institutional atmosphere was dark with shadows. The unit had only one other patient at the time, a tall, well-built man in his thirties. Bob, the son of a wealthy family had been at Las Encinitas for years. For the price of five thousand dollars a month, his family and personal background were matters of absolute privacy. I did learn that Bob was a sexual psychotic and was lobotomized to curtail his behavior. I was told that he was harmless, but he indulged in mild exhibitionism from time to time during my visits with Tom. I wondered how harmless this man really was if he had to continue to be locked up in this special unit. I thought perhaps the lobotomy hadn't worked after all. During this time, the Watts Riots erupted. The TV hanging above the attendant's desk was on constantly. Usually, I went to visit with Tom's mother or Cindi, as I had no car.

I don't recall if he was on medication during those first few weeks, but he seemed much better, more in touch with reality and eager to get back home. He spoke about our future and about getting married the right way. I began to hope that things were getting better again and that he was getting well. Big-time denial was as much a part of my thinking as it was his parents'. They just couldn't account for what was happening to Tom. We spent many evenings going over past events in Tom's life looking for clues to his bizarre behavior. He was now over twenty-one, and the consultations he had with the psychiatrists were privileged communication, unavailable to his parents or me. That was fine with Tom, as he had emerged into full paranoia. Dick and Gladys mined each other's past and families for any nugget of craziness they could find. The fault finding and blame laying became a daily compulsion. The routines of a normal household ceased, and all activities and conversation revolved around Tom.

Finally, I left him. My life was filled with pain and fear. What was there to look forward to, how could I build a life for myself or Jennifer, with a man whose daily behavior ranged from normal one moment to bizarre the next. I didn't understand his illness and I began to doubt my own sanity. He was so convincing at times that even I believed the things he said, the ideas he talked about. After all, what did I really know about the world, about mental illness, and about life in general? I loved him and believed it was wrong to leave him because he was sick. I thought he might commit suicide and didn't want to be responsible for it, and I stayed longer because I was afraid for Tom.

But things changed, and I began to be afraid of Tom. Fear was what compelled me to leave. Throughout the years we'd been together, through periods of kooky, downright weird behavior, I never feared him. Although he would sometimes be aloof or cold, no hint of violence was ever evident. He was kind and loving towards Jennifer. If we disagreed, he would leave my presence. I would be the one who was angry. Before we married and lived together, he would insist on privacy in certain matters but after we began living together, he seemed to change. He kept a small portable box with a combination lock which he would not allow me to open. When he went out, he often took the box with him. This change in his behavior began to make me suspicious. We were renting a small house behind my sister's house. It allowed us to be company for each other. Tom began to find fault with Pat. He claimed she was spying in the windows on him. One day she came and told me that Tom was leaving piles of garbage on her back steps and slamming her windows shut when he passed by to empty the trash. I'd seen him display that kind of petty hostility towards others before and I was on alert. He began keeping irregular bedtimes and getting up in the middle of the night to type letters. I started locking the door to Jennifer's bedroom and lying awake until I was sure he was asleep for the night. I would lie in bed fighting sleep, my mind wandering over dark scenarios, and rise exhausted in the mornings. After one particularly tiresome night I began to think about that box and had strong feelings about seeing what was inside of it.

When he left later that day, I began to methodically work through the three-digit combination, starting at 001. Somewhere around the seven hundreds it unlocked. When I opened the box, I was shocked — a small handgun lay just inside. I thought I remembered him saying he bought a gun, but I wasn't sure. Carefully, I lifted the gun from the box and laid it down on the counter. Underneath the gun were several true crime magazines. I recoiled, my hand covering my mouth, sucking in my breath and holding it. The cover of the top magazine had a title about "killing my wife and..." the next magazine had a similar feature story headlined in bold typeface across its cover too, as did the third one. I stuffed the magazines and gun back in the box and shut the lid.

"He's going to kill me," I thought.

My mind began to go into wild contortions of thought. I was hyperventilating. I ran out to my car, put the box in the trunk and drove to the Alhambra Police Department. The detective who spoke with me said there was nothing I could do.

"It isn't a crime to own murder magazines and the gun is registered, lady."

They say you can smell fear; that in some way we communicate vulnerability. The paranoid's hypersensitivity picks up this change immediately. When he came home that evening, he knew something was wrong, something different about me. I could see it in his eyes. I had made the decision to leave him. All that was left was to figure out how to pack up what I needed and get out. Get out, that is, without giving him a chance to find out where I was moving to or stop me from going. Having to stay even a few more days was going to be difficult. That night I hid the knives from the kitchen drawer before I locked Jennifer's door.

I was up early the next morning, dropped Jenny off at her nursery school and stopped to buy a newspaper. I called the rental ads from a pay phone and found a small apartment on the other side of town. Later that afternoon I went to the Welfare office and reapplied for ADC. Using my small reserve fund, I paid the first month's rent and arranged for the utilities to be turned on. The next step was to find a way to get Tom out of the house long enough to get my belongings out, including Jenny's crib and a few other pieces of furniture. Tom rarely went out without me and now he seemed to even more concerned with sticking close to home and me. Conversation between us was strained. Somewhere I learned how to pull the distributor coil out of a car to make it inoperable and I thought that would be the thing I might do to keep him from following me when I left. Yet, if he physically tried to stop me from leaving, he could. There had to be another solution. I thought I had it.

By this time, my sister was very leery of Tom. I knew if I told her to call the police, in an emergency, she would. I had to get Tom arrested and taken to jail. In that case I'd have several hours, while he was getting booked and bailed out, to pack and leave. Once the plan was clear in my mind, I felt guilty for the dishonesty, fright and anxiety I would be causing to Tom and my sister. However, I despaired of finding another way of dealing with the problem.

Jennifer was staying with my sister that evening. I wanted to make sure that she would not be a witness to the scene I was about to create. I waited until it was dark, turned the outside lights on and without any attempt to conceal my actions I left the house and walked over to Tom's Volkswagen. I opened the engine compartment. After a few moments of hesitation, he followed me. Acting quickly, I located the distributor cap and ripped it and the wires out. I heaved the whole mess over the fence into the tangle of shrubbery on the other side.

It was too late by the time he grabbed me. The distributor was over the fence into the pitch-black shadows. He began yelling and running to retrieve the part. I grabbed the hose I carefully laid next to the car, earlier in the afternoon. The water was turned on at the faucet and ready to spray when I opened the valve. At the same time, I began yelling for my sister, screaming as loudly as I could and wetting my myself with the hose. Realizing he needed a flashlight to probe the depths of the black shadows, Tom ran back to the house. My screaming and the water spraying all over confused him. He tried to take the hose away from me and we wrestled together as I kept it from him and continued screaming, "Pat, call the police."

Tom was now frantic, hearing police, and further confused by what was happening. The squad was in the driveway in minutes." Yes," I said, "I want him arrested." and I would come down to the police department to sign the complaint when I had changed my wet clothes. They took him away in the squad car. The police knew who he was by now from all the complaints over the past years.

I knew his family would be down to bail him out immediately. It was necessary to work quickly to get my things and leave. I told my sister I would get a motel room for Jenny and myself. With Pat's help I moved the crib, dresser, and heavy wooden toy box over to her house. I would get it later. I packed the car and left.

For several months, I hid the car in the back yard of the little house I rented. I found a job, but I stayed on the ADC also. To meet my bare expenses and make the car payments too, I needed the extra money. Even so, there was only enough to take care of necessities, and nothing extra. I didn't see Tom or his family for the following six to nine months.

Into the Wilderness

So what do we do? Anything. Something. So long as we just don't sit there. If we screw it up, start over. Try something else. If we wait until we've satisfied all the uncertainties, it may be too late.
— *Lee Iacocca*

The peace I felt in our tiny home cleared my brain, and for several weeks I relished it. Jenny and I made frequent trips to the local parks and to visit my parents. My ADC paid the rent, but that took more than half of the monthly check. I kept Jenny at home with me, as I couldn't afford the nursery school fees. Her medical care was part of the welfare allotment, so her basic immunizations and any emergency care were covered. Food, laundry money, gas and a few dollars for clothing were all that I could eke out of the remaining $70. The car payments were behind, and I had no auto insurance. I began to worry about losing the car, which represented the only chance I had to get ahead. Without it I couldn't get to the laundromat, night school or the bus stop for work.

A feeling of desperation began to dog my daily thoughts. I don't recall how I got in touch with Dave again, or how I knew he was back from Vietnam. I did know he was married, but I thought that would be a stumbling block I could get around, somehow. By now he owed me back child support, and I thought collecting it might be a way to temporarily take care of the past-due car payments. I thought if he could see his daughter, he might be moved to pay the back support. We spoke on the phone and made arrangements for him to come to visit her at my place. He was to come alone. I had no desire to meet his new wife. Talking about our child and our previous life would be impossible in front of a stranger. In the hours before he was due to arrive, I began to fantasize about our getting back together, remembering the feelings I had when I last saw him. Suddenly I was aware of my neediness. The hand-to-mouth lifestyle I was living seemed bearable after leaving Tom, but the shabbiness of my tiny apartment and wardrobe filled me with humiliation. Looking forward to seeing him provided relief from my feelings of desperation. The woman he once desired was not the image I saw in the mirror before me. The shining blond hair hung in strings from three-inch-long dark roots, the tan was gone, and the figure thickened by my pregnancy still held the unwanted weight. My clothes were threadbare, baggy, and suitable only for scrubbing the floor. I had no resources to remedy this embarrassment.

I had to make do as best I could and hope my words and personality could overcome the other things. Of course I cried, but the water flowing over my hair as I washed it hid the pain from my small daughter. That's how it must be, I thought. I bathed myself and Jenny. We would be squeaky clean and smell like soap. I applied the stale makeup I kept for special occasions and put on clean clothes. Then I set to work picking up the items around the apartment that signaled my distressed condition. I cut fresh camellias from the bushes outside my door, opened the windows to let in fresh air, and swept the rug and sidewalk. Evening came and I turned on the lights. Oh my God, the worn sofa and rug stuck out like pimples on a teenager's face. The wallpaper was faded and dirty. The glare of the electric lights was too revealing. As a final touch, I darkened the other rooms and lit several candles. At least there was a mellowness about the tiny room now.

The sound of the gate being unlocked caused my heart to pound; my breathing became uneven. I opened the door, saw him standing there and felt faint. He wasn't alone. He'd brought his wife. Instantly, I was enraged, and began screaming at him, "I told you to come alone. You promised me you would." I called her some vile name like bitch, and he turned to go. Thoughts flashed through my mind. This wasn't working out at all. I had to decide at once what I really wanted to gain from this opportunity. Above all, I realized, I wanted him to see our daughter. To see his sweet, loving child, his baby. I'd have to swallow my rage, apologize, and beg him not to leave. What I felt didn't matter, Jennifer did. I'd have to appear to be warm and friendly to his wife.

We sat inside, and he held Jennifer on his lap making small talk with her. I began to ask Sharon questions about their life. She dropped her guard and began to talk about how exciting it was to live overseas, and how she and Dave decided that they were going to do just that as soon as they could. She showed me her ruby rings and talked about having silk suits handmade in Thailand.

All I could think about was the back child support he owed me, and the misery Jenny and I lived under without the money he lavished on this bleached blond woman, who wasn't even as good looking as me in my impoverished condition. Years later, I learned that while Jennifer and I were living on $168 a month, Dave was earning more than $1,300 a month.

Nothing came from that visit. Dave never tried to see Jenny again. He never called, sent letters, or even birthday and Christmas gifts. I guess he went back to school then. I filed a complaint to get an increase in child support thinking I could go off welfare, hold a job and with better child support, maybe make it. He went to court, claimed he was a poor student now living on a greatly reduced income. The child support was reduced from $100 a month to $77.50. Mostly, it never came.

Back to ground zero with the failure of that plan, I knew I needed to get a job. Knowing it was illegal to work and continue to collect the ADC, I reasoned that I had no other choice. It was a risk that must be taken if I were ever to improve my living conditions. I signed up for the adult evening high school completion courses. I wasn't qualified at much and hated general office work anyway. My typing speed was somewhere around twenty words per minute, with nineteen errors, and I took one semester of high school shorthand and failed it. The things I had going for me were my ability to talk, and my looks.

I landed a job in the Trust Department at Union Bank, as a receptionist. I was to start work the following Monday.

Our tiny house had a bathroom with a tub, a long narrow kitchen, a living room, and a curtained alcove for a bedroom. The rooms were heated by an open-flame gas heater, which wasn't vented to the outside. The landlady gave me some instructions on its use, and I could light it to get the heat going and understood that the gas had to be turned off at all other times. That was the extent of my knowledge. I had taken my work clothes to the cleaners, and returning home with them, removed the plastic covering that protected the garments. I hung them on the curtain rod that separated our living and sleeping areas. There was no clothes closet. Jenny and I left the house for some errand. When I returned several hours later, I found the tiny apartment covered in a layer of oily soot, including every garment that was just cleaned. Something happened to the heater. My new job started the next morning. After crying hysterically for a time, I realized I had no choice but to clean the apartment and wash something out for wearing. I was angry and exhausted by bedtime and deter-

mined to find another apartment with a less dangerous heating system.

My world was a desperate place in those days. Young, uneducated, living on welfare with my small daughter, and trying to find a way to keep going down that long road of fear and frustration, I was near total despair.

"What I need," I decided, "is some kind of peace and refreshment—an experience of rejuvenation."

I would try something I had never done before.

"Great idea!" I thought.

What could I find to match my meager finances? A transcendent experience—a cheap transcendent experience. I'd climb a mountain. That would do it! Never having camped before, I was truly starting a new experience. As I rented a backpack and purchased my supplies, I worried about what I was getting myself into. Wary of venturing into the unknown by myself, I recruited a friend from the bank to accompany me on the trip, and we departed Los Angeles one late-summer weekend.

Mount Whitney, in California at 14,495 feet is the highest peak in the United States outside of Alaska. The trail to the top follows a series of switchbacks ten-and-a-half miles up the face of the mountain. The sun blazed as we began the trek that morning but within hours rain moved in, soaking me, my pack, and my sleeping bag.

The weather changed constantly: sun, then rain, then sun again. Low clouds obscured the trail and the trail-side thousand-foot drop-offs. This was a popular trail filled with other hikers, trudging over the rocks and stream beds that filled and crossed the steep trail. In late afternoon, my friend wanted to continue to a high-altitude camp, but the weather had me beaten, and I turned back while he continued on. Near dusk, I put in for the night, camping by a lake and laying my soggy bag under a large overhanging rock.

The tiny Primus stove gave me trouble, and the pancakes I attempted to cook burned to charcoal.

"Damn! I messed up again." I looked around to see if anyone else observed my stupidity. A few feet away I saw a man cooking his dinner over a small campfire. I considered the possibilities of that enticing warmth and made my way over to his camp site.

"Hi, I was wondering if you'd mind my using your campfire to warm some cocoa?" He looked up and smiled. Feeling acutely self-conscious I stumbled over my words and rambled on quickly.

"It's getting cold, and well, I burned up my dinner." I stopped and waited for an answer. There was a mortifying silence before he spoke. "Sure, you can."

We talked across the fire until I ran out of small talk.

"Well, I guess I'd better go back to, ah, my place," I spoke with reluctance. As I turned to leave, he called after me.

"Hey, you could share my tent--I mean if it gets too cold and wet."

I felt a rush of emotion, but my pride kept me from accepting. I went back to my rock and struggled into the wet sleeping bad. Another burst of rain sent a rivulet of water off the face of the rock and down onto the back of my neck.

"Damn," I swore out at the sky. "This won't work at all!"

I continued to talk to myself. I picked up my sleeping bag and headed for his tent.

"Knock, knock!" I called out, "I'll take you up on your offer."

We lay next to each other for hours, talking about ourselves. He was everything I wanted but I knew this couldn't happen for me. I was careful to talk about ideas and values and not my failed marriage, my lack of education, and the fact that I had a child. He was single, a college graduate, and handsome to boot. We pulled the tent flap aside to watch the high peaks turn pink and gold — Alpenglow! The sky blackened, more stars than I'd ever seen were sprayed across its wide expanse.

We were in love.

A Quiet Boyhood

Do you know what people really want? Everyone, I mean. Everybody in the world is thinking: I wish there was just one other person I could really talk to, who could really understand me, who'd be kind to me. That's what people really want, if they're telling the truth.
— *Doris Lessing*

In many ways I was an outsider in school. After making high scores on standardized tests in eighth grade, I was slotted in the academic track classes with the popular kids in high school, but I didn't socialize with them outside school. I tried out for football, and managed to make the team, but I still didn't fit in. They largely focused on clothes, dating, sports, and music, while I spent a lot of my spare time reading science fiction or camping. Determined to get into college, I focused on classes, earned straight A grades, and landed two scholarships to the University of California at Berkeley, the only school I applied to.

The world contains countless brilliant students, and thousands of them were my classmates when I arrived in Berkeley, feeling even more anonymous than I did in high school. Seventeen years old and lacking social skills, I joined the college newspaper, *The Daily Californian,* as a photographer. I learned to shoot news photos, and assignments for the paper became my social life. As a staff photographer I attended concerts, speeches, rallies, protests, and athletic events. Usually I was hanging out at the Daily Cal when I wasn't in class. I met a few girls on the Daily Cal staff that I liked, but was too shy to ask them out until my junior year.

In the summer of 1964, the "Freedom Summer," the Civil Rights Movement energized student activists at Berkeley. They came back to campus in the fall eager to take on the world for segregation, racism, and discrimination. The administration responded to their activism by prohibiting them from handing out leaflets and pamphlets on campus, and the Free Speech Movement was born. I spent hours at protests shooting photos for the paper and hearing their speeches, including one sit-down that trapped a police car on campus for days. Confrontations escalated. When protesters occupied the Administration building, police came in and arrested over 800 students, hauling them in yellow buses 30 miles to the Alameda County Jail.

After a darkroom session printing some of my photos of the demonstrations, I met my sociology professor by chance on campus and I showed him the prints. He got an idea for a book about the Free Speech Movement. He told a publisher friend, and the book was born. I worked with them on the project while they pulled in other photographers, and in May 1965 we published *The Trouble in Berkeley*, the first book about the conflict. I enjoyed working on the book, and lost interest in sociology, my major at the time (after majoring in mathematics, philosophy, humanities and French). I wanted to study photojournalism, but UC Berkeley only offered it in graduate school. UCLA had a film school, and somehow I thought that would do. Without asking anyone for advice, I transferred to UCLA to study film making, and left Berkeley in June 1965.

I was in full-blown rebellion by the summer of 1965 before enrolling at UCLA. I drifted into a world of world of underground drug users, dealers, and motorcycle gangs. I bought a motorcycle. In the fall I entered UCLA and my experience was totally different from Berkeley. I felt like a stranger there. I lived off-campus, sharing an apartment with three Iranian students, themselves outsiders on the campus. All but one of my classes were in the Theater Arts department at the north end of campus, and I rarely saw other parts of UCLA. Weekdays I learned filmmaking from Academy Award-winning directors, screenwriters, and cinematographers, and weekends I hung out with bikers. My sense of alienation from society in general fed my discomfort with UCLA. I wasn't happy or comfortable in a life divided between college and rebellion. One Sunday afternoon in late fall I made a trip on my friend Stan's motorcycle to the Mojave Desert, remote from Westwood, to a party in the desert with the Hell's Angels.

Just being up close to Hell's Angels made me feel grimy and tainted, but at first I didn't understand why. An acid trip later in December made me paranoid and anxious, and that mood lasted for months. Eventually my experience with the sordid side of Southern California led me to a conclusion. The Hell's Angels were purely destructive, and threatened the humanity of everyone around them. I watched them use their bare hands to casually demolish an abandoned house in the desert because they were bored, it felt good, and it was their approach to life. They enjoyed destroying things. They were indifferent to the harm they did. The damage they caused outweighed any good they might have done at other times. More sophisticated observers would have recognized that instantly, but various groups saw them differently through their own preconceptions. It wasn't simple. To some degree the Angels represented rebellion and counterculture, yet they acted against antiwar demonstrators in Oakland, a contradictory stance. Having questioned all my principles that year, I was still formulating my own moral code. I needed longer to judge them. I finally realized that they opposed everything I valued, and I left their world.

The next summer, I sold my motorcycle and bought a used car.

I graduated from UCLA in 1966 with a bachelor's degree in Theater Arts. Getting a job in Hollywood was a natural step for a UCLA film grad, but not me. Jobs for new graduates in the movie business went to people who had a gift for networking, or an existing connection like a relative who was already in. I lacked both.

What was I to do? I wanted to earn enough to support myself. The Army was offering jobs, but I did not want to participate in the Vietnam War. I met a guy at a party who worked as a computer programmer. He said if I scored high on a programming aptitude test, I might get a job in the computer industry.

After finishing my last classes I interviewed with System Development Corporation, the world's first software house. SDC had jobs with draft deferments. After passing their screening test and an interview, they offered me a job. I started in January, 1967. I was 21 years old. Programmer training was unlike anything I ever studied before, and I was good at it.

As a young college-educated professional in Southern California I should have been swimming in dates. Not me. Socially inept and shy, a complete nerd, I had dated very few times in high school or college. After a few months I stopped trying to find a date in loud, crowded bars, realizing that I wasn't going to find the love of my life or even a hookup in that scene. To be honest, a hookup was my main goal. I decided to do things that I truly enjoyed as a teenager, like camping and backpacking. One Fourth of July weekend, I embarked on a road trip through Yosemite with a friend from work. By afternoon Sunday, we were driving south through the Owens Valley, east of the jagged eastern Sierra Nevada mountains. The lowering sun lit up thunderheads looming above the crest of the Sierras, and rays of god light streamed into the valley between shadows. The mountains emanated mystery and power. I felt drawn to them, recalling a failed climb up Mount Whitney when I was eleven, fat and out of shape, and altitude sickness gave me a blinding headache the first day on the trail. When the group hiked toward the summit, I fell behind and stopped while they went on. I vowed someday I would finish that climb.

The following Labor Day weekend, at dawn on Saturday I started up the Mount Whitney Trail alone. The friend who agreed to accompany me backed out. I reached Mirror Lake in the afternoon and found a campsite. As the sun began to set, I walked downhill to an overlook to take a photo of the view toward Lone Pine, seven thousand feet lower. Returning to camp, I saw an attractive young woman with blonde hair and sky-blue eyes standing above me on a large boulder, looking at the view. Our eyes met. We noticed one another but didn't speak. I continued back to camp. Later that evening, the same woman approached my campfire. She looked straight into my eyes and spoke in a most disarming way.

"Hi. Do you mind if I heat my cocoa on your fire?"

OUR FIRST YEAR

There is a very big 'college' about how a man and a woman should interact with each other after marriage. However, people get married without 'studying'.
— *DADA BHAGWAN*

The day after we met, Diane hiked up the trail with me. She struggled with the thin air after years of cigarette smoking. We reached 11,000 feet and continued to climb, stopping often to rest, and hug and kiss. We hiked two miles past Mirror Lake together, but above Trail Camp she was too tired to go any farther. She wanted to return to camp, so I left her there and continued up the mountain. Clouds covered the sun, but the rain held off.

In late afternoon I reached the summit of Mount Whitney. I rested a few minutes, then descended to Mirror Lake. When I reached camp Diane was preparing to leave. She agreed to meet David at the trail head, the friend who accompanied her on the trip. He worked with her at a bank in Los Angeles and she assured me they were simply friends. She had to go. After she left, I realized she left a towel and a pillow behind. A pillow! She carried a full-sized pillow up the trail to Mirror Lake! By then I was exhausted. I crawled into my tent and crashed. In the middle of the night I woke up feeling extremely thirsty, but was so tired I didn't have the energy to walk a few steps to the lake for water. I chewed some gum and went back to sleep.

In the morning I awoke refreshed. I packed up my gear and departed. The sun warmed me as I bounded down the trail to Whitney Portal. I looked for Diane's car; she said it was a light blue Corvair. It was gone. I quickly loaded my MG and left.

Diane was gone and I would have to find her somewhere in Los Angeles. I drove home elated, flying down the two-lane highway at reckless speed, passing cars and trucks that kept me from my new love. By late afternoon I reached my apartment next to the Veteran's Hospital in West Los Angeles. I had a problem. It was Monday, Labor Day. I wanted to call Diane, but I didn't have her home phone number, and couldn't call her at work until the next day. As I grappled with that issue my phone rang. Diane was calling.

"I have to pick up my daughter and I wondered if you'd like to come with me."

Daughter? She didn't mention a daughter before. I agreed to go with her.

We drove in her car to Newbury Park, a far-flung suburb of Los Angeles where her parents lived. There I met her daughter Jennifer, who'd just turned three years old in July. Diane's parents lived in a pleasant house with tasteful décor, like the homes of upper middle-class students I had met. I didn't realize they had been living beyond their means for years. I didn't see it then, but I understood later how much their unstable home life damaged Diane. The consequences followed her all her life, but also strengthened her character, resilience, and resolve to make her own life better than theirs.

One evening shortly afterwards I sat at home wondering if I should call Diane, and my doorbell rang. I opened the door and saw Diane. She looked fragile and hopeful, as if the slightest hint of rejection would crush her. I wanted to hold her. She came inside. My roommate was out. We turned the lights down and laid on the carpet in front of the stereo in the living room to listen to music. We kissed.

Nervously I asked, "Do you want go to bed?"

"Yes," she answered.

We walked into my room. The blinds were closed on the large window facing the street, but a streetlight outside lit the room through the blinds, offering little privacy as we undressed. I felt awkward, nervous, and embarrassed removing my clothes in front of her—or any woman—for the first time. She waited on the bed, and I laid down next to her, excited but anxious. We made love. My awkwardness faded as I lay close to her and felt the warmth of her body. In that moment, our lives were bound together on an unknown path into the future neither one of us could predict.

A few nights later I visited Diane in Alhambra. I knocked on her apartment door and she let me into her living room. I looked around and realized her whole apartment would almost fit inside the living room of my apartment. A pile of laundry sat on a chair. I didn't notice that it was clean and folded, waiting to be put away. I thought of my friends Stan's biker buddies and the unwashed laundry, spilled food, neglected toddlers, and desperate wives that inhabited their homes. Jennifer was sleeping on the sofa as we talked. I carried Jennifer into the bedroom and Diane tucked her into bed. We made love on the sofa. As much as I was drawn to her, I feared being drawn into a sordid mess.

Afterwards, we talked. In the darkened room, with light filtering through the drapes, Diane revealed things about herself I wouldn't have guessed from her appearance on the mountain. I already knew about Jennifer, but then Diane told me she was still married. She told me about separating from her husband Tom a year earlier. He wasn't Jennifer's father; that was Dave, Diane's first husband (another husband!). She divorced him before Jennifer was born.

Last of all, Diane revealed she wasn't college-educated as I thought; she had dropped out of high school at seventeen. I was in love with her already, but I felt overwhelmed. She was still married, she was uneducated, a high school dropout living on welfare. Her life was nothing like I imagined. How I could continue this relationship? I broke down, tormented. Soon afterwards I left. At my job the following day I had to learn the details of an air defense system. When I tried to read the specifications, the words blurred on the page.

I called her that night.

She asked, "Do you want to come over?"

"Yes," I answered. Her apartment was twenty-five miles from mine, on the far side of Los Angeles. I began the first of a series of trips to her apartment.

Alhambra was a small town, even though it was surrounded by cities in greater Los Angeles. Even though she was separated from her husband, Diane remained in touch with Tom's family. Eventually he found out I was seeing her. One night, as we sat in her living room, Tom knocked on the door. I let him in. He looked haggard, but determined. I didn't know what to expect.

"You need to leave, now," he said. "She is my wife. You have no right to be here."

I felt overwhelmed by guilt. I couldn't argue with what he said. They were both six years older than me. I was a 22-year old just out of college with little experience and not a lot of backbone. I was ready to leave, but Diane said, "No, stay. I need you here. Tom, you need to go."

Diane gave me a reason to stay. Tom left.

Over the next month, Diane and I traveled to one another's apartments, although I did most of the traveling. I drove to her apartment after work through the worst traffic in Southern California, maybe the whole country. I could afford the drive better than Diane. She called her 77-year old grandmother Anna "Nanny" Christopher, who agreed to watch Jennifer while Diane went to night school. Nanny gave up her apartment in Minneapolis and took a train to California. Diane moved to a small two-bedroom apartment in a newer building so her grandmother would have a room. Tom didn't know where her new apartment was, and Diane could park her car out of sight from the street so he wouldn't find her. Nanny shared a small bedroom with Jennifer. It had a single bed for her and a child's bed for Jennifer, with a white headboard Jennifer soon decorated with her crayons.

At Christmas Diane bought Jennifer a camera that looked like her own twin-lens Yashica. Jennifer loved to "take pictures" with her toy camera. It influenced her life decisively. I remember one weekend the three of us drove out to the Mojave Desert in my MGB. I still have photos of Jennifer in a red jacket, holding her camera, her strawberry blonde hair in a Dutch boy haircut glowing in the golden afternoon sun. She lit up the scene with her smile. Just three years old, Jennifer radiated energy and promise. She was Diane's hope and redemption.

Diane was determined to graduate from high school, not just to pass a GED exam. By October when her grandmother arrived, Diane was attending classes. The classes bored her and she asked me to help. I encouraged her, helped her get to class, and spent many evenings in class with her while she stuck it out.

In December Diane asked me when I was going to ask her to marry me. I was dumbstruck. I hadn't seriously thought that through, and I wasn't ready to answer. Weeks passed. Finally, I asked her. She said "Yes." An immediate obstacle: she was still married to Tom. She hadn't filed for an annulment because she didn't have the money, and she was afraid Tom would try to kill himself if she did. In January I cashed a life insurance policy, and gave the money to Diane for an attorney to annul her marriage.

Every winter the short days and gloomy weather made Diane depressed. One night in January she woke me after a vivid, terrifying nightmare. In her dream she saw someone stabbed in the face repeatedly with an ice pick, and with blood everywhere. I knew about Tom's suicide attempt, when he cut his throat and nearly bled to death. I thought the nightmare was connected to that and might have been triggered because she began the annulment. We didn't know about PTSD, but Diane had classic symptoms. Her nightmares and night terrors recurred until the last few years of her life. After twenty years together she still sometimes woke up from a nightmare, usually unable to remember it, and could not calm down unless I turned on the lights, checked every room in the house, and double-checked that all the doors and windows were locked. It annoyed me to get out of bed and walk through the whole house, but she needed reassurance. Diane insisted I lock all the doors at night until the last year of her life

The drive to and from my apartment in West LA, sometimes at two or three in the morning, began to wear me down. I started to spend nights at her apartment and drive to work in Santa Monica in the morning. I told my roommate I was moving out when the lease on my apartment in West Los Angeles came up for renewal. In March, I packed all my clothes and belongings into the back of my MG and moved in with Diane. Nanny wasn't happy about it, but she never mentioned it to me though she complained to Diane's mother.

A love of nature and a need for recreation we could afford took us into the San Gabriel Mountains near Alhambra. We picnicked at Camp Williams, one of Diane's favorite places, hiked to Millard Canyon Falls, and visited other spots nearby in Southern California. One weekend we planned a backpacking trip to Mount San Gorgonio, but I forgot to pack the tent. We couldn't camp, so we drove through mountains instead. In late afternoon we discovered Oak Glen, a small town with a restaurant that served fresh apple pies from a nearby orchard. We drank strong, fragrant coffee with our pie as the late day sun streamed through the window onto our table, and it rescued our weekend.

Hiking in Millard Canyon one Saturday, Diane stopped to talk to a woman living in a small cabin. She invited us to come in for coffee. Seeing her tiny house we started thinking about having our own little home. We couldn't afford a house then, but thought maybe we could afford an RV. That led us to a recreational vehicle show, looking at different RVs. I sold my MG and bought a used pickup truck and a new slide-in camper, a home on wheels. I couldn't afford it, but I didn't realize that until a year later when the expenses of our new baby came due.

Diane finished her classes and qualifying tests in June, earning the high school diploma she would have had ten years earlier in a normal life. As she prepared for graduation, we also moved on other goals. Diane's attorney filed to annul her marriage to Tom on grounds that he was legally incompetent due to mental illness at the time of the marriage. We delayed filing until we were ready to marry and move out of state, away from Tom and his family's influence. I requested a job transfer from Santa Monica to Colorado Springs, Colorado. The last two weeks in June, Diane graduated from San Gabriel Adult School, her marriage to Tom was annulled, and we married.

During the wedding ceremony I looked down the aisle of the little chapel, and for a moment felt a rush, like the scene in a movie where an astronaut was pulled through space at insane speed to an unknown destination. Was I seeing the future? Then it passed. In early July a moving van loaded our household goods, and Diane, Jennifer, and I began a trip to visit relatives in Washington State in our RV. We drove north to San Francisco, crossed the Golden Gate Bridge, and wandered toward the redwoods. We stopped to pick wild blackberries by the highway, gathering enough for Diane to bake a blackberry cobbler one evening for dinner.

We were young, just married, and living in a dream world.

Wild West

It is easy, when you are young, to believe that what you desire is no less than what you deserve, to assume that if you want something badly enough, it is your God-given right to have it.
— *Jon Krakauer*

I transferred from Santa Monica to SDC's Colorado Springs office to get away from Tom and his family, and not worry about what he might do. We needed a fresh start—but not the kind of "fresh start" that created such a destructive pattern in her family.

Colorado Springs sits next to the Front Range of the Rocky Mountains in an area called the Strep Belt. The winter winds seemed to cause rampant ear, nose, and throat infections among school children. From the time Jennifer was small she had allergies and chronic ear infections. The winter we spent in Colorado, she had several cases of strep throat. Jennifer had an oral thrush infection as an infant, and Diane always wondered if that was connected to her later health issues. Some babies are more susceptible to yeast infections than others, possibly because of lower immunity.

In fall Diane started classes at the Colorado Springs campus of the University of Colorado, determined to get her education back on track. She was ten years older than most of the other students, but made friends quickly with them. Diane met Arielle, a nineteen-year-old who shared a house with two other students in nearby Manitou Springs. Arielle and her friends attended class sometimes, smoked pot and hung out at others. Soon Diane was hanging out and smoking pot with them. She began to tell me about Arielle's sexual activities, studying my reaction, alert for any sign of interest. I had little previous sexual experience besides fantasy, and I was intrigued. Diane asked me how I felt about Arielle as she fed me stories that aroused my interest. She accused me of flirting with other women, but I didn't think I was flirting, even though it was obvious to everyone but me. The problem grew.

Diane felt unattractive because of her weight, so she joined a self-help group to try to lose it. The leader of the group made a play for me at a Halloween party at our house. I wasn't interested in her, but Diane didn't believe me. I think Gloria saw Diane as a threat to her leadership, and flirting with me was a way of undercutting Diane. Maybe she thought I was cute. That didn't occur to me. One night Gloria and her husband Floyd, an Air Force sergeant, invited us to the NCO Club. After Gloria asked me to dance, and Diane thought I was being too friendly with her, Diane poured a pitcher of beer on my head in anger. A few days later we argued about Arielle. Diane ran out of the house, jumped into her car, and raced away. Furious, I chased her in my pickup. Barreling along a narrow street after her, my side mirror hit the mirror of a parked truck. My mirror whipped around and smashed the passenger side window of my cab and broke the mirror on the parked truck. I had to stop and see to the damage. Diane escaped to Manitou Springs.

Winter came, and one grey afternoon I was in the office Diane when called and asked me to come up to Manitou Springs. She was with Arielle, George, and Charlie, sitting around smoking pot and feeling sexy. My imagination was on fire, but I told her I couldn't leave. I finished my workday and met her at home. Diane told me what had happened, in detail, between her, the two men, and Arielle as they alternated sex partners. Diane said she'd had sex with Charlie, and I was inflamed by jealousy and desire.

"Do you want her?" she asked me.

A few days later, Diane and I dropped in on Arielle at her house in Manitou Springs. We agreed to have sex. The three of us undressed and climbed into bed. I satisfied my desire and Diane's dark fantasy as she watched. Diane dropped Arielle after that. For years afterward I regretted not having the strength to resist that temptation. Diane later denied she'd ever had sex with Charlie—claiming she only said it to make me jealous, but I didn't believe her. It left me with a diabolical mixture of unresolved feelings about the whole incident and similar situations that occurred later.

Why did we stay together with such conflict and infidelity? No simple answer comes to mind. The men in Diane's life had betrayed or disappointed her too many times. Her father was weak and ineffectual, and his failures threatened the security and stability of his family. Her favorite uncle, a man whom she admired and trusted, made a pass at her when she was grown, as did other close relatives. She probed and tested me for weaknesses, wondering how and when I would fail like the others. There I was, immature and inexperienced, failing her and myself under pressure. I was ashamed of my failure, but I kept trying to live up to her expectations and my own.

We were both highly intelligent loners and outsiders. Diane's experiences set her apart from most people she met, who could scarcely imagine her past life. In Berkeley, I was part of a community of my peers, students and faculty who were truly exceptional, and I saw Diane had the same qualities. When we met as if directed by fate at Mirror Lake, we felt an immediate affinity based on deep recognition of one another's singular character. I responded to her emotion and her passion, she to my stability and steadfast commitment. Despite how we might wander or fail, we both felt an overwhelming desire to be together.

During our year in Colorado we went to a country western bar in the Springs one evening, crowded with people our age, dancing to a country band and popular records. They played the recent hit from Judy Collins, "Someday Soon." The song is about southern Colorado, where we lived, and it was popular there. It always has been one of my favorites. Whenever I hear it, my mind goes back to that night in Colorado in 1969, twenty-three years old, still young, crazy and full of eagerness for more life, more love, and more of the world with Diane beside me. I feel another burst of sadness for the passing of that moment, the years, and the woman I loved.

The rest of that winter our life in Colorado became tense and tedious. We had little extra money and neither of us was well-grounded in handling what we had wisely. Diane was using for birth control, and she wanted to get pregnant. She stopped using it, and after very intense lovemaking she became pregnant. Realizing that we'd need more money, I asked for a raise at my job without success. I started looking for a job with better pay to support my growing family. In August Control Data Corporation, a large computer manufacturer, flew me to Minneapolis for an interview. I was young, bright, and cheap. They offered me a job. A month later we moved from Colorado to Minnesota. I drove the truck and camper, towing Diane's blue Corvair behind us.

Lauren was born in December. I spent the night before her birth with Diane at the hospital, trying to be her childbirth coach without much success. Shortly after midnight, Diane started having labor pains. She endured pain and anxiety for eight hours, and we finally went into the delivery room on a sunny morning. I'll never forget seeing Lauren emerge squalling from Diane's body, messy and unhappy about it. Before long she was cleaned and nestled on Diane, sweet and vulnerable. I left them safe at the hospital and drove back to our apartment, wild and elated, full of joy, one of the highest points of my whole life.

Lauren came home with Diane a few days later. We lived in an apartment in Brooklyn Park, a suburb northwest of Minneapolis. Two weeks after Lauren's birth, pressed by creditors for unpaid bills, we filed for bankruptcy. Our credit was wiped out and for several years we paid cash for everything. Our truck, camper, and car were repossessed in the bankruptcy. I bought an old red Corvair from my boss at work for sixty dollars. It leaked exhaust fumes from a cracked manifold, so I had to drive in the subzero Minnesota weather with a window slightly open, and I couldn't use the heater. Driving home in the frozen winter nights I felt like Doctor Zhivago, stumbling through snowdrifts across the Siberian steppe. Later Diane's old boyfriend Bob helped us out. He traded us a battered but drivable 1962 Plymouth sedan and an ounce of weed for the tow bar that pulled Diane's Corvair to Minneapolis. That car lasted until we bought a station wagon for our next adventure in 1972. In June 1970, we moved to a duplex in working-class South Minneapolis not far from where Diane lived as a child. As we were driving the old Plymouth to our new home, with clothes piled up to the windows in the back seat, I stopped for gas. The young attendant stood by my window and looked the car over, checked out my beard and shabby clothing, and asked, eyes wide with astonishment, "Are you ... hippies?"

We made the best of our modest income; for recreation the four of us took long drives around the countryside, or went camping. I made a pantry box to carry our dishes, utensils, pans, and food. The box rode next to a large tent on a luggage rack atop our beat-up Plymouth. On one camping trip in northern Minnesota we found a little resort on Everett Lake, and we returned later in the summer with Diane's grandmother to spend a week in a cabin. As we drove north late at night on our way to the resort, we stopped to stretch our legs by the side of the highway. Nanny pointed toward the stars and asked me what I thought they were. She was born in 1890 and had a sixth-grade education. She knew nothing about science, but was curious about the things she did not know. During our week at the lake we spent a whole morning picking wild blueberries in a wide clearing near the resort, staying alert for bears. Nanny used them to bake a blueberry pie. I doubt if I'll ever taste better.

Diane ran up huge phone bills making long-distance calls to her family in California. She had a literal love-hate relationship with her parents. When they were together, they invariably rehashed past grievances, leading to fierce arguments that ended with someone crying. Most of the time it was her mother. That was Gen's last line of defense, even when she started the argument with sharp verbal jabs. Yet, when her parents were distant, Diane kept calling her mother as if somehow she could repair the breach, make her mother reasonable, make her mother love her.

Radicals

Those who profess to favor freedom and yet depreciate agitation, are people who want crops without ploughing the ground; they want rain without thunder and lightning; they want the ocean without the roar of its many waters. The struggle may be a moral one, or it may be a physical one, or it may be both. But it must be a struggle. Power concedes nothing without a demand.
— *Frederick Douglass*

After we moved to Minneapolis we often visited Diane's childhood friend Darryl. As children Diane and Darryl played together while their parents socialized. Darryl contracted polio during an epidemic in the early 1950s, and walked with a limp because of the polio and a later injury in an auto accident. He spoke with a Minnesota twang, and tended to start every sentence with the local phrase "Ya know?" As a closeted gay man, Darryl viewed politics much differently than an average Minnesotan. He was radicalized by his participation in the March on Washington in November, 1969. Diane and I, preoccupied with the last months of Diane's pregnancy and how we'd afford it, didn't pay much attention to politics that fall. When we'd visit Darryl at his parents' home in a conservative Minneapolis suburb, sometimes we would engage in heated arguments about the war. Darryl's strong clashed with those of his father and older brother, who supported the government and the war. We usually sided with Darryl.

The antiwar movement spilled onto the streets of Minneapolis in the spring of 1970, after President Nixon sent bombers into Cambodia in violation of international law. At Kent State University, protesters torched the ROTC building, and after the Ohio National Guard shot and killed four students days later, huge protests erupted all over the country, shutting down almost seven hundred college campuses and blocking Interstate highways in several major cities. On Saturday May 9, Darryl, Diane, and I marched with sixty thousand other protesters from the University of Minnesota to the State Capitol in Saint Paul, thronging past the governor's mansion for hours, shouting "One, two, three, four! We don't want your fucking war!" We joined students at the university, building barricades of trash cans and construction materials to block U. S. Highway 12 where it ran through the campus. About three thousand people participated in the blockade.

My employer had slashed the payroll because of the falloff in government orders as money was diverted to the war. To cut costs further, they cut the pay of remaining staff by ten percent. They gave us ten days off as compensation. I used that free time to spend hours with Diane at meetings, marches, and occasional parties. We met protesters and draft resisters at demonstrations—like Dan, whose wiry red hair and beard would be the first thing you'd notice about him until he spoke. In a soft voice, Dan would tell about his outdoor experiences, like the time he nearly froze to death walking through the Minnesota woods in winter. A talented and intelligent artist, he displayed his abilities in unorthodox ways. Raised in a strict evangelical Christian family, he could quote passages from the Bible verbatim. In 1970 the draft was based on a lottery and when your number was drawn, you'd be drafted. Dan had a low number, and when his number came up, he disappeared rather than go to Vietnam. He joined the community of underground draft resisters in Minneapolis.

An unidentified bomber detonated twenty pounds of dynamite in the Minneapolis Federal Building late one night. A few days later, Diane was talking to some friends and said, "They bombed the Federal Building—Dayton's will be next." She reasoned that leftist radicals would target a symbol of capitalism next. Not long afterward, a bomb exploded in a restroom in the Dayton's department store in Saint Paul. Someone who had overheard Diane's remark called the FBI. The next day, two FBI agents knocked on our door. Diane invited them in for coffee. She called me at work.

"The FBI is here. What should I do?"

"Don't talk to them."

I left for home immediately. It took me an hour on the bus to get there. Meanwhile, Diane sat down with the FBI agents and had a nice chat. By the time I was home, they were gone, satisfied that she knew nothing about the second bombing. We never heard from them again.

A group of draft resistors who worked at the Twin Cities Draft Information Center founded a commune in a large three-story house on South Colfax Avenue in Minneapolis, and called it Colfax house. Dan was sheltered by friends there for over a year, and introduced us to them. Diane was fascinated by the people who lived in Colfax house. Most of them were younger than Diane, like her friends in Colorado Springs, but her adolescence was so severely disrupted that she missed out on much of the social learning she would have had then. It was almost like she was their age. We spent many evenings there smoking pot, talking to them, and learning about their ideas and motives. Dan met a young woman named Cheri at the house, and they fell in love. They married in a civil ceremony at City Hall, and their friends at Colfax house held a reception for them in the dining room that evening. Diane and I stood with them around the ping pong table that served as the dining room table, passing fat joints and a bottle of champagne hand to hand. Dan and Cheri remained our friends for years, and Diane and I visited them in 2011 on their farm in northern Minnesota.

While we lived in Minneapolis Diane and I discussed my adopting Jennifer formally. Her father, Dave Palmer, stopped paying his court-ordered child support and was over two thousand dollars in arrears. He had made no effort to contact Jennifer since she was an infant, and never indicated he wanted to. He made no effort to find us, and we didn't know where to find him. However, his parents hadn't moved since the divorce. I looked up their phone number, called his mother, and pretended to be an old Army buddy of Dave's wanting to get in touch with him.

"I'm on my way north to work on the DEW Line and I wanted to touch base with him while I'm in town," I told her. She gave me his address and phone number.

We passed this on to our attorney and started the adoption in motion. We offered him a deal on his arrears, and he agreed to give up his parental rights to Jennifer. We also asked him to write a letter to Jennifer so she'd have some communication from him. He wrote a letter, but it said nothing. He had no feelings for his own daughter. Hennepin County required me to go through the same investigation as any prospective adoptive parent, and in June the adoption was complete. Jennifer officially became Jennifer Jay Palmer Enfield.

My job was secure at the time, but Control Data's prospects were diminishing. No trace of the company remains today. I saw it coming, and wanted to get out. Because of our association with protesters, draft resisters, and counterculture types, we felt a disorganized urge to go "back to the land." We wondered where to go, and how. Diane was always open to a fresh start. My parents owned twenty acres of unimproved land in Washington State, and our back-of-the envelope plan was to go there and somehow establish ourselves on the land in Whole Earth Catalog, self-sustaining, Mother Earth News style. One evening at a Control Data party I talked about this with a co-worker who'd immigrated from Ireland, and his advice was to take the leap. Five years after uprooting myself from Berkeley with advice from no one, I uprooted my whole family with advice from exactly one person of doubtful credentials. We moved our furniture into storage to be shipped later. We bought a used station wagon with a trailer hitch and set out for the West with some essential belongings in a U-Haul trailer and no idea what to do next.

Journal
Fall, 1970

Jenny went to school—walked alone for the first time. She has gone with her little friend downstairs, for the first month—eagerly, chattering noisily down the stairs and out the door. Now she must walk alone—four blocks of new experiences. So she hesitated, blew kisses, walked backwards waving and shouting softly "Mama" and I hesitated, blew kisses, waved and shouted back "Go on, you'll be late," and I wondered "Will she remember the way? I hope she watches when she crosses the street—does she know other children can be cruel, yet?"

And now I know this kind of fear is just beginning and will become a familiar companion throughout the years.

I look at Laurie and it seems hard to see ahead to the day when she, too will make that first walk alone to school.

Seems school was OK for me until California—it was all new—walking across open, dusty fields—carrying a lunch bag, gone all day. Then it began, all the moving—a new school every year, new friends to be made and never were, living on the edge of the school district, never near enough to other classmates; new teachers, worries about things like the bills my parents always fought over, fights with relatives, mother getting sick and going away, night after she was home—lying quietly in bed and breathing softly so I can hear if she calls or coughs (blood, hemorrhage, chokes).

No money, no clothes like the others, always the new girl in the class, always having to be accepted over and over, others joining GAA and Job's Daughters and I had to be home right after school and somehow never was. They said it was my fault, I was a troublemaker, never did what I was supposed to do and eventually realized they were right—now I am over thirty, have children of my own, bills to worry over and moves to make and I realize they were wrong and I was lost on the way to school—not the first day or the second but somewhere between the fifth and sixth grade—I got lost and stayed lost. I cried for my mother, but my mother was sick and couldn't hear me. I cried for my father, but my father was away at work and it was too far for him to hear me. The teachers were too busy. So, it took me twenty years to find my way home again. How? I was scared but I just kept walking. I stumbled, fell, and scraped my knees bloody, dirtied my clothes, but I got back up and kept walking. Now I'm home. Jenny will walk alone only if she can—perhaps between Ron and I, the bluebirds and my own roadmap of the past, she will not get lost on the way to school.

RETURNING WEST

We all came to Seattle in hopes of building better lives.
No one said we wouldn't have to struggle first.
— *REGINA SCOTT*

We traveled from Minneapolis through several states, arriving in Vancouver, Washington in late June. We spent a summer at my grandparents' house living on unemployment without a plan. I felt disillusioned about working with computers, but I couldn't imagine what else would support us. Our ideas about living on the land never came close to reality, but the reality of living with relatives, with no job, no money, and no independent life drove me to look for a job in programming. Vancouver was a small market and most of the ads listed jobs around Puget Sound. We decided to move there.

In late September we rented a small house on Lake McDonald outside of Renton, Washington. Most of our belongings remained in a warehouse in Minneapolis, so we furnished the cottage from a local thrift store. I found a job working in a bank at the north end of Seattle, commuting 28 miles each way and making five hundred a month less than I earned at Control Data—typical low pay at a bank.

October was beautiful at Lake McDonald, with bright sunny days that brought out the deep green of the evergreen trees around our house. In November the clouds rolled in, and we literally didn't see the sun again until January. Even when the sun finally broke through the overcast, the trees blocked the sunlight all but two hours a day. Water seeped out of the ground everywhere, turning a path through the woods to a neighbor's house into a swamp. Diane's seasonal depression came roaring back. She slept late every day, sometimes barely getting up. Jennifer took a school bus every day to Maple Valley Elementary School where she was in fourth grade, but Lauren stayed home. She was too young for kindergarten and we were too broke for daycare.

One morning as Diane lay in bed, three-year-old Lauren approached her, tenderly pried open her eyelid and asked "Mommy, are you in there?"

The endless gloom and dampness penetrated every aspect of our lives, affecting Diane's mood the most. It wore me down, along with worries over money and the 60-mile a day commute, but it made Diane desperate. A social worker named Jan rented a small one-room cottage next to us. One evening she invited Diane to go out with her in Seattle, to meet someone she knew who was on the campaign staff of Senator Magnuson. Jan didn't want to go alone, and Diane wanted to get out of the deep woods for a while. I stayed home to watch the girls while Diane went out.

In the middle of the night a phone call from Diane woke me up. She said she was at a restaurant in Seattle with one of the Senator's staffers. She wanted to come home, but she rode in with Jan, and Jan was in a hotel room with another staffer. Our car was being repaired. I borrowed our neighbor's car and away I went while his wife kept an eye on the girls. I found Diane sitting in the restaurant with a stranger and she left with me.

I found a better-paying job at the Port of Seattle, got a loan from my grandfather to make a down payment on a house in the city, and in January we moved into Seattle. The Port agreed to ship my furniture from Minneapolis, and we settled into our new home. It was dark, damp winter still, but we had our furniture back and a fireplace to dispel the gloom. A spring flowed from the center of our back lawn to the walkway beside the house, and out to the street.

After we moved into the city Diane made friends quickly. She befriended a neighbor named Julie who lived nearby. She asked Diane to substitute in her place as a volunteer, teaching a sex education class to the students at an all-girls Catholic high school, many from disadvantaged homes. Julie was teaching the class but had to give it up due to a conflict. Diane's background helped her understand the girls and teach them effectively. She did an outstanding job and her students praised her for the way she connected with them. Diane's outspokenness enabled the girls to talk about and understand their own experiences. One girl told Diane she lived in a commune in Seattle where she was sexually abused when she was nine. At the end of the class the girls wrote notes to Diane, telling her how much they appreciated the way she taught the class.

Lauren's personality developed as she grew. One day she showed up in the kitchen, with bright red lipstick smeared on her face like a circus clown. Diane confronted her.

"Laurie, did you go into my makeup?"

"Oh, no mommy."

We began to see she might be difficult to manage.

My cousin visited us from Portland in the spring. She came to Seattle to marry her female partner with officiation by a sympathetic minister. We welcomed them, and Diane enthusiastically pressed them for information about their lives, their thoughts, and feelings, as she did with everyone. That evening my cousin took Diane and Julie to a lesbian bar to show them her world. Afterwards, Diane told me she went home with Julie and the two of them tried a sexual experiment. "It didn't turn me on," she said, "but Julie liked it." Julie was slender, with light brown hair, an engaging smile, and she was younger than Diane—the same age as me. She was exactly the kind of woman Diane feared was the greatest threat to her. Julie dropped into our house frequently, and she and I started noticing each other. Her marriage to her psychologist husband was coming apart, and I was still letting my eye wander after five years of marriage. I tried not to show it, but Diane noticed instantly.

Spurred on by the sexual stimulation that my cousin's visit had stirred up, we drifted toward action. Diane invited Julie to our house one night after the girls were asleep upstairs. We all undressed and began to caress each other's bodies. We moved to the downstairs guest bedroom and indulged our fantasies. Julie would have been a threat to our marriage if I had been motivated mainly by sexual attraction, but Diane and I had a deep emotional and intellectual bond beyond sex. I never considered leaving her and my two girls for Julie. A night or two later, after some discussion, we agreed to stop.

Where was I in all this? Carried away again by lust, my will power neutralized. Julie was a distraction, an indiscretion, a mistake, a repetition of our Colorado Springs adventure. I feared lasting consequences if I gave in to desire, but I was weak. Years later the consequences showed up when dementia distorted Diane's mind and memory. Once, Diane told me I should have been with other women before we met. She was probably right, but it was too late by the time she said it. We had the relationship that was possible, not ideal, and tried to make the best of it.

I didn't marry Diane because she was my dream lover. She was the first woman I ever had a relationship with. She was also the most engaging woman I ever met, and no one else ever came close. Most of her friends felt the same. She needed honest, intimate relationships, and could not tolerate people who would not offer that. She inspired love and devotion, and she was very sexy, but she wasn't my ideal sex partner. From the start of our relationship I knew I wasn't the man she desired most. That was Tom, her husband whom schizophrenia destroyed.

Later Diane retaliated by saying that she was going to leave me and run away to Costa Rica with her English teacher from community college. We were in bed and I was so upset I rolled onto the floor and pounded it with my fist. The solid hardwood floor broke a bone in my wrist, and I ended up with my left arm in a cast for six weeks. At the emergency room, Diane confessed she just wanted to make me jealous, and my reaction surprised her. She was sorry.

Journal
October 1973

Over five years have passed since I began writing in this journal. Five years—filled with what?

One new baby girl—now age 3 soon to be 4

One little girl now a big girl of 9

One marriage—now five years old
one affair—now six years of memories

A house of our own, in Seattle—4 bedrooms, a study, a family room, 2 bathrooms, a kitchen, a basement, a garage, a yard, a fireplace

A trailer which we seldom use but hesitate to sell--(After all—someday)

An annual income of approximately $14,000

A couple of night school classes at a local jr. college

A volunteer teaching job at an all-girls Catholic high school

A king-sized bed

A freezer

A used station wagon

A lot of bills again

A lot of confusion, stress, busyness, frustration. A growing sense of life as narrowing—closing in on me—trapping me into lawn fertilizer, tulips never planted, children's fevers and pin worms, aches in my legs and back that never were,

Thirty pounds of weight I fear I may never lose, skin drying and sagging more each year,

A vast amount of unsaleable knowledge that only creates more dissatisfaction

I have PTA meetings, children's flute lessons, paper routes, freeway traffic, term papers on Assyrian boundary stones, friends that are teachers, lawyers, social workers that are making it

Jesus Christ, have I arrived!

I am 26 going on 50 and I am dying—without options—or choices

I am racing against the clock with jaws set and teeth firmly clenched.

I am being good, but I am dying!

Egypt!
dying—

By November, the sun scarcely rose above the dark horizon by midafternoon, and seldom struggled through the clouds. I spent a week in Colorado Springs at a management training seminar for my job, then I flew home from open, sunny Colorado skies to gloomy Seattle. Dusk covered the landscape in mid-afternoon. Darkness plunged Diane into depression. The first winter we were together, in relatively bright Southern California, she was depressed in January, and every winter was the same. When seasonal affective disorder (SAD) was featured in the media, we all agreed Diane had it. Which major American city (outside of Alaska) would I say was the worst place for a person with SAD to live? Seattle. We started thinking about where to go from there. My parents, Diane's sisters, and her parents all lived near Los Angeles. I started looking for a job in Southern California.

Journal
Undated

Old dreams now face reality—to be kept and nurtured into being or faced as fantasy and buried as the dead are. For so long, I have kept ahold of them, allowing their nebulous forms to dictate my living.

Who, then, am I (now and in reality)

A grown, mature (and I long for my childhood) woman (a man could live differently) married (yes, I sought and yearned for my very own true love—a forever thing)

with two girl children (I never thought I'd have a boy, only blonde-haired, blue-eyed beauties)

with no job or career (but I never saw myself working anyplace other then as an ideal wife/mother)

overweight (never imagined such a curse to be in my future)

in a house (certainly not the one of my dreams and wishes—the beauty of it is nowhere in sight)

in Seattle (while dreams of midwestern humidity and long summer days torment my soul)

What about those dreams—what were or are they?

The house is always first, there is so much time spent within its walls

A white frame house with blue or dark green trim and shutters, two stories with bedrooms upstairs

A front porch with a swing for warm summer nights

A large shade tree in the yard for a old board swing and a sandbox underneath it

A garden with flowers I can cut and bring into the house

Bedrooms with white curtains and flowered wallpaper

In May I had interviews lined up at Hughes Aircraft and C. F. Braun & Company. I flew down for a couple of days and spoke to them and ended up with an offer from Braun. Their headquarters were in Alhambra close to Diane's family, while Hughes was in Orange County some distance away. I took Braun's offer as technical support manager. After returning to Seattle I talked to a Boeing engineer about the job. He asked me if they offered what I asked for.

"Yes," I said.

"You didn't ask enough."

He was right. When we moved to Los Angeles and found out the cost of housing there, I knew I'd made a mistake. It was too late.

We moved to San Gabriel, California in July 1974, and stayed until February 1977. We rented a comfortable two-bedroom house on a quiet street just off busy Valley Boulevard. The neighborhood was majority Hispanic, and our kids were welcomed into the elementary school. It was a pleasant interlude except we were broke all the time. Diane's sisters, so friendly when they came to visit us in Colorado, Minnesota, and Washington, were often indifferent to our presence a few miles away. We got together a few times a year, but otherwise they didn't provide much companionship for Diane and our daughters. Jennifer caught mononucleosis while we lived there. She recovered, and we didn't think about it afterwards until years later.

In June 1976 I flew to Philadelphia with a team from Braun to visit the Burroughs computer factory in Paoli, Pennsylvania. That was my first trip to the area. I was impressed with the luxuriant growth of trees and greenery on the drive along the Schuylkill River from Philadelphia to Paoli. When recruiters from Computer Sciences Corporation, located in a suburb of Philadelphia, passed through Southern California about six months later I contacted them. CSC interviewed me and they made an offer. We were thinking of moving out of San Gabriel at the time, but the Southern California real estate market was too hot for us. A new development of condominiums in Irvine was holding a lottery for chances to bid on a new condominium. One of the recruiters mentioned that his three-bedroom house a few minutes from the office cost less than half the price of a condominium in Irvine an hour from my job. I accepted their offer and we prepared to move to New Jersey.

When the time came for us to move from California to New Jersey we could have driven across the country. Driving cross-country in our small two-door Ford would have been almost impossible for four people and two pets, and Jennifer and Lauren warring in the back seat would have propelled us into the worst circle of Hell. We flew across the continent rather than drive. We had the car driven by a service.

BACK EAST

My home was in a pleasant place outside of Philadelphia. But I really lived, truly lived, somewhere else. I lived within the covers of books.
—ANNA QUINDLEN

Medford Lakes, a tiny suburb of woods and small man-made lakes near Philadelphia, was our home for fifteen years. Diane began a period of intensive reflection and examination of her life history, reporting her impressions in her detailed journal entries.

Journal
Summer 1979

We spent two summers in the old log cabin we rented when we first arrived. The second summer my sister and her two girls came to visit us. That spring Jennifer had graduated from the eighth grade. We celebrated the event on the porch later one evening. The old photographs show the oil lamps lit, my daughters and their cousins at the huge log picnic table. Jennifer opened her gifts and cake and punch. My sister and her daughters stayed about six weeks before returning home to California.

We swam in the cedar-brown waters of the lakes, took a trip to Atlantic city, visited the Amish country, shopping the touristy town of Intercourse, PA and watching the Amish driving their horse-drawn black buggies. One dark evening, Pat and I went down to the lake to swim. The lakes were very shallow, being old cranberry bogs that were deepened. The bottom had a few springs but most of the water flowed from the creeks and lakes upstream, through the woods and cedar swamps. While the water was dark, it was pure and relatively unpolluted, the lake bottom was soft and mushy with silt and mud. In the middle of the long narrow lake, ran a channel, a foot or two deeper. One could walk out to this channel stepping in the muck and then swim the middle five feet of the channel before touching down into the muck again. The darkness of the night and water and the squishiness of the mud made the lake crossing a mini adventure for two thirtyish women who had experienced relatively few adventures in their lives. As the older, more daring sister, I urged Pat to come with me as I crossed the dark waters. At the channel depth, she lost her nerve and I returned with her to the sandy beach.

The night woods were full of natural sounds, new to our ears: a million crickets chirped to each other, frogs sang from the reeds at the waters' edge, small animals pattered through the ground foliage, oak leaves rustled in the occasional light breeze; sometimes we heard a hoot owl in the distant woods. In the late hours toward midnight, the whip-poor-wills began to call. Mysterious black shadows made us wary in the bright full moonlight showing through the tall pines.

We delighted in the crack and boom of approaching thunderstorms, the rain beating on the porch roof, the white lighting that lit up the sky and surrounding forest. We inhaled the smell of the wet forest floor that lay covered with old pine needles and mosses. Safe under the porch eves, curled up on an old sofa, we watched, listened and zoned out—the healing balm only nature could spread over a troubled soul. My sister was in a troubled marriage, even then. Her visit to us was one of three that she had made to us. Though she rarely discussed it, I knew it was never that she yearned to see me but rather a desperate need to escape the painful reality of her life at home. I felt I was offering her a refuge-those visits. She never acknowledged the gift, as such.

Many kids in the Medford Lakes schools knew each other from infancy, and didn't have a lot of experience making new friends, especially kids from the West Coast who spoke with (to them) a strange accent. Jennifer had entered new schools before as we moved from Colorado Springs to Minneapolis, Seattle, and San Gabriel. She was older than Lauren, more mature, and emotionally more resilient. She adapted. Lauren had a harder time. She didn't tolerate teasing and bullying well, and the kids in her school did both. The teachers seemed oblivious. It made an unwelcoming environment for Lauren. In San Gabriel she had been skipped from kindergarten to first grade. When we moved to New Jersey during her second grade, she floundered in school. The New Jersey curriculum was more advanced than California, and by skipping Lauren had missed learning some important skills. She had to repeat second grade.

Other issues cropped up. Diane once complained to Lauren's teacher about an incident in class. The teacher did not like being criticized, and took it out on Lauren, who stopped telling Diane about problems at school. When we moved to Medford Lakes we didn't check out the schools, relying on the real estate agent to recommend a good district. A man I knew at CSC told me he moved into the Lakes, and after the first teacher-parent conference at school he realized he'd made a bad choice, and he moved out. Diane's home life was so chaotic, and her family moved so many times she didn't realize how changing schools might affect Jennifer and Lauren. I had no clue. We could have done better. It caught up with us later.

August brought heat and humidity to Medford Lakes every year. A severe heat wave in 1980 created unbearable temperatures from the Midwest to the Northeast. We had no central air conditioning in our home, just one window unit in the living room and one in the master bedroom. We tried to use them as little as possible because of the electric bills, and we struggled to sleep through the warm, muggy nights. As uncomfortable as our nights were, in Minneapolis Diane's ninety-year-old grandmother was experiencing much worse.

Journal
August 1980

August was cruel that way. The last heat wave of 1980 struck Texas the worst, but the mid-west suffered as well. Grandma died that summer, that AUGUST. The small rooms of her apartment held the heat throughout the night. Sleep must have been impossible. In New Jersey, we bought a room air conditioner and the four of us slept in the same king size bed. Blessed cool relief brought sleep finally. In Minnesota, there was no relief from the days and nights of heat. Her heart struggled to maintain its usual rhythm, the sweat soaked her body and sheets. She put cold water-soaked rags across her forehead and aimed the small fan towards the bed.

In the morning, she called her son and asked him to take her to the hospital. She'd had a heart attack. For years before she complained about the burning that came right up into her throat. She told me it was indigestion, heart burn. I looked the symptoms up in my Merck Manual, and figured she had a hiatal hernia. After she died, I remembered she'd had another heart attack years before. My mother told me gram had a bad heart and refused to take the medicine she had been prescribed. Mom said Gram probably knew she had a bad heart and didn't tell anyone. "She was stubborn like that." My parents called me to tell me she was in the hospital. She was 90 but I thought she would be ok, she'd pulled through colon cancer and lung cancer. I called the hospital and they told me she was ok. Well, not exactly ok but stabilized or something that didn't really register the seriousness of her condition. Somehow I spoke to my uncle who was at the hospital, he was crying and told me she was probably not going to make it. Then I got panicky, this was for real. I called the hospital and begged the nurse to tell her I was coming — to tell her to hold on — I'll be there.

I got my husband and daughters packed up and we took off a few hours later. It was still steaming hot outside and night was blackening the sky when we set off. Five miles down the road I was seized with the idea of calling the hospital again. I needed to tell them I was on my way. A female voice answered the call and told me to hold on so I could talk to Dr. Olson. I still didn't have a clue. The telephone booth was like a sauna, sweat dripped from my face, down the arm holding the phone to my ear. He told me she was gone. My knees gave out and I sank to the dirty cement screaming and howling. I saw my uncle' s face, wet with tears, my husband and children stood next to the car, Ron tried to hold me and a stranger passing by thought he was beating me. The kids were crying, I continued to scream. She's gone — my mind kept turning the phrase over and over, attempting to understand what gone meant. I wasn't prepared for GONE. My family tells me I was inconsolable that night. It was one of the few times in my life when I was unaware of myself, not self-conscious. We returned home and I wept through the night hours.

I flew to Minneapolis the next day. My husband and the girls drove back.

Diane never hesitated to speak out on issues she cared about. She cared often. Some people disliked her outspokenness. Others admired her for it. In the spring of 1981, gypsy moth infestations threatened the forests in South Jersey, and many Lakes residents worried about their trees. They wanted to use aerial spraying to combat the moth larvae, using the pesticide Sevin. Diane opposed spraying the town with Sevin, listed by the EPA as a potential carcinogen, and she voiced her opinion loudly and often. That angered several prominent Medford Lakes residents, and some children parroted the inflammatory rhetoric of their parents. Kids whose parents supported spraying taunted Lauren about her "crazy mother." Many residents hired private contractors to spray Sevin on their trees, and after much controversy the Medford Lakes Borough Council passed an ordinance setting out regulations governing commercial pesticide sprayers. In the next election the anti-spraying faction won, and we were invited to join the Borough Environmental Council.

After leaving CSC for the MITRE Corporation, I eventually moved to MITRE's office in the Federal Aviation Administration Technical Center near Atlantic City. My life improved. My commute was only half an hour instead of the previous hour and a half. The facility sat next to the Atlantic City reservoir where I could run at lunchtime through quiet woods on sand roads. I had more time at home, our family was calm, and we enjoyed one another's company. That summer we rented a house at the Jersey Shore for the last week of August. Remnants of a hurricane passed hundreds of miles to the east, roiling the surf and spoiling the bathing somewhat, but we still enjoyed our vacation away from the house and my job. One night as we ate hamburgers at a restaurant on an amusement pier, we smelled smoke. Diane stood up and announced in a loud voice, "Everyone stand up and walk slowly to the exit NOW." Then we walked out. We stood on the beach and watched while fire destroyed the pier, including the restaurant where we just were eating.

Journal
August 1981

August, the heat — always the heat. The dog days of summer, the height of the hurricane season, nights filled with the incessant whirring cicada's (ugly bugs). On the forest floor lays a thick mat of fallen dry yellowed pine needles, when crushed underfoot scent the air. The pine barrens of New Jersey often burn now, raging fires that fill the blue skies with grey smoke that filters the sun to a red ball. Lawns wither while people flee their suburban homes for the cooling shore breezes "down the shore" time in New Jersey. So we went to a rented place in Ocean City. The girls took friends.

Ocean City is known as the family beach resort. There are no bars, clubs or liquor stores within the city limits. Those looking for night life go to the adjacent beach towns to get drunk and raise hell. I don't remember much of that week, a storm had passed and eroded much of the beach. We walked on the boardwalk and in one of the arcades, a metal bar fell from the ceiling just after I passed under that section. I thought I was lucky, then.

I recall Lauren and Jenny having some kind of a dispute. Jenny seemed to sleep a lot that week. She complained of a hard lump on her neck, in the hollow above her collar bone. I think that was the first time she mentioned it but I can't be sure.

Mostly it was a quiet week. One night we played a joke on Laura who had been sleeping during the late afternoon into the early evening. When she awakened, we all went down to the beach for the moon rise, telling her it was early morning and we wanted to see the sun rise. We all got a good laugh out of her believing it. On Sunday, Lauren and a friend went to visit a Catholic Church without telling us where she was going, except for a little walk. We went to the museum and saw a huge twenty-pound-plus lobster they had hauled up from the offshore waters many years ago.

Several days later, after we were back home, I took Jennifer to see a doctor in Haddonfield (this was a referral from our family doctor). The diagnosis was a jolt for me when he said I should be thinking of something more serious than a mere swollen gland. I think he suggested some possibilities and mentioned Hodgkin's Disease, which I knew nothing about. He scheduled Jennifer for some kind of a test, but the facility's machine was down. Some time went by before she saw Dr. Ansel, an ear, nose, and throat specialist, who admitted Jennifer to Burlington County Hospital for a biopsy.

Something seemed to tell me this was going to be what I feared most—cancer. I recalled that mother told me years before when Jenny was little that she should protect her throat. When she was about two years old, I noticed a small pea sized nodule on her neck cord. The pediatrician examined her and said it was nothing to be concerned with. I am not sure it was even on the same side as where the tumor appeared. Mother dabbled in as-

trology and was always giving the family advice about problems and weaknesses associated with our astrological birth signs. She would tell me that Jennifer was born in July, and that her birth sign was Cancer, the crab. She warned me to protect her against illness. I didn't believe in astrology and couldn't see how I could protect her anyway, beside the usual daily precautions and generally nutritious diet I fed her. Yet, my mind fastened on the idea that she would get cancer one day. The thought was so horrible that I brushed it off whenever it came up. I felt that my mother had planted it in my mind, and it made me angry to think about it. However, she was right in the end.

That afternoon, Dr. Ansel called me with the results of the biopsy. Inside, a voice told me that everything was fine, that I was being my usual overly dramatic self and that nothing was wrong. Again, I felt electrocuted with shock. I remember Ron came home from work soon after the call. We left the house and walked down the street. For once in my life I could not talk — my throat was knotted with pain — my eyes filled with blinding tears. I sobbed and retched but I could not get the words out.

We visited Jenny at the hospital that night but decided not to tell her until the morning. She introduced us to her roommate, Robin, a young unmarried girl who had just had a baby and was upset about her future. We spoke together in the room and tried to be light-hearted about the evening. I spent the rest of the evening practicing how I would tell Jennifer she had cancer. My family had always called attention to the way I dramatized things. It was a bone of contention between us as I felt they never took things seriously, particularly my reactions to painful personal crises in my own life. I thought about this when I was preparing myself for the next morning. Perhaps, they were right, that I needed to downplay the seriousness of things and that this was certainly one case where I should. it must have been one of those life crossroads for me. The most important person in my life was in serious trouble and how I behaved might be critical to her survival. I had to be in control of myself, my emotions, my language. I had to portray a positive attitude. All of this was the opposite of my real self, but I could act, and I would.

We scheduled Jennifer for exploratory surgery in November. It was a staging laparotomy, a major surgery with an incision from the bottom of her abdomen to the sternum, removal of the spleen (the main organ in the lymph system) and excision of lymph nodes in the chest and abdomen to determine how far the disease had spread. At the same time, her ovaries were moved within her abdomen out of the path of radiation therapy to come later. Jennifer spent several days in the hospital for surgery and afterward for recovery. She was afraid she would die. The scar from that surgery remained for the rest of her life, a vertical track half an inch wide from chest to groin, forever reminding her of what she had endured (and alerting medical professionals that she had had a laparotomy and her internal organs had been rearranged).

In August that year, the air traffic controllers staged a nationwide strike, and President Reagan began firing the striking controllers. In October, Reagan reduced the budget of the Federal Aviation Administration by forty percent to punish them for the strike. In turn, the FAA cut MITRE's contract by the same amount. My job with MITRE at the FAA Technical Center was eliminated. I received a month's notice and a month's severance pay, and I had to find another job. I could have accepted a transfer to another MITRE location, either in Maryland or Massachusetts. We discussed it and naively assumed Jennifer should continue her treatment in the local hospital.

I could have returned to my old job at CSC, but Diane urged me to become an independent contractor. I accepted my first assignment at an AT&T office in Morristown, New Jersey, 75 miles away from home. I drove Jennifer to her radiation therapy sessions during December, and once I began work in January Diane took that over. During the next seventeen years, I worked as a contractor for several AT&T divisions, never less than 65 miles from home. That affected all of us.

Jennifer's cancer was caught in stage 1a. The best treatment at the time was radiation therapy. Jennifer received 4000 rads of high energy radiation during the next six weeks, pinpointing the areas where the cancer could spread. Lead pads covered areas of her body to protect her heart, lungs, and other vital organs. In spite of those precautions her heart and lungs were damaged. Because of the radiation, she recovered completely from the cancer. Without it, the cancer would be fatal. She was pronounced clear of lymphoma five years later and never experienced a relapse.

Looking back, I sometimes wonder if her treatment would have been better in Boston or Baltimore, possibly less damaging in the long run. It was a standard protocol, so any competent facility could administer it. I will never know, just as I will never know if somewhere in the past, a different choice might have resulted in a different life-or-death outcome. Sometimes I wonder what the other choices might have yielded. If we had stayed in Seattle, would Jennifer have avoided mononucleosis? If she had, would she have avoided lymphoma? If we moved to Boston, would her treatment have been better? I know there is no way to change the past, but why this outcome?

Jennifer finished her radiation therapy in January and was discharged. She began another struggle to understand and deal with her new life as a cancer survivor. In those days we knew nothing about counseling and support groups for cancer survivors and their families, and none of the medical professionals we dealt with provided any information. Another father might have searched tirelessly for support, but I didn't. My proud, stubborn parents and their families came from a tradition of neither seeking nor accepting "handouts" and not relying on help from other people—even from family. Jennifer finished her senior year at Shawnee High School with home assignments from her teachers. She graduated with her class in June, and as she recovered from her surgery and radiation, she prepared to enroll in the fall at a women's college in Maryland.

Jennifer and Lauren

Sister.
She is your mirror, shining back at you with a world of possibilities. She is your witness, who sees you at your worst and best, and loves you anyway. She is your partner in crime, your midnight companion, someone who knows when you are smiling, even in the dark. She is your teacher, your defense attorney, your personal press agent, even your shrink. Some days, she's the reason you wish you were an only child.
— *Barbara Alpert*

Jennifer was fond of saying she taught Lauren how to walk. There was a bit of truth in that — I have a photo of her holding Lauren up by her arms, her stubby legs not yet ready to support her. But she would have walked anyway. When cancer struck Jennifer, Diane and I focused our attention on her, and for several years Lauren didn't get the attention she needed. Lauren didn't share her feelings about Jennifer's cancer, and while our attention was on Jennifer, we didn't understand how upset Lauren was.

Jennifer's cancer hit Lauren hard for two reasons. She was terrified Jennifer would die, and she often was pushed into the background while we gave Jennifer the treatment and care she needed. Lauren was on the brink of adolescence, just eleven years old when cancer struck her sister. She rebelled against the school, her peers, and us. We worried about her behavior. We realized something was wrong, and we didn't know how to fix it.

Lauren didn't tell us how unhappy she was at school. She didn't like her classmates and she thought they hated her. Like Diane at the same age, she made friends with other girls who were outsiders. They kept their activities secret, covered for each other when they snuck away from where they said they'd be, and generally tried to do the opposite of what they were allowed to do. A lot of that was normal teenage rebellion, but because of Diane's past, she had little experience of how a normal parent would react. When Diane was the same age as Lauren, her mother was in a tuberculosis sanatorium, and her father was a Greyhound bus driver who often left Diane alone, unsupervised for long hours. Diane had no model for handling Lauren's behavior. My own background didn't help. I was away from home most hours of the day, commuting to jobs miles away, and I didn't take an active role as a father. I repeated my father's behavior raising me, which wasn't a lot different from his childhood with no father at all for years.

Lauren grew older and her misbehavior led to confrontations, which usually provoked more acting out. Later, she said our family discussions revolved around "let's fix Lauren." We all went to family therapy together. When the family therapist said that Lauren was a "lightning rod" and a scapegoat, Diane quit. She would not accept blame for any of it. To her, we were different from other Lakes families because we were smarter, more educated, came from a different background. We talked about things. We were open about things. It made Diane angry when Lauren said our family was dysfunctional.

But Diane's own family was beyond dysfunctional. It was broken. She was already hyper-vigilant from her ordeals and traumas, always anxious just below the surface. Jennifer's cancer changed her more. She lost her spark of fun and joy. She developed phobias about crossing bridges and riding in elevators. Lauren remembered earlier times we all played together, badminton, splashing in the lake, water fights in the yard that spilled into the house. After Jennifer's cancer we worried more and played less. Lauren remembers a time when she purposely fell down the stairs to get Diane's attention, to care for her and comfort her. In her memory Diane wouldn't soothe her when she was sick, but got angry instead. It was how Diane's mother treated her. Genevieve was hampered by her tuberculosis, of course, so she feared if she came in close contact with her children, they would be infected. More than that, Diane's mother was narcissistic, and she would be angry when Diane made demands on her that she couldn't meet. There were times I could have stepped in to offer love and support Lauren needed then but I didn't, leaving her to find her own way.

Jennifer had yet to face the aftereffects of her cancer treatments. She enrolled in a women's college near Frederick, Maryland. In the first month she had problems with her dorm room. We felt that the college wasn't paying attention. She began to feel ill, and to avoid serious illness as she recovered from her cancer treatments, we withdrew her. She returned home and spent the school year working part-time jobs in local shops, miserable and unsure what her future would be. During that year, I worked with her to apply to another college, and she was accepted at all-women's Goucher College near Baltimore. She enrolled at Goucher in the fall of 1983, majoring in Political Science, hoping to go to law school after graduation. During the school year she lost interest in her classes, became confused and didn't finish assignments. She still could not accept that her life would never be what she expected. In May, Goucher advised her to withdraw for a year and reapply after proving herself through work experience and studies elsewhere. She returned home, feeling a failure again,.

During that year at home Jennifer excelled in photography classes at Burlington County College. Her internal struggles continued. Driving home from the store one day, she pulled out from a stop sign into the path of an oncoming car. The car door was smashed, but she was unhurt. A few weeks later, while I was working at home, Jennifer wanted to use my computer (the only one in the house) to print out an assignment at the last minute before class. She was procrastinating again, and I was working on a deadline, and refused. She left for class upset and angry. A few minutes later a neighbor about a mile away called, asking if Jennifer lived here, because she had been in an accident. I didn't believe it was her at first. It wasn't on the route I would have taken to the college. Jennifer didn't take that route. She usually drove a different route past her boyfriend's house, and it was her. When I reached the accident scene I saw the car rolled over on its side, the front end smashed by hitting a telephone pole. Jennifer sat next to it on an embankment, bruised and dazed, but not badly injured. An ambulance took her to the emergency room.

Later, I wondered if she intentionally ran into the telephone pole. It was possible. Her internal struggle had reached its climax. She was unhappy with political science; it dwelled on abstractions that meant little to her. She wanted a creative career and asked for my advice. I told her to do what she loved. I wrote her a letter then, to try and express my advice the best way I knew how. I wrote:

> "You were my introduction into fatherhood, and I learned from you as I tried to teach you. I was a slow learner, and I

had a late start on top of it. My talents were in other areas up to that point.

"It's harder for me to write about how I feel about you, partly because you're so close, and partly because it's more complicated. You were already there with your mother when I met you, and already three years old. I didn't know then how little that was. I think I may have seen you as a short grownup. It took me awhile to figure it out. I'm really sorry that I didn't understand sooner and learn to feel and express that precious brief experience of your being little.

"You are, of course, one of the three people in the world whom I love without reservation and who can piss me off the most. I helped you to form that "always right" attitude, possibly by serving as a model of trying to be always right... It can be annoying, but there's an important truth behind it. The desire to know and understand and speak the truth is a splendid, shining example of good moral conduct. We all have our lapses, you and me included, but you are a moral and ethical person at your core. To me, that is a trait deserving the highest respect, and for that I do respect you.

"Now that you are embarking on your vision quest, I feel confident that you are fully prepared to find and follow the true path where it may lead you, and to decide how to handle what you may encounter along the way. When the time comes that you must walk along that path without us, I believe it you will know how to do that. I didn't always teach you well, but you have learned well. Now go and do what you can do, and don't doubt that you can do it. I love you and I will always love you, and I want you to follow your dream and find it."

I majored in film at UCLA, but it was not my love—it was hers. She changed her major to Communications to learn filmmaking.

Lauren spent the next few years in all-out rebellion. Looking back, I see that she was trying to get attention, and she did. I was preoccupied with commuting to a job 75 miles away and working freelance jobs on the side for extra income. The burden of dealing with Lauren fell on Diane. Because of her own troubled adolescence and her parents' failures, Diane was ill-prepared. I neglected to take an active role in guiding and disciplining Lauren. She and Diane had fierce arguments during that time. Once Diane shouted at her, "You're an evil creature who crawled out from under a rock!" She never forgot that.

Lauren started Shawnee High School with mixed results. She loved art classes and got along with the teacher, but not math and history. She sang in the school rock band, giving a stirring solo in one show. By the end of the school year Lauren had a disciplinary folder an inch thick, and faced expulsion if she was in any more trouble. We tried to transfer her, but failed to find another school that suited her, or wanted her. After a search for information on home schooling, we enrolled her in the University of Nebraska's home study school.

We taught Lauren at home for a year, finishing courses in English and chemistry, among others. During that year we traveled with her to Maine, Nova Scotia, and the Virgin Islands to supplement the courses. She began to learn. At the beginning she tested at college level in vocabulary, and sixth grade in reading comprehension. Her first English assignment was to read and report on *The Great Gatsby*. Diane and I sat with her one whole day, forcing her to read, reread, and analyze the first page of that book. She learned how to unpack a sentence and derive the meaning of it. Lauren learned how to focus on subjects she once disregarded. She got our undivided attention after years of feeling ignored. She liked the attention, but despised the control. She rebelled even more furiously.

In fall 1987 we enrolled Lauren in a different high school in the district to complete her junior and senior years. At the new school she met Jeffrey, whose father was away driving trucks most of the time, giving Jeffrey free rein to run his own life. He dropped out of school, and sometimes borrowed his dad's Corvette (without permission or a driver's license) to cruise the area. Over the next few months Lauren's behavior worsened. One boy she dated said, "She is the most rebellious girl I ever met." She had no interest in him except as a cover for seeing Jeffrey, the boyfriend we didn't want her to date. I realized she was sneaking out at night to meet Jeffrey when I found bits of mulch inside one of the ground floor windows from the flower bed outside. To keep her from climbing out the windows by her bedroom, I screwed them shut. She slipped silently out the doors, instead.

One night as we were all preparing to go to bed, Jennifer walked into Lauren's room to check it, and she saw someone's leg hanging inside the small window at the back of the room. She gave a bellow that echoed through the whole house. I ran down and she told me what she saw. I ran back up to my bedroom, grabbed my two-foot-long Mexican machete and rushed to the back door in time to see a dark figure leap over the six-foot fence, race away down the street, and disappear into the shadows. We called the Medford Lakes Police. They came quickly, checked out the area, dusted the wall for fingerprints, and offered the advice that night-time break-ins were rare and dangerous. We were on edge for days until the truth came out.

Jeffrey's father kicked him out of his apartment and he had nowhere to stay, so Lauren offered to let him sleep in her room. He was hiding in her closet when he heard Jennifer coming down the stairs, and decided to leave by crawling out the window. He nearly made it without being spotted, but his leg was still inside when Jennifer entered the room. He wasn't breaking in—he was breaking out. As he ran away from our house he passed a neighbor's kid down the street, said hi, and continued on. The kid wasn't surprised because he already knew about Jeffrey. In time, Diane managed to ferret out the details. We had a big sit-down to confront Lauren about it. We forbade her to see Jeffrey again. That didn't work.

Twice we found bicycles abandoned outside our lot. Jeffrey stole them near his house and rode over to see Lauren. Later, he borrowed a friend's old green station wagon. It had a leaky muffler and we would hear the car rumble slowly past our house at night. That signaled to Lauren that he was there and wanted to see her. We finally caught on. Then one night Lauren slipped out to be with Jeffrey. Diane, Jennifer, and I sat on our screened porch and waited all night for them to return. About four in the morning, in the dim predawn light we saw a green station wagon rumble into a driveway across the street. We dashed over to it. Diane headed for the driver's door and I jumped into the open back tailgate. We all carried big, thick hiking sticks.

A terrified newspaper deliveryman gaped speechlessly at us, his eyes wide. Instantly we realized it was not Jeffrey.

"Sorry. We thought you were someone else," I said, and we disappeared into the night.

The drama reached a peak shortly before Lauren's eighteenth birthday, when she ran away from home. We had no idea where she went, but suspected Jeffrey. We found her and brought her home. We gave her an ultimatum. Knuckle under or move out. As a minor, she would have to stay in a shelter. She went to the shelter, and returned home after a few weeks.

Jennifer finished her courses at Goucher in January 1988 with a bachelor's degree in Communications. I knew there was no clear path to success in the film and video industry unless you know someone, or you start at the very bottom. Jennifer didn't know anyone in the business. More to the point, neither did I. She'd have to work as a production assistant and do grunt work on jobs, fetching and schlepping to prove she could understand and follow directions, and show dedication and loyalty to people who would hire her for more jobs.

Jennifer moved into an apartment in Baltimore with two friends who graduated in her class, planning to work in the film business there. Within a month she was in trouble. When Diane talked to Jennifer on the phone one evening, she knew something was wrong. She sounded incoherent. Diane insisted that we needed to go get her that night. We drove to Baltimore, picked up our very sick daughter, and drove her back to Burlington County Hospital. She was admitted in critical condition with kidney failure from a pathogenic E. Coli infection. With constant care, her condition slowly improved. After ten days in the hospital, Jennifer was discharged and came home. In May, we drove to Goucher College for Jennifer's graduation ceremony, and celebrated the second time she survived and finished.

I bought a desk and added a phone line for her in my office so she could start looking for work as a production assistant, or PA. She began calling every production company in the Philadelphia Film Office directory. She got jobs: camera operator for a low-budget company doing horse show videos—sometimes she had to share a motel room with the woman who owned the company; camera operator for Comcast, shooting high school sports; and backup studio camera operator for the New Jersey Lottery every night in Trenton.

Over time, her calls to local production people got her jobs as a production assistant on local shoots. On one location shoot, two of the other PAs were named Jennifer. Determined to stand out and not be just another Jennifer, she began to use her middle name, Palmer, in her work. From then on, she was Palmer Enfield to the trade. Over the next few years Palmer was a production coordinator, location scout, location manager, production manager, producer, and finally director. That was her goal in college. She was relentless about reaching it, always reaching out to people, staying in touch, and helping those starting out to take the next step. She set up training for new PAs, to teach them what she learned from experience.

Lauren always was a singer. She literally sang before she could talk. In grade school she signed up for talent contests and loved to appear on stage in front of an audience. In her brief career at her first high school she stood out as lead singer for the school rock band. When we pulled her out of high school and home-schooled her, we enrolled her with a voice coach to learn singing technique. When Lauren sang "Ave Maria" at her teacher's showcase recital, it inspired Jennifer to write in her diary, "I know what the voice of an angel sounds like."

Diane wanted Lauren to participate in contests where her singing could give her an advantage, but Lauren resisted until her senior year. Diane firmly believed in feminist principles, but pressed Lauren to sign up for the Miss Burlington County contest, part of the Miss America pageant. She won. Next up was Miss New Jersey.

When Lauren reached the interview for Miss New Jersey, she was asked:

"Did you graduate from high school?"

"Yes," she said.

Lauren had just failed her last high school class and would need to finish summer school to graduate. They knew the truth. She went through the motions in the pageant with the gnawing feeling that she would be disqualified for lying. She was. It was probably best. Lauren was so disorganized I doubt she could have fulfilled the responsibilities of Miss New Jersey had she won, much less Miss America.

After Lauren wrapped up her stint as Miss Burlington County in 1990, the four of us took an evening to walk through a Halloween haunted house at the nearby Y camp. We separated as we wandered around the event, planning to meet at the end. When it was time to go home, Lauren was not there. We started asking around. We bumped into Ivan, a Russian national Lauren befriended that summer while he worked at the camp. He said he saw Lauren with "that Mexican guy."

What Mexican guy? We knew nothing about him. Neither did Ivan. Lauren had vanished. For the next few days we tried to find out where she went. We were frantic, but her friends were unworried. She shared her plans with them, but they were not sharing with us. All we knew was that she was gone, and no one had seen anything unusual that night. As we mulled over whether to file a police report, we got word that Lauren was safe but did not want us to find her. After about a month, we learned Lauren was staying at the ISKCON temple in Mount Airy. "The Mexican" was a Krishna devotee named Joaquin who met Lauren at Govinda's restaurant on South Street during the summer. She enrolled as a prospective initiate and began to live at the temple.

After a few months as a not-too-diligent Krishna devotee, Lauren was asked to leave. Joaquin moved out with her, first to a friend's house in Germantown, then to an apartment over a pizza parlor on South Street. There followed months of subsistence. Joaquin's pay at Govinda's wasn't enough to pay the rent, and Lauren found jobs to make money off the books to survive.

DIANE'S EARLIER JOURNALS

Journal writing is a voyage to the interior.
— *CHRISTINA BALDWIN*

January 3, 1984 - Medford Lakes, NJ
Dreams

I was in a house where my parents were supposed to be living. At first, I simply walked around examining it, then I began to get confused over something I couldn't quite figure out. Suddenly, it was clear, I realized the house was unfamiliar, and it was not the mobile home they were supposed to be living in. Not the place Ron and I bought this past fall, for them.

The house was dim, lit by candles, very diffused lighting. My parents were not present at the time, but my grandmother Nanny was and assured me they'd be along soon.

I remember focusing on gentleness, kindness and thinking I must understand emotional pain in others the way I felt it myself. I recall gentle smiles and a feeling of peaceful reconciliation. I felt commanded to empathize and this feeling was associated with Ron. I felt I was being advised to treat my parents' follies and goodness as Ron has treated me in our life together, always making me feel worthwhile, secure and loved. There were other elements which I cannot remember. I woke up and within a few minutes I seemed to understand the dream was about my parents' death. I thought the house, unfamiliar as it was, represented a place where they would soon join my grandmother. She seemed to be saying "nice" things about the house in spite of the fact that my parents shouldn't have been there, but in their mobile home. I was confused by this. I think the room in the house that I was in resembled a mortuary with the kind of soft light they usually have.

December 9, 1985 - Medford Lakes, NJ
I felt frightened and wondered if I was experiencing precognition.

I was planning to begin this diary on the New Year; however, I feel like writing now and I must record Merlin's (our cat's) death before it fades. Having begun other such diaries and then quit, I am leery of this one but I recently read about a famous diarist who urged people to record their daily lives and family events for posterity and I thought, perhaps what our life has been might one day be important to someone. So, I'll begin with the "why" I am writing here.

Attempting over the last twenty years to get information on my own family, I've found very little besides dry facts — birth & marriage or death records, scrambled memories from my parents and a few other relatives, but very little about day to day living: how tragedies were handled, important decisions made or goals achieved. I have wondered ceaselessly how the events of the larger world affected the lives of my family's "little world." Mostly how did they feel about growing old, their own eventual death, their children, their loves and romances, the truth they discovered about the world, about life. Recently I read excerpts from diaries kept by women pioneers of the American West and it helped me feel more at home with myself, hearing about their daily living and personal struggles. We were not so different. As I have always felt different, odd — cut from cloth that escaped the ordinary mass production of human beings.

I want my life to mean something to someone else as they live out their own. As I have looked for purpose, goals and identity, in what others have written — so I wish for someone else to do with my words.

On Saturday morning (Dec 7) my husband Ron took the family cat (Merlin) to the vets to be put to sleep. It was so sad and I have tried to keep myself from thinking about it. I feel that so many sad things have happened to our family over the past five years that I cannot bear any more. I want to put the sorrow away as quickly as I can and think only of happy times and future plans.

I feel so guilty about Merlin — about making a decision that God or someone like that should have made. Not us. Not Ron and I. Yet over the past month, Merlin grew worse, lost weight and was hardly more than skin, fur, and bones. The week before Thanksgiving we took him to the vet who discovered that he had a mass in the stomach area, his bowels were liquid, his appetite was gone and he would barely move himself from one spot. I suspected the worst while others called me a pessimist. We asked the vet for medicine to keep him alive through my daughter's homecoming from college. He was most special to Jennifer.

Merlin got better for a few weeks, I lied to myself and put off a decision. Before we gave him the medicine, Merlin took to sitting on the desk next to Ron or he would lay in Ron's lap as he worked on the computer. He would barely move and stopped responding to his name being called. He'd lay almost motionless in Ron's arms at night as we sat together on the sofa. Merlin seemed to need warmth and comfort. We, (Ron, Laurie and I) cuddled and stroked him as much as we could. Then with the medicine, Merlin got better, began eating and mewing to go outside. After Jenny returned to college, he got worse as the tumor in his gut grew larger.

We had the option of surgery but the vet told us the chances were not good at all. Merlin was too thin and weak and the cancer would probably have spread by now. It would be expensive and probably wouldn't save him anyhow. There was no way to justify the expense in order to spare us the guilt and sadness.

So another part of our family was gone. Another part of the family that Ron and I had put together. Grandma Nanny (Christopher) in 1980, Jennifer's cancer in 1981, then Pushka (our Lhasa Apso) last summer and now Merlin.

January 3, 1986

I've been smoking since I was thirteen and in ninth grade (Minneapolis.) I remember the first time I smoked — my first cigarette. A Pall Mall, red package w/ white letter — long, king-size thin things with no filter. I must have continued smoking though its impact seems lost among the other memories. The gang I hung with smoked — Pall Mall, Luckies and Camels. In small greasy safes that tolerated wayward youth, we drank coke and coffee and puffed away over conversation that concerned itself mainly with boy/girl relationships.

Undated

As for me, I was diagnosed with cervical dysplasia six months after my daughter's radiation treatments were finished. A complete hysterectomy was advised by my doctor, but I didn't feel I could take on the additional burden of artificial menopause and all the problems of hormonal changes. I decided to go "piece by piece" with cryotherapy, conization and several D& C's over the ensuing years. While the fear and depression over my daughter's cancer put me in bed for many hours of the day, my own condition received little thought on my part. I still managed to get the housework done and meals cooked and maintained as cheerful and positive an attitude as I could under the circumstances, but only because sleeping revived me. Attempting to overcome the depression, I took classes at the county community college while my daughters were in school and studied in the evenings when the house was finally quiet.

Emotionally I was a wreck, depressed and anxious every waking hour of my day. I developed phobias to elevators, bridges, highway speeds over 45 mph; crowds and closed spaces elevated my heartbeat and breathing rates to the point of near faint. Our younger daughter was doing very poorly in school, truancy, her room was filthy and her personal appearance unkempt. Any attempt to discuss any of these problems resulted in violent arguments between the two of us.

In her sophomore year we took her out of school and using University of Nebraska correspondence courses for high school students, we began teaching her at home. She reentered school in her Junior year, changing from one high school in the district to another. Her behavior worsened and her grades continued to be poor.

MIDDLE AGE

She was wishing that whatever stage of her life she was in now could be got through quickly, for it was seeming to her interminable.
If life had to be looked at in terms of high moments or peaks, then nothing had "happened" to her for a long time; and she could look forward to nothing but a dwindling away from full household activities and getting old.
— *DORIS LESSING*

In Diane's chaotic childhood, her relatives engaged in endless bitter arguments, screaming and crying, arguing repeatedly about the same issues without settling them. In contrast, my parents didn't argue or even talk openly about what bothered them. Sometimes I'd hear muffled voices behind the door of their bedroom as they apparently worked something out. They never told me what they argued about. Diane wanted to settle issues in our family by talking them through calmly in open discussions. With such different backgrounds, she and I agreed that we had to talk about our disagreements if we ever hoped to solve them. She was driven to break the tension by airing all the issues and talking them through. I often felt that we needed a period of calm and quiet to let things blow over. Usually I wanted to avoid the discussion, hoping it would go away. Diane feared that quiet was the ominous prelude to another blowup. To her, peace and quiet often meant a disaster was brewing. She adopted the same approach to problems with people outside the family. They were usually unwilling to engage in discussions on that level, and Diane grew frustrated and angry at their reactions, while they felt she was nosy and pushy.

Her zany, enthusiastic side created legends among the children who knew her in Medford Lakes. She would invite any friend of our daughters to stay for dinner and join our conversation. We talked about anything at the table. One neighbor banned his kids from coming to our house after one dinner conversation touched on topics of birth control and abortion, offensive to his conservative Catholic views. We joked that we were excommunicated. Sometimes Diane would pull pranks, like calling a jalapeño pepper a "Mexican pickle" and delighting when she convinced one neighbor boy to try it. Diane organized a group of kids to come along to the edge of the athletic field to look for a Luna moth. No moths showed up, so Diane had them line up, bend at the waist, and see who could fart first. They loved it. The neighborhood kids liked coming to our house because it was fun.

Diane didn't go quietly into middle age. When she turned 40, I bought her a red MG, like the one I had when we met. She drove it to and from class at Burlington County College, where she was taking courses for a psychology major. She drove it around Medford Lakes with the cassette player blaring her favorite song, Gloria Gaynor's "I Will Survive." She earned two speeding tickets in one day driving forty miles an hour in a twenty-five zone, on the way to the Seven-Eleven for cigarettes and sodas.

Diane met Julie when both attended Burlington County College. They were opposites in as many ways as they were alike. Both were highly verbal, bright, curious and rebellious. Julie's upbringing was as conventional and stable as Diane's was chaotic and disrupted. Julie grew up in one house, married a local man, and after some years moving about while her husband served in the military, settled a few miles from her childhood home. Julie divorced her husband, becoming a single mother and caring for young children at home. Her older daughter Renee stayed with Diane after school while Julie worked and attended classes at Rutgers University. Julie and Diane made a formidable pair. When we decided to put a swimming pool in our yard, it was covered by scrub pines that needed clearing, some of them with trunks four inches thick. Diane and Julie cut them down together. Their most daring unsung exploit was the "ecotage" they did on dark nights, dressed in dark sweats and caps, delivering "justice" to wayward neighbors. They gathered ripe roadkill carcasses along Tuckerton Road and chucked them into the backyards of the offenders.

Diane's father Jack Christopher never attained any success or satisfaction with his life that would keep him happy in one place. When his dissatisfaction reached a certain point, he'd start an argument with his boss or the landlord and get fired or thrown out. Then he'd move somewhere else and try again. We bought a mobile home for Diane's parents in Hemet, California, so they couldn't be evicted by arguing with their landlord as they had done in the past. We wouldn't go along with that ploy, so they had to stay in Hemet. We flew to visit them in 1990. We saw some signs that Diane's mother was losing her memory, but Jack tried to hide it. During our visit, I fixed a few things in the mobile home that needed repairs. The sink and tub in the bathroom were missing stoppers, so I replaced them. I thought it was just carelessness and didn't guess at the real reason. Jack took them out so Gen wouldn't leave the water running and cause another flood.

Later Diane flew to California and brought her mother back to New Jersey. Once Genevieve was with us, she clearly had advanced dementia. She could not talk coherently, she was incontinent, and she could not dress or care for herself. She stood by the front door trying to get out so she could catch a city bus (there are no buses in Medford Lakes) and return to her old home (in Minneapolis). She couldn't work out how to unlock the door. We tried to persuade Jack to move near us so we could help, but he wouldn't consider it. He continued to care for Gen at home, but his health was also deteriorating. In 1991 when he was no longer able to care for her, Jack agreed to put her into nursing home care. In 1992 he was hospitalized with metastasized bladder cancer and not expected to survive. Diane and I flew to Hemet to move him from the hospital to a hospice and to clean her parents' belongings out of the mobile home. Jack never left hospice, and he died there on July 16, 1992.

Journal
March 15, 1992 Medford Lakes

It's Sunday and thank God or whom ever- it's sunny though much too cold to please me. Ron went to Philadelphia to look at apts. for rent and Laurie is off on her own doing the same thing. Jennifer is in LA, today she will actually be in Sherman Oaks taking the DGA test for the third time. Later this afternoon she will drive out to Pat's house and Chuck and Ginny will be there, Cheryl and her boyfriend Walt as well. Then Pat will be bringing Mother over there for the visit. Suddenly now I have a pain in my chest, rather like pressure, straight in the center and above the breasts slightly. I have had them off and on for several days now again. I think it's indigestion, the same stuff I took the Pepcid medicine for several months ago.

Anyway, the house is very quiet now and I certainly need the peace. Actually, I need a vacation more than anything but too much is going on with selling the house, packing boxes and with Dad's cancer. It's been a hell of a month for all of us and I am desperate to find ways of dealing with the stress and worry of it all. The usual tactics I have used are too unproductive, sleeping—like I have slept away a lot of my life dealing with depression and finding the same problems right there to be deal with. This time I am trying a different tack.

We returned to Medford Lakes, where we were in the process of selling our house. We felt as though our life was disintegrating. I still don't know how to explain why we did this. We went off the rails that year and spent about a year coming back. We closed the sale on April 20 and moved into an extended stay suite to figure out the next move. Like another turning point twenty years earlier, we had no plan. We were unconsciously reenacting the earlier scenario. Our furniture and belongings were in a storage unit until we knew where we'd be going. We rented a house on Long Beach Island, New Jersey for the summer and moved in. Summer stretched into fall and we found a house to rent for the winter about a mile away at the north end of the island. I bought Diane a word processor and she started writing about her life.

Journal
April 17, 1992

The white U-Haul with its orange stripe sits in the driveway loaded and ready to take our belongings to the storage space we have rented to store things. Then on Monday, the house sale will be completed. The house that has been our family home for the past thirteen years will belong to strangers. Lauren has insisted on having her own apartment in Philadelphia. Jennifer will remain with us for the present although she intends to get her own place also.

We've added Dad's dog Winky and a tiny stray kitten to our family over the past months. One hot August evening, a starving calico kitten appeared in our backyard. We bought a doll bottle and hand fed her for several days. She survived and Jennifer claimed her, naming her Margaret Sanger. As for Winky, I brought him back from California this month after clearing out my parents' mobile home. When Dad was transferred from Hemet Hospital to the Ramona Convalescent Home, it was clear that he wasn't coming back to stay in the mobile home again. He was dying and it wasn't going to be long from then. My sisters left Winky in the mobile home for over three weeks until I went out and rescued him. The neighbor, Midge, fed and watered him and they left the radio on to keep him company. He also had his doggie door and could go in and out when he needed to. However, my sisters refused to take the dog, claiming they had tried to find a place for him. Yet my sister Pat had taken in two very large dogs, a great Dane belonging to her daughter Kim and a golden retriever belonging to the boyfriend of her daughter Lisa. Later, she found a stray and took it home also. But she flat out refused to take Winky even in the interim. I didn't want another dog after we had Pushka put to sleep but I felt that abandoning Winky after he had been such a beloved companion to my parents, was another example of the kind of dysfunctional family behavior I had come to observe and abhor over the years. Ron and I took him home to New Jersey.

In 1980, my beloved grandmother, Anna Christopher, died. In the year following, my oldest daughter, Jennifer was diagnosed with Cancer. With Gram gone and Jenny seriously ill, I was overwhelmed by depression and severe anxiety. During the five years that followed, my daily life held little pleasure. I held my breath waiting for disaster to strike again as I knew it would. When my parents became ill, life was an hour by hour hell.

Within that same five years, the marriage of my youngest sister failed and ended in divorce. Her children moved out on their own and apart from each other. They rarely visited their mother and made no effort to stay in touch with the rest of the family. The ties to their grandparents were tenuous at best, riddled with painful memories. Nevertheless, duty, obligation or something should have motivated them to at least visit on occasion.

June 8, 1992

How do I feel about our present situation? I'm afraid I can't lose weight and that I'll end up the summer in the same physical condition I began it. I am afraid I'm just deteriorating faster than

I can recuperate. That I waited too long. That the struggle ahead is worse than the struggle of the years behind us . . . of moving away from the girls and losing contact with them. I am more afraid of life now than I was when I was alone with Jenny and on welfare, had no education, no money, no car and no one to help me.

June 16, 1992

I am continuing to feel depressed and having nightmares. Things bubble up to the surface of my mind and I try to ignore them — at least I feel I have for many years. Like?

Things like how I really feel about my weight and looks. For many years I told myself it didn't matter how I really looked and wanting new clothes was a weakness of vanity, a failure in women and in our society. When others in the world couldn't get enough food to eat or medical care. I recall that shortly after Ron and I were married and living in Colorado Springs, I was young and felt old then, unattractive and useless — like it was too late to do what I wanted in life. I was jealous of younger women I saw walking on the street or in the stores. They were more beautiful than me. I was ashamed of my teeth and my fat and my not having any clothes to wear to look good in.

I guess I rationalized even then. I should have gotten therapy and faced whatever that problem was then because it's still here with me. Maybe much of my depression is about my self-image? Even as I say that I think how stupid of me — most people's problems are about self-image or self-esteem.

I tried to handle it by becoming educated and being a good mother. But now my mothering job is over and I feel bad and need to stop the feelings.

During the summer Diane started to experience autoimmune thyroid disease, which lowered her thyroid hormone levels, and caused her to become depressed. Later it affected her heath in other ways. In the fall, while we were living on the island Tom Allard's sister Cindi called. She told us that Tom had committed suicide at his mother's house in Cardiff, California. In late afternoon Tom's mother Gladys told him she was going to the store with his wife, Angelina, leaving him alone. No one knows what went through his mind in that quiet Southern California beach community, usually disturbed only by yard crews with their equipment, distant traffic noise from the afternoon rush, and surf crashing along the beach to the west almost out of hearing. Apparently Tom was upset because Gladys told him she was planning to sell her house and move. He was alone in the house and increasingly agitated.

According to the police report Tom slipped into Gladys' bedroom and pulled his 30-30 rifle from under the bed, then found a box of shells. He loaded the rifle with one bullet, walked into the bathroom, pointed the rifle at his chest, and fired. The bullet hammered his chest, tore through his body and passed through several walls before stopping. Still alive, Tom walked back into the bedroom and loaded another round. He walked back to the bathroom and shot himself again in the chest. The bullet passed through his heart and lung and lodged in the medicine chest. Tom walked to the living room and collapsed, hitting his head. Blood poured out of his wounds and spread across the floor. After more than thirty years of torment from schizophrenia, his inner voices fell silent. Perhaps, as he lost consciousness Tom felt peace at last. He bled to death before Gladys and Angelina returned to found him lying on the living room floor.

Journal
November, 1992 A Few days after Thanksgiving

You're wondering, aren't you, what it's like for me

Of course you are, why not? It's easier to answer why? Some of you have already lost a great love of your life and today, you will remember again and feel some of that past great pain. You will wonder and compare your experience to mine (ours). Others of you will think of your future losses, wondering if I am about to reveal to you what lies ahead for you. You will ask yourself, will I behave in this fashion or is there some other mode I can or must affect? Others will deny me the expression of my full feelings, they fear awakening the buried anguish of their hearts. Of course, you wonder and rightly you should. For it is that wondering that leads to empathy, without which we are less than full human beings. It is empathy, not sympathy, that is appropriate today. Sympathy is a feeling or expression of pity or sorrow for the distress of another, while empathy is a far deeper emotional connection, one identifies with the others' pain more completely. The stinging lash of the whip cuts our own back, the piercing stabs to their heart double us over, their weeping closes our eyes and furrows our brows. It hurts so much, we fear it but if we avoid it, our skies will never be as bright a blue, our sunsets as purple and pink, summer breezes never as refreshing, and our love for each other never as sweet as it could be. Cold and frozen in defense against life's great drama's, believing the myths about composure, true grit and stiff upper lips, we deny life's fullness.

What I remember about my mother, the earliest memories:

Watching her put on her lipstick while getting ready to go out for an evening occasion. She was so upset about not looking right. Right to her eyes, because I told her "Oh mother, I think you're beautiful."

"No, I'm not," she replied, "don't be silly." Yet, as the years passed and I grew older, I still thought my mother was an exceptionally handsome woman. Perhaps, my child's eye beheld a beauty born of love, but my wiser, older sight saw that I was more right than she. In the last years, she fretted constantly over the brown spots of age and sun that had spread themselves over the backs of her hands and forearms. She tried to rub them off with a towel, wondering aloud where they suddenly came from.

Her confusion and sad disappointment with this disfigurement burned into my mind. Over the years, she'd point out each and every physical flaw to me; she had bunions on her feet, her hands were too big and raw boned, her skin too white, a mole here and there. I have no doubt that she knew quite well every weakness in her mental character as well as she did the physical anomalies of her body. What she did not know were the marvelous differences, those personality traits that were unique to her. She did not know well enough, the self-wonder that brings confidence, esteem, and fulfillment to the human spirit.

February 7, 1993 Long Beach Island

We were frozen or paralyzed, as my husband would say, with fear, indecision and boredom, as I would say. Nothing seemed to appeal to us, no action or pathway seemed possible. Life was unbearably unsatisfying to us both at this moment. Also, at the moment before this one and at exactly the same time yesterday. Life, our life, was at a complete standstill. Could we make any kind of a move that would feel like the next twenty years were worth living? Had we just given up the struggle? And if so, why?

There seemed to be an answer in the two words that kept bouncing around in all our conversations with each other, with our friends and in our own heads. Those two words were life and struggle. Life — Hmm? What does it really mean? I tried to think about it like I was answering an essay exam. Searching my memory bank. "Tell me everything you know about life," one side of my brain demanded.

"Well, life is what they told you was going on when you were at some young age in the past." Oh, nobody actually said, "Hi there, what you're doing is living and before you did this you were not alive. I don't know where you were exactly, but it wasn't here and it wasn't called Life. But forget about that for the moment and look at what's happening."

Usually you were introduced to this LIFE idea with someone saying to you, "Hey, this is life," or maybe it was, "That's Life!" This response was usually given after you had expressed disgust, discovered injustice, felt serious disappointment, or got dumped by some significant other which could have been a parent or a lover.

Ok, life moves. It may simply stand in one place, firmly rooted like a spring flowering weed or a Pacific Coast redwood, but it cannot change its location except to sway back and forth when the wind blows. Now and then it feels sun, rain, fog, temperature changes and occasionally, in the case of the redwood, snow. So, its life is just to stand and grow straight up out of the ground towards the light. A number of things can happen but only one thing for sure will happen. That thing is death. It will die one day.

Now in considering what CAN HAPPEN is to consider the time between its beginning and its death. In the case of the spring weed, there is the possibility that some small child will come along, admire its beauty, pick it from the ground for a bouquet and then it has death. Maybe it escapes this happening and remains in place, feeling the sun, rain and changing temperature and just swaying in the wind. One day it experiences pollination and drops its seeds into the ground besides itself. The days grow shorter towards fall and the first frost. AND THEN IT DIES. Maybe one day this giant beast lumbers into the weed, trammeling the stalk into the dirt and then the beast just pees on it. Toxic waste death! JUST DEATH!

Back to the redwood. The days of its life are greater in number than the one season weed. It also seems to experience at least one other condition, more than one season. It stands in the forest until either a fire, storms or old age brings it crashing to the ground. DEATH! Yet, perhaps in its early prime the loggers come and admire its particularly good health before they lay claim to its life. The sound of the death machine, the chain saw rings through the forest and DEATH!

Ok, ok, so death is the end of life. So, the time in between is a matter of chance occurrences. But what about things that move and can do so willfully? There are fish, birds, insects, animals and maybe some things I forgot to add to that list. So, what about them?

Take domesticated animals like horses, cats and dogs. Yeah! Take dogs. Those pedigreed breeds people sell at very fancy prices to other people. Well now, how many choices do they really have? Or aren't their lives just as much a matter of chance/luck? They don't have a choice of partner, as they are bred to increase some specific trait that seems to increase their marketability. The Shar Pei for its loose folding wrinkles that necessitate surgery so it can see. The Persian cat's smushed-in-face that makes it impossible to breathe. One day a nice middle-class couple comes into the kennel and selects Fido for its family pet.

Fido goes to a big white colonial house with green shutters in a quaint small town in Connecticut. He has a soft red and green plaid covered cedar stuffed bed from LL Bean and his own ceramic water bowl and a matching food bowl. Every morning and evening its owner takes it for a dutiful walk, so Fido can take a shit on somebody else's green, well-kept lawn, and then retires for the night.

Now, Duke on the other hand has an entirely different life after leaving the kennel where he was sold for just a much money as Fido, and the couple seemed not much different than the people who put Fido into the back seat of their Mercedes. Once at home in his new household, Duke meets the rest of the family — two very bratty young boys who promptly fight over who is going to take Duke for his first walk. Out the door they go, all three of them but without a leash. Down the block and around the corner, they continue to where the main flow of traffic exists and in a flash the dog bolts away from the young boys who have momentarily forgotten their mission and are preoccupied with newer events. In a flash Duke is several blocks away and completely out of sight of the boys. His surroundings are new and confusing to him, so different from the fenced runs he was raised in at the kennels. The boys rush home with the alarming news — he ran away from us.

By the time the more mature (but not very) members of the family jump into the Mercedes and return to the area the boys claim they last saw Duke, the dog has been picked up by the driver of a passing semi-truck, who realizes the dog is an expensive breed and without a collar.

Duke is bound for North Carolina, sitting in the front seat with the half-drunk driver who ignores the young dog's whimpering cries to relieve itself.

Diane's mother lived in a nursing home until she died from advancing ovarian cancer exactly one year after her husband Jack, on July 16, 1993. That night we were staying in a rented cottage on Cedar Bonnet Island. I was in asleep in the middle of the night when I thought I heard Diane say clearly with a tone of finality, "I'm leaving you now." It was so distinct that I woke up and checked Diane to see if she said what I just heard. She was still in a deep sleep and didn't stir. Then I thought I must have dreamed it, so I rolled over and went back to sleep. Four or five hours later, about seven in the morning, the phone rang. Diane's sister Pat called to tell me their mother died in the nursing home a few hours earlier. We hadn't talked recently to Pat about Gen's condition and weren't expecting any news. Gen's voice was similar enough to Diane's that it could have been her voice I heard in a dream. I can't explain it. I was so struck by the experience that I wrote it down in my journal that day. I still have that journal. People have asked me why, if it was a communication from Diane's dying mother, did I hear it and not Diane. I have no answer. Diane was still recovering from severe hypothyroidism and colitis, and in a state of exhaustion. Maybe I heard Diane talking in her sleep. If so, why? Did she receive a message from her mother? I know only what I heard.

After a year on the island, we planned our return to the mainland. We didn't want to return to Medford Lakes. They aspire to be a quaint resort village in the woods, but in reality they live in a small, crowded bedroom community at the outer edge of the Philadelphia suburbs. Jennifer lived in a small apartment in Haddonfield, New Jersey. We wanted to be closer to Jennifer and to Lauren, who lived in the city. We found a house to lease in Haddonfield and moved there in August 1993. We spent the next few years recovering from the threat to Diane's health from her autoimmune diseases and re-establishing ourselves in a new town:

finding new doctors, learning the fastest routes to my job, making new friends and reconnecting with a few old friends from Medford Lakes we still wanted to see.

DIANE'S LATER JOURNALS

We live in a youth-obsessed culture that is constantly trying to tell us that if we are not young, and we're not glowing, and we're not hot, that we don't matter.
I refuse to let a system or a culture or a distorted view of reality tell me that I don't matter. I know that only by owning who and what you are can you start to step into the fullness of life. Every year should be teaching us all something valuable.
Whether you get the lesson is really up to you.
—OPRAH WINFREY

My mother never drank and hated to be with people who did even if they could handle it. Her life with Jack Christopher was filled with instability, crisis, financial problems—bankruptcy, constant emotional upsets and vicious arguments. She also was diagnosed with TB and sent to a sanatorium in California. Her children, myself and my two younger sisters were farmed out to relatives.

She must have thought about her own mother's leaving and the disastrous consequences to her and her brothers then. Perhaps, that is why she never left my father, even when it became apparent to her that she had made a very bad choice. At least, she must have thought, he doesn't drink.

The irony of her TB and her brother's TB, was the fact that the woman her brother, Francis married had been a nurse at the Minnesota sanatorium and then again, was the Head of the Nurses at the sanatorium my mother went to. The irony of marrying a man named Charlie, like her father, and of being pregnant out of wedlock like her mother had been. She shared many of her mother's qualities; attractive, well built, artistic interest and ability, friendly, uneducated and unskilled, with no family to help her. She had married the man who made her pregnant and probably regretted it most of her life. He moved the family over 100 times, losing two houses to failing finances, and their children's schooling was constantly disrupted. They were constantly in debt and countless times had to ask for help from friends and relatives. The stress of her life was too great, she became very depressed in her later life, began to suffer from hardening of the arteries, experienced mini-strokes and mentally deteriorated.

Several years before her death, she lost her abilities to write, read with comprehension, speak, bathe, control her bladder and bowels, feed herself or even dress. My father could not give her the daily care she required because he could not handle it emotionally, mentally. After my mother left their mobile home to stay with my sister while she found a place for her, my father refused to go see my mother. He knew he could not stand the pain of seeing her and knowing how he had failed her. She was put into a nursing home where she stayed for about two years before dying in July 1993. My father was diagnosed with bladder cancer about two years before Mother died. He mentally denied his condition as long as he could. At last, he began bleeding from the bladder, was hospitalized for a surgical procedure and declared terminal. He went into a nursing home and died within three months, in July 1992.

April 1994
Who I am

I am 54 years old but for the last few years I've been telling myself and others that I am 50, over 50, 52 and avoiding the fact that my 55th birthday is this coming October. It's true, you have heard it before, "I don't feel (fill in the blank)." Since I was thirty, I felt old, like in Senior Citizen kind of old. Then, I had a child five years old, was newly married for the third time and pregnant with my second child. Perhaps what I felt was not "oldness" but sentenced (like a prisoner, a lifer) to a lifestyle that I had not consciously chosen. That is, I had been shoved into a slot by society and my family's working-class status, but mostly by my parents' neurotic relationship. In the dreamlike world of my childhood, I had experienced several awakenings and made several decisions with clear sight, though they were too few and my aim too low. What were those decisions you ask? I was nineteen, unskilled, without financial support and having no direction in my life, I found myself pregnant. Then, abortion was illegal and physically dangerous in this country, but the risk seemed the only answer to my predicament. So, I aborted MYSELF. That's part of the story I will save until later. Another decision came after I married for the first time, having known my husband for three days. We eloped to Las Vegas to be married and ended up in San Jose, California where he was registered to begin his junior year of college. About a month after we were married, I got pregnant. I can't recall the thoughts I had about this decision, only that I wanted a baby, knowing that it would change my life, slow me down and help me focus my energy. What I knew about life, marriage and motherhood was largely from observing my family and their extended circle of friends and relatives. Women married, had children, stayed home and did housework while the men worked and took care of the financial dealings – paid the bills and got the money to support the family. Of course, there were women who were exceptions to this pattern but if they were young, they always seemed to be unattractive. The older ones, like my paternal grandmother and a few of her agemates had either been divorced or their past was never spoken of. So, my decision to have a child was indirectly a desperate attempt to survive, a way to make a living but never consciously understood as such. No doubt the reader will fault me for weakness and deceit, given the climate of the present times but I plead that you stay your judgment for the moment.

That first marriage ended in divorce and a second husband entered my life. That marriage (but not the relationship) was brief and ended in annulment (which is also something I will tell you about later). Shortly after I left my second husband I returned to school, attending nights. I quit high school in my Jr/Sr year and though I had made other attempts to return and finish, I failed.

At the time, I was living on welfare, Aid to Dependent Children—ADC, and was at home during the day caring for my daughter. The decision to return to school was again a desperate attempt to find a way to make a living. The monthly welfare checks barely covered our rent and food. Medical care for my daughter was part of the ADC package but there was no provision for me. I illegally took several part time jobs during this period and saw that there were other women working at jobs that paid more money than just clerking or typing. The employment applications I filled out always asked for the date of your high school graduation. I also I began to hear about girls who went to college and I began to consider that I might (MIGHT) be able to do that. I was sure that I'd have to lie and con my way in as I had a very poor background in actual learning. My family had moved many times and I had attended many different schools, sometimes as many as three in single school year. Compounding this awareness of what I didn't know about math and grammar, was the blackest blot on my record — SAUK CENTRE. Shortly after I began my sophomore year of high school I was committed to the Youth Conservation Commission girls' school for breaking my probation with the Juvenile Court. As a temporary ward of the State of Minnesota, I was placed in this home-school situation and subsequently lived at the facility in Sauk Centre, Minnesota for two years. When I came out, my school records reflected this status and would follow me to wherever I applied for additional education. I was sure this would result in refusal of admittance and I could not think of a way around this damnation. Compounding the problem was my lack of required credits as well as the prerequisite college preparatory courses, I learned that these things were absolutely necessary and would be reflected in those "holy school records" I was already terrified about. Without answers to these obstacles. I forged ahead as I had in the previous decisions I have already written about. Hoping I'd find a way to subvert the system through my own cunning. I gave no thought to the funds I'd need to pay for that college education, only because I was unaware that the need would exist.

The bare bones existence that welfare afforded my daughter and me along with a deepening fear for her future drove me to return to finish my schoolwork. Though the path was unclear and full of doubt, the years of poverty stretching ahead were more frightening. I graduated at age 27.

Shortly following graduation, I got the annulment from my second husband and remarried for the third and final time. The birth of my second daughter came two years later. How I met my third husband and made the decision to marry him was another one of the calculated risks to which I have referred.

Many years have passed, last June we celebrated our 25th wedding anniversary, and many other struggles, problems dogged our footsteps. Many of my friends and acquaintances tell me that I am very lucky to have the life I have now, the kind, loving husband and the beautiful daughters. However, the sorrow, the illnesses, and misfortunes that I have experienced over the past ten years has left me in a state of deep depression. The enthusiasm for life, the fighting spirit, the risk-taking actions I was so good at are gone. This is the year I turn 55 and I am filled with fear, with loneliness, without energy, my body is filled with signs of aging. The future looks like a downward spiral. Even my sisters and my closest women friends are mired in misery and facing the kind of serious poverty so common to elderly women in this country. Not only are they besieged with personal problems, but our society and the country seem to be equally in trouble.

So I am 55 now, my body is telling me that time has passed ever more quickly than I thought it was passing. I recall my mother telling me quite often, "Life is short, you'd better get busy." And there were those ubiquitous homilies, ". . it's later than you think," ". . . where has the time gone." Relatives who'd meet again after long absences saying, " I can't believe so many years have passed." Oh, there were warnings about this terrible truth, but youth cannot understand its own mortality and time is the best example of relativity. As a child, Sunday afternoons stretched on forever, January and February were twice as long as any other month and yet, there were those anticipated events like Christmas Eve and growing up that seemed forever in the future. Time is a trickster for sure.

But I am still 55 and the list of problems needing resolution are long and difficult to resolve. The work needed is more clearly forbidding and the path still filled with mist, more murky now than when I began so many years ago.

I should soften this writing with claims of being satisfied, more fulfilled by marriage and motherhood, like so many women do in their conversations and novels. I cannot do that. It seems to me that if I had been so satisfied with my life at those other decision points that I have written about here, I'd have risked nothing and life would have been even bleaker at this point. I know that I must not lie to myself or to you, dear reader. While I admit that I have known happy times, moments of pure gold, joy beyond the reach of many, I know also that my nature is greedy and I wish now for other treasures, some of them never within my reach but yearned for with burning envy. I am not so different from others, others who would be honest, accepting the pain that such knowledge brings. An old friend of mine, once my anthropology professor, asked me if I thought " women could have it all." She meant marriage, children, home and a career that was a challenge to one's abilities. At the time, she was married and had two children but wanted tenure and a secure college post. I told her, "I didn't think so." She was visibly distressed and responded in an acidic tone, "Why not, men do!" She got tenure, a house in the suburbs and a devoted husband. She also got a child with learning disabilities and last week, I spoke to her husband about his surgery for brain cancer.

September 22, 1994

In speaking to my sister Pat, (California) over the past week, I discovered that her husband, Ron has continued to threaten and frighten her. His drinking continues and his behavior when he is drinking becomes physically violent. While he has not touched her person, he yells, curses, calls her filthy names and smashes in doors and cupboards. The last episode he picked up her computer and threatened to smash it onto the brick patio.

Upset about the possibility of increasing violence by Ron, I called Cheryl to ask her to talk to Pat about calling the police the next time something of this nature happens or getting the divorce started. Cheryl told me she knew that these confrontations had gotten worse since Pat's daughter and granddaughter had moved out (about three weeks ago). She said she would try to talk to Pat, get her to call her and she would call the police next time.

Today we've had a light rain, overcast grey skies and a breeze pushing the still green leaves towards their yellow, orange, red and brown perfective. Fall began its melancholic descent yesterday. I miss the smoky blue mist that rose from burning leaves and gathered in the roadways' distance. Those early sensual memories of a season's change. A year now since Mother's death, two since Dad's. Autumn in Minnesota, Home at Last.

Sept 26, 1994

Just talked to my cousin Kathy. She said she has six months of withdrawal time left on Xanax and feeling very impatient about it. "I am more at peace with myself," she said. As for her marriage to Marco, "I don't want to die in his arms," but, ." . . he's not a dog I picked up at the pound, where you can just discard him."

"I should have never left Brent — I live 30 years in the past and 30 years in the future but I can't be here in today."

October 1, 1994

The project Ron has been working on was presented in the Wall Street Journal and Byte magazine, so he is elated. They also had announcement celebration at work, which he attended.

Ron's father went into the hospital for colon surgery which was successful and the cancer was excised and the colon resected. He never told us before hand as he didn't want us to worry. Ron told his mother, "Next time to tell me before and let me decide if I will worry or not."

I began my Creative Writing evening course at Haddonfield HS. The teacher is currently teaching at Rutgers, has recently published a book of poems and seems to be quite knowledgeable. I submitted the piece "A Pair" that he read at the second class after reading the class a short story by James Joyce. The "Arby" was about a young boy who has a crush on a girl a few years older than him and how he comes to see the folly of his obsession. I knew when he was reading it that it was done for me to illustrate an excellent example of what I was trying to do with my work. He said I have a story worth working on — revising. He then read my story to the class and they commented. Mostly, that it was interesting. So, while I felt good at first, I now feel disappointed about my abilities.

Jennifer has been having problems, hyperventilating. Some days up to six or seven times a day. She saw her primary physician who did an EKG that was fine, a blood panel that showed her cholesterol level was below 170 but her HDL's were too high and she needs exercise to bring them down. Her thyroid level was ok and the only item out of normal range was a liver titer which he said could be an error and should be retested in three months or so. She forgot to show him the plantar wart on her foot. He also gave her an antibiotic for her ear infection. She feels greatly relieved hearing the test results. He further suggested that she get a chest x-ray later if the breathing and coughing problems don't go away. She had a chest x-ray in April or May when she saw her radiologist. How about a Mantoux test?

Laurie gave her poetry series on Tuesday night which Jen attended. She said Laurie was dressed nicely and looked good, "like she was the owner of the coffee house." She was nervous about being the MC but did fine. Jen enjoyed the evening but thought Lauren's friends were generally weird.

January 17, 1995

Cloudy morning, temperature above normal — expected 50s today. The house is quiet as Ron is up in north Jersey. Winky and I are alone. Jen is working on NFL project and is in Chicago until late tonight. Lauren was here for a few days (with Sal) as they both had some upper respiratory illness. Ron took them home.

I am off to a late start this morning, feeling tired, sleepy and body sore. Yesterday, Gina (cleaning lady) was here and got things back to order. Started the laundry but not finished yet. I am wearing the nicotine patch but continue to smoke. I started off with it and did well the first three days, but then Lauren came home and then Sal, both smoke a lot, and it was too hard. Then we were on our way to Alice's and I knew it would be impossible to not smoke because she does. To top it off, now Joel has taken up smoking also. So, I am trying to stop again.

I am so confused about what I should be doing with my life. I wake up each day with no definite commitment to anything. The grief over my parents' death has passed from my conscious mind and some of my health problems have been resolved — the hysterectomy, the abscessed tooth and bone graft, the thyroid problem. The overall soreness in my connective tissue remains a problem, as well as the swollen inflammation of my left Achilles. I need to go further with that problem but feel resistance. I am trying to tackle the smoking because I want to see if I'll feel better. I am hoping that the back pain and the problems I feel in my chest every late afternoon and evening will go away. Besides, my cholesterol will drop if I stop smoking and perhaps, I will stop worrying about having a stroke. The other thing is that I should be able to do some exercise without being out of breath and exhausted. I thought that even if I didn't quit forever, I might at least see how those other problems were affected by stopping. I know those things should be addressed first; however, it doesn't take up my whole day and I get bored.

I still need to clean up the art stuff in the basement, the boxes that are packed in the basement, the gowns and other clothes that need to be taken to the consignment shop and the files in Ron's office. Almost forgot the remaining junk and mess in the garage although that's mostly done. My papers and files in my office need to be gone through.

For fun and recreation, here is where I have a problem. Mostly we have gone to the movies and out to dinner, but it gets boring. I watch the tv news shows which Ron doesn't like, but I feel I must if I am to keep abreast of what's happening out there in the larger world. Ron wants to ski and although I wish I could, my bad heel and sore muscles, poor physical condition make it impossible. I have all my equipment and it just sits there. I have my bowling ball, bag and shoes but I hate the people one has to league bowl with. We have our camping equipment but haven't used it in many years, yet I feel I can't give it away or sell it. I can't give up the ideas and dreams I had for years about camping, backpacking, etc. Now this is where my mind gets cloudy and my thinking starts to fuzz, frustration sets in and all the projects, plans, travels, dreams for a brighter future start to crowd in on each other. Each demanding to be satisfied, each resisting their death and demise.

There is the family genealogy, my writing, my watercolor painting, a house of my own to decorate, the cabin in Vermont, the life for Jen and Laurie. Now then, it begins to spiral downwards, with my sister's problem, Laurens' lack of direction, Ron's inability to do something about his plans to become a consultant that earns more money, the 60 lbs. of fat I can't lose so I can buy jeans and sundresses so I can go places and feel like something besides an elephant or a whale. My sex life is unsatisfying and Ron must surely be in line for the first aggressive younger woman that comes along. About this time, I get overwhelmed, like Dorothy in the field of red poppies and I take a nap, staying in that warm, cozy bed until it's dark outside and my eyes refuse to stay closed any longer.

Writing here makes it seem clearer somewhat to me. So, I shall quit now and make an effort towards the path that is appearing before me.

Bittersweet (1995)

I found some bittersweet today, Mother
Growing, viney, up a tall oak tree
Near the creek,
in the town park.
I wanted to gather it up in armloads, but
The red-orange and yellow berries were too fragile
So I only kept a small branch.
I was full of joy;
I thought I might send it to you by mail, but
It was too fragile.

I stuck it in the philodendron plant
In my kitchen, on the cool white cabinet top,
Where the morning sunlight will touch it,
and me,
and you.
The dark, bare branches cast shadows.
The orange-red and yellow berries
Touch memory spots in my mind.
Each day the berries fall
Spilling onto the floor,
Are swept up and thrown away--
It is too fragile.
Once, I bought some bittersweet from the florist
But it was not the same
As a country ride, on a Sunday afternoon,
One Minnesota autumn,
Years ago,
Your mother crying out,
"Stop, I think I see some bittersweet."
You didn't, So I found it
In the park today,
for us, Mother.

April 1996
Exercises from Dreams Into Action by Milton Katselas
Exercise: State your dream. Just let it out. Write it down.

I want to be a very successful author. I want to write the stories of my life as a way of encouraging other people to fight back, struggle on and overcome the obstacles life puts in their way. I want to teach lessons in how to do this.

With the money I earn from this (late life) career, I want to buy a house for Ron and me that is on a lake, where we can work from home. I want this house to have a large window with a distant view of the lake and the surrounding beauty. I want a wood burning sauna, a fireplace, bookshelves, a black grand piano, a leather couch and chairs, appropriate lighting and other creature comforts. I want it to have a large garden and maybe some fruit trees. I want it where there are not a lot of people living. I want it paid for with proceeds from my books, so only taxes need be paid each year.

I want the brass bed I saw in Pennsylvania that cost $1700.00.

I want a pale blue large, cushiony chaise/lounge type chair for my bedroom.

I want a white eat-in kitchen where we can both cook together.

I want him to have a top of the line sound system.

I want another dog or cat or both.

I want a pink climbing rose arbor, a screened porch with a porch swing.

I want a wooden boat dock and a swimming raft in the lake.

I want to travel all over the world and not budget class.

I want to get down to 150, quit smoking and get fit again.

I want to snow ski, play racquet ball, hike up a mountain and swim in the ocean waves.

I want to be able to help Jennifer and Lauren realize their dreams.

I want them to be able to travel with us on some of our trips.

Exercise: Write down anything that makes your dream more defined, by relating it to a specific career.

I think I already did this. I want to be a best-selling writer, lecturer and through these avenues teach people how to manage their lives, fight their battles and live more fully.

Exercise: Write out your career concept. Be bold but be specific.

I needed the equipment for writing and the space. I have the time but don't use it well. I need more energy and more determination to do it each day and not let other jobs, people and events deter me from my writing time. I got the equipment, the space and the time. It's the energy, determination and the freedom from negative thoughts about myself.

July 2, 1996

My father told me, years ago, that I should leave the family, go to another city and find a life for myself. He said he didn't mean it in a hurting way. Of course I did that after Ron and I met, but I continued to try to make connections with my sisters, cousins, aunts and uncles. I guess there won't be anyone at my funeral but my daughters.

Travels and Travails

Spiritual crises happen to us every day. Most of them are sufficiently low grade, devoid of enduring consequences, so we pay no attention and keep on rolling. A spiritual crisis occurs when our identity, our roles, our values, or our road map are substantially called into question, prove ineffective, or are overwhelmed by experience that cannot be contained by our understandings of self and world.
— *James Hollis*

Alaska—remote, mystical wilderness—home to glaciers, caribou, brown bears, dogsleds, Inuit people . . . Diane and I both felt the magnetic pull of that place. When we lived in Seattle, we read that our city was the jumping-off point to the Alaska wilderness, and we almost felt like we *were* in Alaska. One fall morning, we watched a newly-launched crab boat depart from the Fisherman's Terminal in Seattle, headed for Alaskan waters, and we read in fascinated horror when that same boat was found drifting in the Gulf of Alaska, covered with ice and abandoned by her crew, who were never found. Diane's brother-in-law Ron spent several years climbing mountains in California, Washington, Ecuador, Mexico, and finally in Alaska on Denali, where he was forced by a blizzard to shelter in a snow cave for days, a storm that killed several climbers on the mountain. For years we wanted to see Alaska. Finally we decided to do it.

In 1996 we researched traveling the Alaska Ferry through the Inside Passage from Bellingham, Washington to Juneau, Alaska. In January 1997, I booked a stateroom on the ferry for four people the last week of July. Our room measured about nine or ten feet wide and had light brown metal walls, two metal bunk beds on each side, and a wide sealed window looking out on the water.

We passed incredible scenery that beggars description in words: white-capped mountains whose steep forested slopes plunged thousands of feet straight to the water's edge; whales breaching a hundred yards off the side of the ferry; small icebergs with topaz blue facets drifting past; islands with eagles perched on every treetop. Before dawn one gray morning we walked through a totem pole museum in Ketchikan, Alaska. At that hour the town was closed except for one building, now a gift shop (open for souvenirs), once a thriving bordello.

Juneau looked more like a logging company town than a state capital. We drank a beer in the Red Dog Saloon, crowded with patrons like a six-and-a-half-foot tall Russian who wore a nickel-plated revolver on his hip. We rented a car and drove to the foot of fog-shrouded Mendenhall Glacier. Sometimes I study a photo of Jennifer standing framed by the mist and the glacier, gazing absently into the distance as though contemplating a future beyond our knowledge. We returned our car to the airport and boarded a flight to Anchorage.

In Anchorage we took a taxi to a hotel for an overnight stay before our train left in the morning for Denali National Park. We wandered around Anchorage, passing the starting line for the Iditarod dogsled race on 4th Avenue. At lunch we sampled reindeer stew. It smelled like Alpo dog food. The train pulled away from Anchorage, past whistle stops at highway crossings where the only man-made objects were the railroad, a highway from nowhere to nowhere, and a tiny coffee stand in a gravel parking lot, all surrounded by impenetrable forest. The train stopped once to pick up a passenger standing next to the track, miles from any sign of a station. Our route passed boreal forests, braided rivers, and mountains stretching to the horizon. We strained to catch a view of Denali to our west, but it remained hidden by heavy clouds the whole time, except for one brief glimpse of a white peak gleaming in the sun that may or may not have been Denali. The train cruised slowly alongside a crystal-clear river fifty feet below us, where two-foot-long salmon slowly swam parallel to us.

At Denali Park we checked into our hotel, a no-frills row of one-story buildings near the park headquarters. The curtains in our room didn't block out the midnight sun that kept us awake through the night. Jennifer, Lauren and I took a whitewater rafting trip, on a river filled with gray glacial runoff. Diane refused to go. Before embarking the guide gave us a detailed safety lecture that boiled down to this: Don't fall out of the raft into the river. It's really cold. You'll die. The park was swarming with tour buses and RVs, where a ranger shared his pet name for the tourists who arrived that way: The Great Gray Wandering American Geezers. I thought that was funny. I never expected to become one.

Why does this trip live so vividly in my memory?

Two reasons: the obvious one, that the sights and experiences were unforgettable, unlike anything we'd seen before or since. The second, more important reason — it was an interval in our lives where all of us were together, healthy, and fully cherishing each other's company. We functioned as a family and we were happy being together. It stood in contrast to other times and places when we were separated by distance or disagreement. Our time in Alaska was one of those periods we all shared full enjoyment and appreciation of one another and the world around us. I shot a lot of photos then and used many in the memorial service we later held for Diane. They were us at our best.

Lauren's experience as a pageant queen earned work as a fashion model for an agency in Philadelphia. She became a local success, featured in the Philadelphia Inquirer and billing out for a top rate. She became disillusioned with that, too. She gave it up and enrolled at Community College of Philadelphia. Using her intelligence in classes for the first time, she earned a place on the honor roll, then was admitted to a transfer program that prepped CCP students for transfer to elite colleges. In 1997 Lauren was admitted to Bryn Mawr College as a transfer student.

Journal
1998

The creative artist exercises from the book Lynn loaned me has me thinking about the negative thinking I do, the fears I have and let confuse me. I don't feel good today, tired, was very tired after grocery shopping yesterday, unloading all those bags, unbagging and storing all that food. I feel good about having stocked cupboards—our pantry at home was always nearly empty. Mother never planned ahead, and we seemed to have the same ground beef patty and boiled potatoes most nights. I don't remember much about what we ate until I was about twelve in California. I suppose Mother was depressed about having TB and afraid. She certainly couldn't do anything fun. Not that there was much money for such things. We never took a family vacation.

Never planned much. Maybe they were both depressed for years. Why wouldn't she be, probably having never recovered from the grief of her mother's death ten months before I was born. Then all the trouble with Dad over marrying and Gram over Dad and it just went on and on. It makes me tired to think about it now. I just want to crawl back into bed and sleep. Of course the sky is cloudy and gray and only about 50 degrees, high for Feb but I yearn for sun and warm, blue water, beaches and temperatures in the seventies or low eighties. I could go alone, I have the money saved in my travel account but there is so much on the To Do List again. Especially Jenny's moving in here. I refuse to digress into list making when I write. Maybe the problem is not starting this writing exercise early in the morning before the urgency of my personal life's needs get in the way. There is always so much to do and shit it makes me angry that my parents never did any of it and Ron's parents had some of this stuff but far less than we do.

Maybe I should take the Serotonin affecting prescription that my Dr. gave me. Long enough to see if it does anything for me besides leaving me feeling flat like the Zoloft and Paxil did. I took the Zoloft the longest. I am better than I was in 1992-94. I can walk more than a laborious block and I don't hurt as much, however I could not run with the dogs yesterday and I was so tired from shopping. I did have a big sugar diet yesterday and I am sure that didn't help. I don't want to continue thinking and focusing on my health. If it's not my health, it's the girls and Ron's health. End.

Journal
February 23, 1998

Fatherless households are poor, mother and children suffer. Dad was malnourished and got Ricketts, who knows what else, my sister Cheryl had chronic throat infections which made her sick much of her early life and affected her schooling. Couldn't afford the doctor bills. My poor dental care and losing my teeth seriously affected my self-confidence and whatever that effect caused. My mother's fear of dentists came from her mother and ended up being a major part of her own lack of social life and part of what helped to kill her in the end. The sins of the fathers, can I say the sins of the mothers, but they had no economic means to remedy these problems. The society was run by men, a patriarchal world. Yep, the sins of the fathers!

It leads to questions about women and their need for adornment vs. money spent on medical and dental care, psychological counseling, education — I think people need vacations, recreation, how can we endure the wear and tear of life unless we have time to rest. It's worse today, people are being driven too hard, the stress level of our lives has skyrocketed. The water in the kettle is about ready to boil the frog.

A reviving trip for Ron would be fly fishing. For Lauren, a place in the sun where there are other young people and she could go snorkeling, swimming and hiking — That Windjammer cruise might be just the thing if we can fix the sea sickness thing. It might be good for Jenny too. I guess it's time for them to go alone or alone together without Ron and me. This is a big thing for us to decide on or maybe to take action on. Yes, definitely taking action is the thing that has to be done

So, my head aches and I have to critique those pieces for The Borders group' meeting tonight so I have to go now. End.

February 25, 1998

"MOMENTUM CAN LEAD TO FRENZY" — a bit from a TV ad for pitching a traditional stock brokerage approach vs. online e-trade — threw me into thinking about frenzy, and momentum and how those concepts defined the way my life had moved. (I'll come back to this). I flashed on thoughts about all the unfinished business I had left undone throughout my early years. After all, when you are magically picked up from one place and transported into an entirely different place, it eliminates the need to plan, to finish anything, to be honest, for there do not appear to be any possible consequences.

With all that moving my family did, one apartment to another, a house to an apartment, a different school, new classmates. My God, people who read about this girl's life must wonder what it was like for her and how did it hurt or damage her. Did it?

I wonder myself, how are the problems I have had or have today connected to the chaotic environment of those years. Momentum, moving — the force of a moving object, a concept of physics.

February 26, 1998

How easily I am distracted! Perhaps I was always that way, even when I was a child. But I think then again, it was all the chaos that entered my life after my parents decided on moving to California. I was only ten years old then and my life in that old basement apartment in Minneapolis seemed ok, even, thinking back, adventurous. I suppose life at ten is adventurous because so much is new and the world around one is within exploring reach. Then, I had a grandmother whom I adored living within walking distance of our place. She had an interesting house with a screened front porch where I could sleep on hot summer nights (Did she ever think about some pervert coming in there and taking me, raping me and killing me like Megan in New Jersey?) Her friend Albert lived upstairs and provided entertainment like Rummy and some dice throwing game Grandma always got excited over, and a cold green bottle of Seven-up or Orange crush.

Grandma was to be counted on for Saturday trips on the city bus downtown, maybe lunch at Forum's Cafeteria where I always picked the Chow Mein, Cherry pie and chocolate milk. My Uncle Barney lived at Grandma's and he was funny and teased me. He was affectionate, not like my father, who hardly ever kissed me or had anything funny to say to me. He was always too busy arguing with my mother, listening to sports on the radio and scowling at me over the dinner table when I drank all my milk before the main dinner had even begun or when he discovered I had hidden the Asparagus on the ledge under the kitchen table. Grandma and Barney planned Sunday picnics at the river in Wisconsin or long drives with a stop for an afternoon beer or two.

They could be counted on, that was for sure. They laughed and talked to me and lifted my heart like my parents didn't.

I knew my way to school and back. I walked slowly so I could learn about everything that was happening in my neighborhood, like what they sold at the candy store, what I could buy for my family on Christmas at the dime store, what made the shoe repair shop smell so interesting, where the prettiest flowers grew — there were so many interesting things to investigate then. My days were full of things to do even when the cold, gray days of winter came.

I got my feelings hurt when the Valentines went to girls who were the cutest in the class, though I still had no idea what I really looked like to myself. I cried then, hot tears that made the desk smell. I cried the same way only harder when I couldn't attend the class Gold Star Picnic because my mother didn't get my dental work finished on time.

I could understand the seasons and I looked forward to each of them. There were special events, activities. colors and clothes to be worn with each. Summer meant Camp Manakiki, going to the lake, Sunday picnics, bathing suits, bare feet in the grass, cold shade under the tall elm trees that lined the block, craft classes in the basement of the Jr. High School at the corner of my block. Root beer popsicles, evening trips to the custard stand, the chance to go back outside after supper and play Hide and Seek until the stars came out. Summer was the best of all. By the middle of August, I looked forward to fall. The weather began to cool and the air smelled different, school was soon to begin and there were new clothes to buy, plaid skirts, navy blue knee high stockings, sweaters and scarves. Dark colors now.

The trees turned colors and Sunday drives were excursions to see those beautiful trees along the river, around a lake, the marsh grass burnished gold and the cat tails to be gathered. Wienie roasts began instead of picnics, in some woods where the leaves lay carpeting the ground and the smell of the wood smoke in the crisp air was new. Evenings grew dark and mysterious when I was allowed to venture out with some family friend or Grandma. My birthday came in October and bright blue skies were followed by Halloween's orange and black cats, pumpkins, witches, owls and ghosts. Planning a costume and finding a large paper bag for holding the candy. Fall ended with Thanksgiving, its wonderful turkey dinner, a chance to be the one who said the ritual "Thank you for..." prayer and going on like a preacher, my uncle always said. So many guests at the dinner, family friends who were different than my mother and grandmother. Like Vera, who smelled of fancy perfumes and cosmetics, wore perfect hair and spoke in a high almost squeaky voice. The women wore fancy aprons for these holiday dinners — white organdy with fine narrow gathered lace edges, monogrammed or decorated with some special symbol. Everyone dressed up for these holidays. I looked forward to brand new knee-high socks and my patent leather Mary Janes, a silky kind of underwear that was different than the heavier cotton things we wore every day and the dress would be made of some fine fabric like velvet or taffeta. Yes, Thanksgiving was a small glass of sweet port wine like the adults, a rich, thick liquid that stayed in one's mouth and throat.

So much the better if it snowed.

Winter's first snow was catching the star-like flakes in your mitten and admiring the cap of white stars accumulating on one's hair — magical stuff. Dark nights came early, city lights, windows in houses brought a sense of mystery to my mind. The black and white of winter, the red, green gold and silver of Christmas, the meals of heavy soups and stews, Sunday roast and stuffed chicken smells. Sunday dinners served at three o'clock and easy suppers of grilled cheese sandwiches with tomato soup or white rice boiled in milk with cinnamon and sugar. Preparations for Christmas, shopping trips downtown where Salvation Army Santas rang brass bells and collected the nickels I always put in their black kettles. The store windows filled with toys and animated animals dressed in flashing metallic trims and bright colors. The dark shadows on white snow, blue snow and long silvery, dagger shaped icicles hanging from roof edges, patches of ice on sidewalks good for a short slide, tiny dull brown sparrows that flocked and pocked the white snow pecking at the bits of old bread spread by a toss of Grandma's hand. Red and raised bracelets banding wrists and ankles where lumps of snow had found bare skin and burned cold.

Oh God, I am nearly sick with yearning for those intense times — the anticipation and thrill, now gone, covered with calluses and the thickened whiteness of scar tissue. I feel so little joy now. It is a time of sorrow, anxiety and such is wisdom. Can it be different?

Christmas, oh Christmas, now you are gone from my life. The myths of a savior, son of a God — in whose image I am made defied my logic and reason. Challenged the very process by which I survive, tried to swallow the fable, the parable, its beautiful simplicity but I could not abide your flock. Their hypocrisy — too blatant, their simple ignorance too great, their worship of false idols too idolatrous. Jim Jones, Tammy Fay and Jim Baker, the Texas guy.

Yet, the memory of peppermint, new evergreens, cinnamon and cold, crisp wood smoke filled air strains my resolve. A STAR shinning bigger and brighter in the midnight blue-black night sky grabs at my throat and gives rise to wonder. Mankind's attempt to find purpose in the chaos of heavenly infinity and I am sad.

March 2, 1998

Later than my usual "morning pages" stuff but anyway a thought popped into my head about what Mother might have been thinking whenever she seriously contemplated leaving Dad. Precipitating this is the fighting that has been going on between Ron and me. I think we just don't get along; our personalities are at odds with one another's. I didn't really know him when we married, why did I marry him then?

Well, I guess I was trying to find a way out of the miserable poverty I was in, for one thing but that was the situation before I met him. Then he came along in those mountains and I was attracted to him that first night we met. He was good looking, tall, seemed kind and gentle, had an education and a job, he was doing his "own thing," climbing that mountain and camping out, alone and that seemed self-sufficient, which was important to me. His history seemed peaceful enough, stable and accounted for. Then too, he was attracted to me but actually, I think he wanted a woman, any reasonably attractive woman with a brain would have done. His sexual innocence appealed to me because I had so little regard for men, especially men who had a history of non-commitment and sexual promiscuity. If he had been separated or divorced, it would have been a no-no for me, with kids? Never have done more than talk at tent width's length and on my way in the morning.

March 6, 1998

Near waking this morning, a clear piece of advice from my subconscious (dream life) on advice for my life, for getting myself together — get rid of stuff, throw it away or give it away or do the garage sale stuff. Be strong, swift and keeping in mind there is not enough time left to do the things you have stored up to do. Free up the girls, Jen and Laurie

Nanny and the end of her life — what did she do — how did she prepare for it?

She gave away to Pat and me the few things she had, the wooden heart shaped box that held her hankies and few pieces of cheap costume jewelry. She gave her diamond ring to Pat, it was very tiny, the diamond. Her pearls, which she got during the WW2 years. She stopped accumulating everything and pared down her dishes, pots and pans. She didn't own any furniture by then and the small two room apt. with the shared bath and alcove kitchen was pretty spare in the years before. When we tried to give her anything, she'd say, "No-no Diane, I don't want to keep anything around, anymore." She had never had very much anyway.

When Harold, her youngest son finally got married at age 35, he took the furniture there was, a 3-piece sectional couch, a few end tables and a couple of lamps, maybe a dining room table set, a bed and dresser. There wasn't much else. After he left, she lived in small rented rooms, always spic and span, she bought some towels and a pair of curtains or two. The Salvation Army was her favorite place for getting the few things she needed including a few clothing items like skirts, which she always took to the seamstress to be hemmed and fitted to her own peculiar shaped waist and lower body, which had suffered a number of surgeries over the years. She took underslips and nightgowns to be fixed for the same reason.

She had two small credit card accounts which she used to buy a winter coat, a hat, shoes, stockings and more intimate underwear like undershirts (she did not wear a bra) and the long, loose, legged bloomers we always made jokes about.

Oh God, this is so painful to remember, to think about everything I never asked her about, how much I didn't know about this woman I so admired and deeply loved. I think about how she used to say she got so "blue" and didn't think about the past because it was "too hard" and "she didn't know how she got through everything, being so sick so much." She lived to be ninety, outliving most of her friends, her two sisters, her employers, Mr. and Mrs. Larson (not a very generous woman). Many of her extended family were gone by then too, though she never seemed to show any particular sorrow when she had attended one of those funerals.

She walked to the supermarket to bring home cardboard boxes, one at a time, carrying them about six blocks, a small bag of groceries in the other hand, stopping to rest a few minutes here and there when the pain in her chest got to her or she got out of breath. Her heart was bad, but I didn't really know that was her problem. I thought it was a reflux problem — hiatal hernia, I used to tell her. She brought the boxes home and stored them in the attic, telling me in a kind of offhanded way, "They are to put my stuff in when I go, I am not going to live forever, Diane." This always upset me to hear it and so she never spoke about it any further. The attic was quite bare, she'd given the two old Victrola's that had gathered dust for years to a young friend, Marcia. Marcia had formed a friendship with Gram and visited her and taken her places. I never met her, but she must have been very kind to Gram.

Yes, the attic was bare, Gram used to hang a few things she had laundered on a clothesline up there. She swept and dusted for cobwebs regularly, the wooden floor was spotless.

The last time she came to visit me, in New Jersey, she was 87. She flew and I think it was her first airplane ride. We picked peaches from a south Jersey roadside U Pick farm, and later the same day, she insisted they be peeled and canned that night, though we were all very tired from the day's outing. She worked until the last peach was processed in the "boiling water bath."

Her sister-in-law Martha Moen lived next door to Grandma's last place. They ate together occasionally. Gram took care of Martha's dog Penny when Martha went fishing or away for a weekend up at the lake. Martha gave Gram one of the funeral plots she had. Grandma was relieved to know where she would be buried and that she'd lie next to Martha. It was good not to have to be alone, she'd say. She had two insurance policies worth about $500 each, never knowing that a funeral would cost $5000. She didn't have a checking or savings account, there was nothing to manage or save. She paid her bills with cash at the special counter in the supermarket set up for people to pay utilities, gas and electricity and phone. She paid the landlord her rent in cash too. Her small credit card accounts she paid at the store, in person on one of her weekly Friday or Saturday trips downtown. She took the bus downtown, spending a half day there, purchasing the few items she needed, thread and needles, gloves for winter, an Easter Hat, a new pair of white shoes for the Spring-Summer season. An item from the dime store. Sometimes she treated herself to a light lunch at Forum's Cafeteria. When she *returned home, she always made herself coffee, reserving the extra coffee in a glass jar in the refrigerator for later.*

She always had a few dollars set aside for emergencies, usually loans to her sons. She bought my sisters and I underwear or stockings at Christmas time, also her sons. Always telling us she was sorry she couldn't afford more. She sent birthday cards with dollar bills to us, too.

March 9, 1998

I can hear the fire house siren in the distance over the drone of traffic for mornings rush hour and the rain against the window. Why does that "rain against the window" always sound cozy in novels? And feel so dreary and hopeless in real life?

It's been said, life is what you make it. Well, I tried to make it good for my family and then the shit hit the wall, like in Shit Happens. Shit happened over and over in those years between 80 - 95, fifteen years of battering cruel storms. I hate Ron's parents for doing so little then and for the whole course of our marriage, my own parents for being so steeped in their own endless personal harangues. My sisters for such little concern, my neighbors for the same.

I always wanted to plant hundreds of bulbs, all varieties of daffodils and grape hyacinth and maybe even tulips to welcome spring. I loved the lilacs, snowballs bushes and hydrangea in blues and purples. In Medford Lakes, the sandy soil wasn't any good for that and I never could depend on living any place long enough to believe I'd get anything out of it but wasted money.

What I would do if owned The Tea Shoppe in Haddonfield? I'd have a gas fireplace and small sitting /waiting area with an oriental rug and easy chairs, a grand piano and a pianist to play classical stuff. The flower shop in the front with unique arrangements for takeout buying. Scones and tea for takeout sales, Better curtains on the walls and more, larger paintings on the walls, more colonial blue paint as Wedgewood implies that color blue and a barrier between the entryway and the tearoom. Clotted cream, Devonshire cream, scones with currents and toasted almond bits. Fresh strawberries and the best strawberry preserves available, also blueberry and blackberry. I'd serve my Lotus ice cream with coconut drizzle. I'd sell teapots and teacups and small elegant spoons, dishes for lemon wedges, sugar cubes that were decorated, shortbread wedges (freshly baked) for lunches, tiny baked quiches, dense white bread w/cream cheese or butter and water cress, cucumbers. Cups of soups in cold weather, like an elegant cream soup, — pumpkin, bisques of scallops, crab, lobster. Tall frosted glasses of lemonade in the summer or pale green limeade, apple cider tea with tiny plain doughnuts in the fall. I'd lower the lighting and have all the best of the classical music stuff.

March 10, 1998

I think I will have to actually leave in order to get my family to believe I am serious about what I say needs changing in our life. I have threatened enough and that hasn't worked. Lauren still takes advantage of us, Ron continues to — what? So many things he needs to take seriously and plan for and does not. I suppose he is overwhelmed by all that has happened to us in the past fifteen years.

I keep thinking things will get better, we'll get a break somewhere — to Jen and her career — directing and more money. Lauren and her getting organized or getting Bryn Mawr scholarship money, Ron and his job — more money, an opportunity to do high paid consulting. It's not just the money, but the money would bring some relief in the form of a vacation, savings for the pension, a house down payment, a new computer for Jen, a car for Lauren.

Mother must have stayed with Dad for some of the same reasons — she thought things would change. It did get better when she went to work and had some money of her own to spend and some friends, even though none of us thought Jane Deming or Naomi were what she needed, not her level. At least she could get out occasionally with them, a movie or dinner. Small changes for her but she could also dress up and get sale clothes to wear. If only they could have stayed in one place — one of those new apartments they lived in — why were they always moving???? I mean, there were a couple of apartments in Alhambra, but there was always the complaint about the dirty laundry room. Mother hated doing her laundry where other people left dirt.

April 1, 1998

This nagging anger and dissatisfaction keeps hanging on. I have to break through this stuff. I am just worried over everything.

I don't want to be in Jersey in the humid heat of July and August. At least a month and a half away from here, someplace like a lake in the northern climes, Maine, Minnesota or the Adirondacks. Is this impossible and a pipe dream or could I find a way to do it? Could I be alone? Need a gun, if I am alone.

I am so distracted by problems and my interests. Getting a house, making money for my travels, getting my teeth fixed, my hair cut and dyed, the dogs need shots and Winky a teeth scaling, Laurie's summer classes, getting rid of old clothes, having a garage sale, doing eBay jewelry and stuff, clearing out basement and attic, losing weight, stopping smoking, getting exercise, work for my Borders class, writing my story about Tom and I. Getting away to clear my head and the list goes on, every day, all day the list interrupts my activities again and again. I have to find a way to deal with it more peacefully.

At Bryn Mawr, Lauren's emotional life began to interfere with her classes. She still brooded over her breakup with Sal, her boyfriend between modeling and college. She'd left him behind but hadn't recovered from it. In May 1998 as she struggled with a difficult philosophy course, she became depressed. After the end of the term, she learned that she would not be eligible for financial aid the next year, and she would not be able to return. She transferred to Temple, a public university located in an area of Philadelphia vastly different from the cloistered, landscaped, suburban Bryn Mawr campus. The classes at Temple failed to match her experiences at Bryn Mawr or community college. She got more depressed and stopped going to class. The rest of the term she floundered. Memorial Day weekend she was admitted to a psychiatric hospital in Philadelphia for depression. After discharge she moved back in with us. Still depressed, she attempted suicide by swallowing an overdose of her prescription medicine. The next several months Lauren began healing. She'd been rail-thin during her depression, and when she took a course of steroids for an infection her appetite returned. She regained her normal weight and a healthier outlook. After that she was never severely depressed again. Her life wasn't back to normal, though.

For several years Lauren endured one bad relationship after another. First it was an Irish Catholic from North Jersey she met online. Despite everyone's advice he convinced her to move in with him. She learned he was an alcoholic, a closeted homosexual, and a sexual deviant with a taste for sadism and masochism. He became progressively more abusive, and she began drinking. They went through cases of wine together. When Lauren started to mistrust him, she hacked into his computer and learned he was secretly meeting men from Craigslist. She said later, "There was so much fucked up about him it would take an entire day to go into all of it." After she left him, he threatened her life. Terrified of him, she cut all communications and went to counseling for a year through a state program for victims of domestic abuse. She told us some of that, but not all of it at the time.

Diane struggled with her weight throughout the time we were together. In the 1980s her weight peaked, affecting her health. Her cholesterol levels climbed to twice the recommended upper limit, her blood glucose to well beyond safe limits. She had a history of autoimmune disease that first presented as psoriasis when she was seventeen, then as Hashimoto's thyroiditis and colitis at fifty-three. Added to her lifelong smoking addiction, it meant long-term health consequences. By 1999 Diane was taking prescription medications for type two diabetes, hypothyroidism, severe colitis, and high cholesterol. That all affected her cardiovascular system.

In October, Diane turned sixty years old and we threw her an unforgettable birthday party. Jennifer hired an Elvis impersonator to sing Diane's favorite song, "Can't Help Falling in Love," and bought her a bottle of Dom Perignon champagne. Several of her old friends from Medford Lakes came. Three weeks later, Diane woke up in the middle of the night with chest discomfort. She said she knew it was a heart attack. She was not in pain or great distress, and did not want to call an ambulance. I gave her an aspirin and drove her to the emergency room two miles away. Blood tests and EKG confirmed she had a mild heart attack, and she was admitted to the hospital. We transferred Diane to Jefferson Hospital in Philadelphia, where a cardiac catheterization found she had blockage in a small artery in the back of her heart, too small to perform angioplasty. She was prescribed a beta blocker and an ACE inhibitor and discharged after a few days.

Later that year, the owner of the house we leased began to pressure us to move so she could sell it. Jennifer and I started looking for a suitable house, and by summer we found a one-story ranch house about two miles from our house in Haddonfield. It had ample windows and skylights, higher ceilings, and hardwood floors throughout. More like a California house than typical Haddonfield Colonial houses with their low ceilings and stingy windows, its open, airy style appealed to us. In October 2000 we moved in and there we remained. I wasn't planning for a time when Diane couldn't walk on her own, but when it came, the new house was well-suited. I could move her around in a wheelchair without going up or down stairs.

Journal
August 2, 2001. Exercises. My first love

After I was married to Ron, we moved back to Minneapolis. I had Jennifer and Lauren by this time. I called Bob, on a whim. I wondered if there was any attraction between us any longer. I found out he'd continued his life of petty theft and friendships with his old felonious reprobates. Guys I knew by name and vague association in the past who'd been on the path to a criminal career then. I met his wife, who seemed to be a straight and narrow kind of woman, much like his mother. She worked full time and he ran a towing and junk car business. He had, in fact, repeated his father's history (which neither of us knew until this time). He had two young sons and lived in a very small house near my apartment. Once I saw it and thought it shabby and cheaply furnished.

One night I met him, and we went out for a drink at a local bar. Afterwards, we parked. He tried to kiss me and put the make on me, but I was disgusted by him. When that didn't work and I insisted I wanted to talk about us and the past. He told me, "you were too smart for me . . . we would have ended up killing each other." I think now that he was referring to the Josie incident when his excuses did not keep me from leaving. Somehow, he knew that I could not be conned by him. Strange, I didn't know this about myself. He didn't have much else to say, I think he wasn't very verbally sophisticated. I never saw him again.

Over the years I occasionally called his mother to seek out information about Bob's life. This probably had more to do with finding some continuity with my own past and keeping people in my life with whom I had an intense, personal association with, as it included others also. The last call I made, his mother paused and sighed, when she heard me ask how Bob was. "He's gone, Diane." I asked her what did she mean 'gone'? He was killed in an accident, a hit and run, in Arizona. Shock took my breath away and I think I cried a little. It was over, for him.

Did I love Bob? It's a question I grapple with now to understand what Jen and Lauren feel about A____ and D____. I wonder what it is that I think about loving men, loving the men I have loved in my life. Does what I felt for Bob equate in any way to what I felt for Gary, or Tom? What I feel for Ron? In some way they all feel different, they seem somehow weighted by the amount of time I spent with them.

2001 Reflections

It's 1:30 am and like many nights I can't sleep, my mind races over every mistake I made in my life, every worry I have over my daughters, the regrets and fears. Sometimes I can calm myself with slow breathing but other nights nothing works. Tonight, I feel a loneliness which I cannot define. I think about the ideas I have read about, that everyone is lonely at times, that there are many, many lonely people in the world and that loneliness is The Human Experience. I guess it's like if you are a human being, you're going to feel this thing called loneliness. I think I have no right to feel sorry for myself and I cry into sleep. So, I compare myself to others I know and to their lives and I think, I have more people who love me — a husband and daughters. I think of my friend Julie. being single and living all alone down in coastal South Carolina, or of my sister Pat, her husband Ron's drunken loneliness, my poor mother in her dementia and my father with his cancer alone in his mobile home and in serious denial about his life and his health condition. So many people I know have loneliness and have no partners to love them and be with them. So, I think there is another kind of loneliness that I am feeling, and I ask my husband, Ron. He tells me the loneliness he feels is like needing help and having no one to help him. Then, I think I can understand that as I experienced so much of that in my childhood and early adult life. All the moving my parents did and all the different schools I went to. All the problems I faced in school and my parents never helped me solve any of them.

September 26, 2003
(Diane's last entry)

When a problem happens in the business of daily life, with family or friends, I cannot begin to deal with it unless I have a chronology of the events leading up to the problem.

It makes me crazy in my mind and I want to just lash out at the person who is telling me about it.

I realize this is because of the chaos in my childhood and teen years.

So many things went unexplained and so much unhappiness was caused by the lies and irresponsibility of the adults who were supposed to interpret the world and teach me to understand life.

So many of the adults in my immediate family, as well as, those in the extended family refused to "own their own mistakes" and tried to cover their shame and guilt with lies and omissions.

This then, is the reason for my telling my life story. Instead of being given an opportunity to give the world and the society I live in, the best of my intelligence and abilities, I seemed to have been doomed to a kind of obsession with the past and with the people who raised me and the people who raised those people.

Like most of humanity, my parents and their parents were poor, under-educated and ashamed of this. To make matters worse, they were above average in intelligence. They bitterly resented this station in life but could not see how to improve it for themselves. They did try to "improve things" but the actions they took made things worse for them and for their children.

Now then, what kinds of mistakes or actions did they engage in that caused those results?

I think the relatives of my parents' generation were very much like actors in a play or movie. They wore the costumes of the role they wanted to play in the world, dressing in whatever clothing they could afford to buy. They bought the things that the economy, as it grew, could provide with the small monies they came by, often going into heavy debt for cars, TV's, stereos, pets, sometimes a house in a cheap development. Mostly, they bought the set props to go with the costumes.

What they didn't buy was education, dental and medical care, insurance of most kinds. Behind the actors and the sets was nothing and the slightest storm would blow it all down.Mostly they could never speak for themselves, they outright refused to answer when, as an adult, I asked direct questions about their choices, their thoughts and their feelings. Sometimes the resistance was bred of shame, other times it was "psychological denial" and much of the time to was to avoid the pain of knowing they had failed themselves and their children. Yet, I know the ground is full of the same dead bones and untold stories of the generations that have lived such lives and I did not want to go to my grave without telling at least one true story.

Dementia

We must make haste then, not only because we are daily nearer death, but also because the conception of things and the understanding of them cease first.
— *Marcus Aurelius*

Our population is aging. The oldest Baby Boomers turned 73 in 2019. Cases of Alzheimer's and related dementias are predicted to more than double in the coming years as we all grow older. Many more husbands and wives will care for their spouses with dementia. The disease is devastating. So is caring for someone you love who has it. Anyone who becomes a caregiver can benefit from a look ahead, to learn what to expect and how to plan for it. The less resources you have available, the more important it is to reach out for advice and support. I didn't know about many sources of help at the time, that could have improved our lives as I cared for Diane. You must go to them; they will not come looking for you.

Many different diseases can cause dementia, with different symptoms and effects on behavior. In general, common caregiving tasks apply across all types of dementia. You need an expert diagnosis to determine what type of dementia is affecting your loved one, so you can get a care plan that fits their needs. Even specialists can be fooled by some people who skillfully mask their symptoms until the disease progresses and they can't keep up the façade.

Diane said that when she had a toothache in grade school, she walked herself to the dentist and asked to have the infected tooth pulled. The bill went to her parents. She never knew if they paid it. Her parents were too distracted by their emotional and financial chaos to give her proper care, and never took her to a dentist. When she had her heart attack, Diane's cardiologist told her that she must attend to her dental health for the sake of her heart. She was afraid of dentists because of her childhood history, but I managed to get her to a dentist in Philadelphia. He referred her to an oral surgeon. He said she needed her upper teeth completely removed. We discussed implants but the expense, lengthy process, and finally, her ability to care for implants were factors in choosing a denture instead. Diane had the surgery in 2003.

In the winter of 2004, she slipped on ice outside the house and sprained her left leg badly. No bones were broken, but it kept her off her feet for days. A month later as Diane was exiting a cab in Philadelphia, she slipped again and re-sprained the same leg, aggravating the injury. She went to physical therapy for one visit and refused to go back, and she never fully recovered from the sprain. The next year the four of us traveled to Belize for a vacation. Jennifer, Lauren, and I took an afternoon tour of the Monkey River while Diane stayed behind at the resort. After lunch, Diane stumbled when she stepped off a low platform at the restaurant in the resort, falling and re-injuring her leg, further limiting her mobility. The injury kept her from walking, another problem affecting her health.

During those years Diane frequently argued with her sisters in phone calls. Later we learned that Diane's youngest sister Cheryl began developing dementia around the same time. Cheryl was a heavy cigarette smoker, although she quit a few years before her health declined. She also drank alcohol to excess. Diane and Cheryl both had traumatic experiences in childhood, and talking to each other apparently triggered those emotions, leading to bitter arguments and a lasting breach. Cheryl stopped talking to Diane and would not answer phone calls or return messages. Diane also argued with her sister Pat and stopped talking to her, though Pat continued to keep in touch. Diane argued bitterly with a cousin over events in the distant past that probably never happened, and she insulted her younger friend Renee, who stayed with her many afternoons as a child. Diane broke off most of her relationships with old friends and relatives, isolating herself as her condition progressed and she lost her capacity to function socially.

I retired when Diane's dementia was serious enough that she needed full-time care. We had enough money saved that I didn't need to keep working to make ends meet. A movie like "Still Alice" tells the story of a woman with dementia, but critics point out that Alice could afford care that is out of reach for an average family.

One of the most difficult decisions you may face is whether to care for your loved one at home or place them into an assisted living facility (if you can find a way to cover the cost). As the years passed while I cared for Diane, I was haunted by wondering whether I would need to move her from home. I heard discouraging stories from others in my Alzheimer's support group. Some people became so difficult to manage that their caregivers couldn't cope and had to move them into a facility. What you decide depends on your physical, emotional, and financial resources, and on how their dementia affects their behavior. I was lucky that my wife was not disruptive. Some people are.

In my situation I could care for Diane at home until the end. I was six years younger, in good health, and was strong enough to pick her up if she fell rather than call for emergency services. I could keep Diane at home because as her disease progressed, she remained fairly calm and even-tempered, and pleasant most of the time. Some members in my dementia support have much more difficult situations than mine, and some have had no choice but to put their spouse in assisted living.

Diane experienced many traumas that affected her for her entire life. She had many symptoms of post-traumatic stress disorder, or PTSD, but she was never formally diagnosed. She clearly had an anxiety disorder, and developed a variety of coping mechanisms. Yet Diane gave herself fully to friends, though not everyone could tolerate her directness. In time, dementia diminished and distorted her personality. Her memories of our life and our family faded, her exceptional intellect slowly disappeared, and physical problems kept her from enjoying ordinary activities like going for a walk on a pleasant day.

As her caregiver I was responsible for managing Diane's health. I had to understand how she was feeling even when she couldn't tell me. I had to work with her physicians to deal with any health problems. I began taking an active role managing her health when her autoimmune disease first flared up in 1992. Over the next several years we saw gastroenterologists, endocrinologists, cardiologists, dermatologists, oral surgeons, and an internist. When a problem arose, it wasn't always clear who to call. Sometimes no one was available to respond to an immediate need and I had to decide what to do based on my own knowledge of her history. At times that was nerve-wracking, especially after she fell and hurt herself badly the year I retired. The consequences of that injury played out over the next thirteen months. No one, including me, knew how severely she was injured then.

Diane's family medical history had a direct bearing on her health and her dementia. Diane's mother Genevieve Christopher died at the age of 82 from ovarian cancer. By then she was unable to walk or speak, totally disabled by vascular dementia. It was a mercy when cancer ended her life after two years spent ill and alone in a nursing home. Diane's mother showed symptoms of what we called "hardening of the arteries" as early as 1970 when she was in her late fifties. Aside from possible inherited factors, other significant risks for Diane were obesity, high cholesterol, and an addiction to Winston cigarettes that began when she was a thirteen year-old girl.

Diane became depressed after her father died in July, 1992. We consulted a psychologist, who agreed to counsel her for the depression, but only if Diane had a physician prescribe anti-depressant medication. We went to a family practitioner near our house in December, who wrote a prescription for Zoloft for Diane. He failed to order a blood test to assess baseline functioning, particularly her thyroid hormone levels. The association between depression and low thyroid hormone levels was well-known, and his negligence probably contributed to what followed.

The following April Diane suffered an onset of severe colitis with uncontrollable diarrhea. I took her to a gastroenterologist, who ordered a complete blood workup. The lab tests found that she had extremely low thyroid hormone levels, a result that could have been found earlier by the family practitioner who saw Diane in December. Thyroid supplements restored her functions and mitigated the depression as well, without the need for antidepressants, but by then the colitis was established as a chronic condition that endured for the rest of her life. Diane also had chronic inflammation from abscessed teeth, a consequence of her parents' neglect when she was growing up. As a result, she had a heart attack in 1999. By then, the insidious effect of cardiovascular disease on her brain was well along. Gradually, over the next few years, her personality and behavior changed subtly. She became more irritable, engaging in arguments that alienated old friends and family.

Her lapses of memory occurred more often.

DIAGNOSIS

While no one can change the outcome of dementia or Alzheimer's, with the right support you can change the journey.
— *TARA REED*

In 2007 Diane and I traveled to England, staying in London for a week. Diane never quite overcame her jet lag from the flight to London and slept a lot during our stay. Later, Diane said she couldn't remember much about the trip. She was showing memory loss in other ways, like struggling for words, unable to recall the word she wanted to use. Jennifer and Lauren both noticed her memory problems. We used to joke about the earliest sign of that problem a decade earlier when she'd often say something like, "Hand me that *thing*, will you?"

Diane agreed to a consultation at the Penn Memory Center of the University of Pennsylvania, a leading research center for Alzheimer's disease. Months passed as they performed tests and imaging studies, including a CT scan of the brain and tests of her spinal fluid. In January Diane wouldn't agree to an MRI because of her claustrophobia, then she refused to participate in more imaging studies. By February, we had the results from the completed tests. Her CT scan showed damaged areas in her brain indicating micro-vascular ischemic disease, and her spinal fluid contained two significant substances: amyloid beta and phosphorylated tau protein.

Her overall diagnosis from the cognitive tests was mild cognitive impairment, or MCI. Dr. Jason Karlawish, the director of the center, told me that the presence of the two substances in her spinal fluid was a risk factor for Alzheimer's disease. He said fifteen percent of people with mild cognitive impairment with those indicators exhibit changes (i.e. deterioration) in any given year, but forty percent don't change in ten years. His phrasing was cautious, but I understood what it meant: there was a sixty percent probability that Diane's condition would deteriorate within ten years, and would lead to Alzheimer's dementia.

My father and mother were both in assisted living then, where they had been since a court in Washington determined that they were no longer capable of caring for themselves and invoked their power of attorney. My brother took over their care and transferred them to a facility near his home in Columbus, Georgia, where they stayed until their deaths. I visited them in their assisted living center. By then they were content to live in a memory care unit. When they were first placed in assisted living, my father escaped twice because he wanted to go home. He was found sitting outside in the parking lot of the facility. In January 2010, he choked on food, he collapsed and his heart stopped, and he was not resuscitated. He was 93 years old. After he died, my mother's dementia progressed and she spent more and more time sleeping. She followed him a year later in 2011. She was 91.

Diane changed slowly after her MCI diagnosis. In 2011 she and I traveled to Southern California to visit her sisters and an old friend of mine. Stan was a friend who lived two houses up the street from me when I was young. Our lives were like a quote from Truman Capote about one of the characters in his book, *In Cold Blood*: "It's as if Perry and I grew up in the same house. And one day he stood up and went out the back door, while I went out the front." By 2011, after surviving heroin addiction and prison, he had insulin-dependent diabetes, and he already had suffered one stroke. Two months after our visit, another stroke left him in a coma, and he died a month before his 65th birthday. In March I flew alone to Vancouver, Washington to hold a memorial service for my parents with my brother and relatives. When I left on a Friday, I left Diane some notes about things to do, and an envelope with two hundred dollars in case she needed any cash.

When I returned on three days later, Diane imagined that I had flown to Seattle for a week-long rendezvous with a former neighbor. By then, Diane had exasperating gaps in her reasoning ability. Logic was useless. I showed her my plane tickets, car rental receipts, motel receipts, and even photos I took of the Columbia River Gorge the last morning I was in Vancouver, but nothing shook her delusion. It persisted for several years afterward. I started to realize how her mental condition was changing. I never learned what she did with the cash.

That summer we flew to Minnesota and visited old friends and family there. We drove to the north-central part of the state to see

Dan and Cheri, friends of ours from antiwar demonstrations and communes in Minneapolis. We drove back to Minneapolis via scenic roads through the north woods. When Jennifer asked if she enjoyed the trip, Diane answered "It was boring. All we saw were trees and more trees."

In December we took a cruise to the Caribbean. We docked in Costa Rica, where Diane and I took a boat tour through a rain forest, returning to the ship afterwards. As we were about to re-board, I realized that I forgot to buy some denture cream for Diane when we passed the market at the end of the dock. I asked her to wait for me, and walked into the open-air market to buy it. When I returned to the pier where I left her, she was gone. I felt rising panic, not knowing whether she boarded the ship or wandered unnoticed through the market. I asked a crew member attending the entrance if she was on board. She was. Diane was somewhere on the cruise ship, but I didn't know exactly where. The crew found Diane after a search, and we returned to our cabin. I realized she could just wander away and disappear if she was not supervised.

While we were on the cruise, Diane had an onset of diarrhea that lasted most of the time we were on board. It could have been a stomach virus, or a recurrence of her colitis. After we returned, I tried a treatment that I read about in a study in England, using bismuth subsalicylate (Pepto-Bismol) for six weeks to treat colitis. I set up a treatment schedule in January and followed it strictly for six weeks, and it worked. We tried all the available drugs for Diane's colitis during its eighteen-years course, with mixed results. The only clear-cut result, which was not an improvement, was that Diane became less willing to take pills. The Pepto-Bismol treatment seemed to resolve that bout of diarrhea. Maybe it simply would have resolved itself in time. I believe her colitis affected her mental condition from the time it began in 1993.

After the cruise I continued working at Oracle. Fortunately, they had a liberal policy allowing employees to work from home, as I did two or three days a week. On days when I was in the office, I assumed Diane was taking care of herself at home. Later, Jennifer told me that she visited a few times on days when I was at work and Diane did nothing but sit, waiting for me to come home. She still had a car to drive and a valid license.

I didn't realize she might just drive away and go somewhere on her own.

FULL-TIME CAREGIVER

There are only four kinds of people in the world.
Those who have been caregivers.
Those who are currently caregivers.
Those who will be caregivers,
and those who will need a caregiver.
— *ROSALYN CARTER*

I kept a journal to record everyday life caring for Diane as her condition changed from mild cognitive impairment to dementia. I had no idea how long I might be caring for her, or how it would end. I based this narrative on that journal. I didn't expect anyone would ever read the journal, but writing helped me to keep my own sanity, and I hoped it might have some value for others. I wish I had been more diligent about writing regularly in the journal. There are gaps in this story, but they were times when the same events happened repeatedly without much change.

I hope this story will help others cope with their lives and the challenges of caring for loved ones with dementia. I occasionally refer to *The 36-Hour Day*, the go-to resource book for Alzheimer's caregivers. It is available from many sources. I have listed it along with some other information in the appendix of this book. The list is far from comprehensive, but it's a starting point to begin learning. A vast amount of information is available, and it can be confusing to anyone just starting on this journey.

Diane no longer did most things for herself—what medical professionals call the activities of daily living: dressing, grooming, bathing, cleaning, shopping, and cooking, for example. There are more detailed lists available. One winter before her diagnosis, Diane suffered two serious leg sprains from slipping on ice. A year after the falls, at a resort in Belize she missed a step, stumbled, and fell again, spraining the same leg. Her sprains weren't severe, but they were bad enough to need medical attention. She refused to do the physical therapy exercises that would have helped her to recover. After each injury she lost more function. By 2012 she couldn't walk unassisted. Walking is critically important for maintaining the health of your heart, lungs, muscles, and brain. Above all else, Diane was a lifelong smoker since the age of thirteen, and would only smoke Winstons, a brand with high tar and nicotine levels. Eventually, she sat most of day and her health deteriorated faster.

I took up the slack. I picked out clothes for her to wear and helped her dress. I gave her a shower if I could get her to cooperate. She seldom cooperated. Bathing people with dementia is a common problem. The few times she showered were usually a result of having soiled herself with diarrhea. Caregivers often need to deal with incontinence. Writing about it is not disrespectful to the person with dementia. Everyone poops; we just don't like to talk about it. When dementia incapacitates people's control of urine and stool, we take care of them. It's a health problem that we need to deal with, and doing that is an act of love.

I shopped for food, cooked the meals and cleaned up, cleaned the house when it got too dusty to function, washed, dried, folded and stored the laundry, fed and walked the dogs—everything. I took her to medical appointments while she still cooperated with that. Eventually she stopped cooperating. When I could persuade her to get in the car to go to an appointment, usually she would refuse to get out of the car when we arrived at the doctor's office. She was always self-willed: incorrigible, as she once put it. Later I found a physician who made house calls, and this worked well when she occasionally had an infection or a virus.

When I took over Diane's care, she was taking several prescription medicines, some in the morning and some at night. Eventually I switched all her pills to morning dosage. Forget about evenings. She balked too much, refused to take them, and the dosage became inconsistent. Her doctor agreed that taking the medications regularly was more important than taking them at the optimum recommended time of day. As time passed and her condition changed, I worked with her physician to eliminate pills that weren't critical, such as vitamins and a statin for high cholesterol. Near the end of her life, the only pills she took were her daily thyroid medicine and occasional anti-diarrhea pills. Sometimes she needed anti-anxiety medicine, which usually I could crush and mix it into a food she liked, such as ice cream.

A word about doctors: get the best medical advice available to you. Some family doctors aren't well-versed in the issues of dementia care. I live in an area with ample health care resources, so I could find an internist who specialized in geriatric medicine to be Diane's primary care physician. In southern New Jersey near Philadelphia, the Institute for Successful Aging at Rowan University deals specifically with geriatric issues, and provides treatment plans and continuing care. The Penn Memory Center in Philadelphia, a leading center for Alzheimer's disease at the University of Pennsylvania, conducts research and offers resources and information for caregivers. Many diseases cause dementia, and the proper treatment can be vastly different depending on the underlying cause. It is critically important to get a competent diagnosis as soon as you suspect you may be dealing with dementia. You usually need to obtain a diagnosis only once, so it is worth traveling if you have to do that to see a specialist. If you reach out to The Alzheimer's Association in your area, they can give you information about providers and sources of help. (See the **Appendix: Caregiver Resources** for more information.)

In March 2012, I went on a weekend ski trip to Vermont with a local ski club. We left on a bus on a Friday afternoon and reached our motel next to Okemo Mountain Resort late at night. I shared a double room with another skier—a man. We skied Saturday and Sunday and returned home late Sunday night. In Diane's mind I was again gone for a whole week, and where would I go? To Seattle to see my old girlfriend of course! All the local ski areas closed at the end of the weekend, so the season was over for me. I dropped off my skis at a shop to be tuned and waxed for the next season. A week later, the ski shop called and Diane answered. The man at the shop told Diane my skis were ready to pick up. Diane used that bit of information to embellish on her delusion, claiming that she knew I couldn't have been skiing because a man called from the train station and told her I left my skis there. She held on to that delusion for years, and sometimes threw it back at me when she was angry.

One morning in April, Diane saw me writing in my journal and wanted to know what I was writing. I told her I was journaling so I could get back into writing when I retired. That was partly true. Morning was my time to write, read, or do whatever I needed while Diane slept. In the evening she demanded my full attention and got upset if it wasn't given. I was just feeling my way, trying to find a method and style of living from day to day that worked and satisfied both of us. By evening Diane was often in a crappy mood. She wouldn't watch TV, read, or talk. If it was overcast during the day, it made her more unbearable. Later I learned that many of the members of my spouse support group go to great lengths to engage their husbands and wives in activities to keep them physically and mentally active. That has been shown to slow the process of deterioration in dementia. Some spouses enjoy this and cooperate. Some don't. Diane didn't.

Diane was often angry at me for things I did twenty, thirty, or forty years ago—or things she imagined I did. Distant memories can be more real than recent ones as dementia impairs recalling recent memory. *The 36-Hour Day* mentions this effect. The book is depressing to read, but it full of vital information for caregivers. It tells you what you might need to know starting in the early stages to the most severe forms of dementia. The chapters are organized by stages of dementia, so you can read as far as you want for the stage your loved one is in, then put it down until later, when things change and you want more information. Things change. In dementia, they usually get worse, not better. Unlike many diseases, there is no recovery in the future.

Diane's daily habits changed as her energy levels declined. She started going to bed earlier and wanted me to go to bed at the same time. I had to work out a way to live with her early-to-bed zeal. By then, I was taking care of everything in the house—shopping, cooking, cleaning, maintenance, and of course, Diane—and I couldn't drop it all at 7:30 PM to go to bed with her. It was frustrating. However, she did have a point. I could feel the soreness in my back muscles and know that I was tired. She probably could tell by looking at me. I thought maybe I could get up earlier in the morning to make up the time.

I posted to Facebook that I was changing my personal goal from satisfaction to happiness. For years, my goal was satisfaction—satisfying my own wants and others' expectations. At last, satisfaction wasn't enough. During the previous years I satisfied many of my life goals, but that alone didn't bring me happiness. I worked at my tasks fast and aggressively—moving, shopping, driving, or other activities—and that blocked me from happiness. It got things done. It satisfied my need to check off things on my list. But it induced a state of tension and stress that prevented enjoyment. Striving to reach those goals made reaching them unsatisfying, a paradox.

I believe the movie "The Way" spoke to that issue. The main character is a man who is accustomed to achieving and satisfying his goals. But during his pilgrimage, undertaken spontaneously, he begins to realize this about himself: that achieving is not fulfilling. At first he believes his son's death to be a senseless act of nature, but it becomes meaningful by transforming his own awareness. Now I see the parallel. Diane's illness was likewise bad luck, a random combination of heredity and lifestyle, that forced me to confront what was left of my life and to ask myself what is important. What brings happiness? What is happiness when goals like achievement and intellectual prowess become irrelevant, if you can't think and you can't remember anymore?

Sometimes painful experiences result in lessons learned, in growth, and emotional pain leads to emotional growth. Maybe that's what I felt—irritated and annoyed when I had to walk step-by-step through an explanation for Diane that most people would grasp at once—that she once would have understood with no explanation. But Diane wasn't most people. That's where the pain came in. I loved her, and it hurt me to realize how diminished she was. As her time horizon and her breadth of understanding contracted, unbeknownst to her, she became more demanding for an explanation of what I was saying. Sometimes I felt trapped, caged up inside the house taking care of her. If I said that to her, she would have replied in fury "Then go!" I couldn't do that. It would have hurt me too much and it would have left her unprotected and vulnerable. Who would care for her? The motto of the modern Army: leave no man behind. We are in a war with the forces of Nature. Ultimately, we all lose, and the only thing that matters is how well we fought, how we took care of our casualties, and how well we cared for each other. I was determined to live long enough to care for Diane for the rest of her life. After that who knows how I'd feel?

One afternoon in early May, I was at the office when Diane wandered off in her car. When I returned home I discovered her car was gone. At five o'clock we made a call to the Cherry Hill Police Department. We already had checked the parking lots around the mall, at all the stores, restaurants, and hospitals where she might have gone. We called the police in Cherry Hill, Medford, and Mount Laurel. We drove around all the streets in the neighborhood looking for her. I called Jennifer. She and her fiancé Mike drove out to search in their area, in case Diane got lost on the way to her house. I sat in the house with Lauren, trying to devise a plan to find Diane and waiting for someone to call with news.

While we wondered frantically where she might have gone, Diane was meandering around South Jersey between Hammonton and Salem, enjoying her drive on a sunny day in the country.

She couldn't have gone any further southwest without driving into the Delaware Bay. We were lucky that she didn't wander north into densely populated areas and cities and disappear. I wondered anxiously how we would get through the night if she didn't turn up, knowing every hour that passed made a tragic outcome more likely.

Finally a call came in at 8:17 PM. Diane was in Lower Alloway Creek Township near Salem, New Jersey. She stopped at a house, said she was lost, and asked for directions. The two schoolteachers living there recognized her condition and called us. Lauren and her fiancé Kevin were here. Jennifer and Mike were on the road headed toward us, and immediately turned to go get Diane and her car.

I ended the day feeling emotionally drained, nervous, and exhausted. The next day Diane chattered about what a great time she had the day before—so relaxing. We told her she was the only one who was relaxed.

A couple of weeks later as I worked at the office, Diane called at three o'clock. She wanted to know where her keys were so she could go to the bookstore.

I told her, "I have them." She asked me where that was.

"They're in my coat pocket along with me at the office," I said, "I'll come home and take you to the bookstore."

When I got home she was asleep, and once awake of course she didn't want to go to the bookstore anymore. She wanted her keys back.

I told her "I don't trust you not to disappear like you did two weeks ago." By the next day it was forgotten.

The next morning Diane demanded her car keys back .

"Give me my keys or I'll call the police. I'll tell them you're keeping me prisoner in the house."

"I'm sorry, but I don't trust your driving after that stunt you pulled two weeks ago. I will drive you anywhere you want to go, any time."

She didn't call the cops. Eventually she stopped asking.

Not long afterward, Diane told me she was walking along the sidewalk near our house when a large, ugly man kept her from going into the neighbor's house. She said he was bigger and taller than me, he was combative, and he didn't speak English. He assumed a martial arts stance to block her way. Diane said she knew that he kept his wife locked up in the house and wouldn't let her go out. I didn't believe her story, but thought I should check it out, and find out what actually happened, if anything. Awhile later

Diane and I walked over to the neighbors for a visit, and talked to the boy who lives there. He said she might have seen his uncle who was visiting them. We never met the uncle.

Later, Diane told me her primary care physician, an unmarried woman, was being held prisoner by her husband in her own house. Diane believed she lived in Medford, not far from where we once lived. Diane refused to admit that there was no truth to it, and she was so worried about her doctor's situation that she called 911 to report it. Two officers from the Cherry Hill Police Department came to our house and listened politely to her confused explanation of the emergency. Out of earshot, I explained Diane's condition to one of them. They pretended to take the information and said they would investigate. Diane was satisfied she'd done the right thing. She stopped worrying about her doctor.

On May 14 Diane was experiencing chest or abdominal pain, and I drove her to the emergency room at Cooper Hospital. Tests showed no sign of a heart attack. After six and a half hours waiting to be examined and waiting for test results, she refused to stay for more tests. We signed out and left against medical advice. Later that day, I was in the garage when our neighbor came to the front door. As Diane walked to the door to answer it, the dog got underfoot. She slipped and fell against the corner of a small table near the door, hurting herself badly. She refused to see a doctor. After two days Diane's back hurt so much she couldn't get out of bed. I called 911. The EMTs lifted her onto a gurney and carried her to an ambulance, and we returned to Cooper Hospital. They examined her injury from the fall and took imaging studies. She'd crushed a vertebra in her back and sustained deep bruising around her duodenum and pancreas. The images showed thickening of the duodenum that was concerning. Concerning. When a doctor says that, the unspoken word is "cancer." The extent wasn't known but she needed to follow up with her cardiologist and gastroenterologist.

Our calm, mishap-free days were overtaken by days of trouble and drama. We spent ten-and-a-half hours in the emergency room that week. Pain in the middle of the night brought the fear of another heart attack. With some cocoa and calm, the stomach pain subsided. Was it due to Diane going almost a day without much to eat? I had to see her in the morning before leaving for the office to make sure she got what she needed. Otherwise there was no way to know. An office visit with Diane's cardiologist ruled out heart problems, She needed a GI workup for abdominal pain. The pain seemed to travel around, maybe from inflammation in the bowel. How much better would Diane be if she stayed at the hospital on May 14th instead of coming home and suffering that fall? Diane was at the ER for stomach pain; the staff tended to patients first who were in critical condition, and Diane was last in line. If we stayed and waited, we would not have been home when that neighbor rang the doorbell, and she would not have fallen... "What-ifs" are futile.

We spent the next few days trying to book an appointment with her gastroenterologist. Diane's pain distracted her even more and she could scarcely remember anything. The gastroenterologist who saw Diane at the hospital recommended an endoscopy. That would need to wait a month until after her duodenum healed. She also had a thickening of the esophagus that must be checked out.

A whole host questions rose my mind. Would she recover from this condition, or was it the state of her health from now on, or only the prelude to much worse? Where did this path lead? How much of her mental confusion was from sickness, weakness, and nausea? There was little joy in her life, and she could do or to look forward to doing much at all. I tried to keep going from day to day, but I was doing it alone, and loneliness is a heavy strain, but I didn't reach out to a support group until two years later.

The days after May 14th were grueling. Diane slept a lot because her nausea medicine made her drowsy. We were just enduring the days until her upper GI exam. One morning Diane woke up at 4:30 AM complaining that her back hurt, and that woke me. I gave her an acetaminophen. She went back to bed and fell asleep while I remained awake. Finally, I got up at 5:30. Our house was a virtual infirmary. I was a medic and Diane was the patient. I hoped for clarity from the results of the endoscopy but feared it would bring more bad news. Medications, surgery, chemotherapy... What? The prospects weren't encouraging. We all know that no one gets out of here alive, but when we're young, we believe that the settlement date is far in the future. At this stage it seemed, the date grew near. On May 31, I retired from Oracle and became a full-time caregiver.

Every time she ate Diane felt a lot of nausea. Her gastroenterologist recommended pancreatin capsules, but it was unclear whether they helped or hurt. I discontinued them temporarily. On a typical morning Diane was up for about an hour. Prior to eating I gave her a ranitidine tablet. She was also taking omeprazole. She drank some cranberry juice and a can of tomato juice. She ate about a quarter cup of Cheerios with soy milk. Then she started to feel nauseated. That worried me, given the gastroenterologist's concern about the esophageal thickening. Her endoscopy was scheduled for July third. It couldn't come soon enough. I believed she had some very inflamed tissues in her stomach, esophagus, and duodenum, and eating anything irritated it. My approach was to give only antacid for the nausea. Meclizine seemed to help but did not completely resolve it. I was just muddling through until her scheduled endoscopy.

Finally, the endoscopy was completed and the results came: the esophagus looked normal. The previous CT scan result wasn't accurate. Her stomach looked inflamed. They took lots of biopsies. They tested for h-pylori bacteria, which can cause nausea. They went into the duodenum to the area where the scan showed diverticulosis. The opening to diverticula can be tiny. They were unable to see anything. The test for H. Pylori was negative.

Diane's back pain continued to bother her for months after her fall. We went miniature golfing one afternoon with Jennifer and Mike, Lauren, Kevin, and his son. I gave Diane two 500 mg acetaminophen tablets and she still had to leave the mini golf course and sit down. She groaned every time the car went over a bump as we drove home.

One night, Diane said she thought we should separate because I was still in love with Julie. I told her I was never in love with Julie or anyone else but her. That seemed to satisfy her, and the mood passed. I resolved to be more affectionate to her. It was bothering her and that was cruel. She needed my love more than ever. The next night she wanted to make love in the middle of the night. She was feeling better and the intensity was wonderful.

We had an appointment with Jason Karlawish at the Penn Memory Center. We discussed Diane's stated feeling of boredom and lack of interest in activities. He gave her a depression screening test and the results led him to prescribe a weekly Prozac—weekly, based on her aversion to taking pills. He also recommended she get involved in senior day programs. I called to get some leads to check it out and started searching online. I found two places with adult daycare programs and we drove to look at them. One was situated in an old red brick building in Moorestown, formerly the site of the YMCA. Diane saw the institutional appearance of the building. It must have looked a lot like one of the buildings at Sauk Centre. She refused to get out of the car to look inside. Another program was in a new, one story office complex, but the main entrance had a cipher lock on the door, announcing it as a place of confinement. Diane went into the waiting room and sat while the manager explained their program, but she had no desire to be locked into any facility. I couldn't persuade her to participate in any day programs.

Diane slowly recovered from her injuries due to the fall. Her back continued to cause pain. That never completely went away because of the permanent injury to her spine.

In September 2012, Lauren and Kevin married. Lauren and I did the planning and we included Diane in as much of it as possible. Lauren and I found the location for the ceremony and reception at the Valley Green Inn in Philadelphia, and arranged for the food, decorations, and rooms in a nearby hotel for out of town guests. Jennifer, Diane, and I helped Lauren pick out her dress at an event held by Brides Against Breast Cancer, a nonprofit group that resells donated wedding dresses once a year in return for a donation. After the wedding she donated the dress back to the organization so another bride could wear it. The event was important to Lauren, but because she worked as a model for several years, she didn't attach much significance to the dress she wore for just a few hours. Diane attended the entire event — an outdoor service by the Wissahickon Creek, followed by a reception in an outdoor pavilion attached to the inn. She participated the whole time and even gave a short speech to the guests during the reception. Diane still could meet and socialize with a large group of people and enjoy the experience. It was a high point. We all enjoyed it.

Later that fall I rented a camper for a week. I had an idea how we could spend our time, now that I was retired and had leisure to figure out the next stage of our lives. I planned a trip to drive through Vermont and visit my college roommate Gene, who lives on his Christmas tree farm at the northern end of the state. We took our two dogs with us and left the cat in a kennel for the week. We drove to Vermont through New York and Massachusetts along winding two-lane roads through woods turning to fall colors. I thought it was a pleasant drive, but to Diane it was "nothing but trees, trees, and more trees." Still, it was less boring than just sitting at home with not a lot to do. Later, as caregiving became more demanding, finding things to do wasn't much of an issue. I hoped that the trip would remind Diane, as it did me, of the times we traveled in our own camper the first year of our marriage. Gene was glad to see us, and Diane enjoyed his company. Afterwards, I felt like the trip was a success. Even if Diane didn't remember much of what we saw on our trip she was comfortable in the camper and somewhat entertained most of the time by the passing scenery. So was I, and that was important to me. I wanted to enjoy our time together.

The Vermont trip convinced me this would be a good activity for us, a way to spend time together and reconnect with our past. I hoped this mode of travel would feel familiar so she could at least be comfortable even if she did not recall previous trips. I felt like this experience confirmed it, and decided to go ahead and buy a camper so we could travel more. We could take the dogs with us and avoid big boarding expenses, she could smoke whenever she wanted, and we'd have as much privacy as we needed. I started looking for a camper. I settled on a type B camper, built from a standard van and fitted with beds, cabinets, stove, refrigerator, toilet, water supply, holding tanks, and more. I started browsing Craigslist ads and found one for sale from a local couple, schoolteachers at a private Quaker academy north of Philadelphia. In a couple of weeks, I took delivery, we signed the papers at my bank, and I was the owner of a 1995 Roadtrek camper with a whole bunch of repairs in my future. I became good friends and a returning customer at the Dodge dealer, a local mechanic, a body shop, and a local RV dealer.

I won't go into detail about all the repairs I made to the camper, but they added up to more than the initial cost. After the first three months of ownership the body work was done, it was repainted, mechanical repairs done, and almost ready to go on the road when another disaster struck.

LIFE AND DEATH

Illness is the night side of life, a more onerous citizenship. Everyone who is born holds dual citizenship, in the kingdom of the well and in the kingdom of the sick. Although we all prefer to use the good passport, sooner or later each of us is obliged, at least for a spell, to identify ourselves as citizens of that other place.
— *SUSAN SONTAG*

In March, Diane had a recurrence of colitis and I tried treating it with Pepto-Bismol as I had the year before. That was an extremely serious mistake. Pepto-Bismol turns the stool black. Her chronic colitis caused diarrhea, but so did internal bleeding. The chronic diarrhea started in late March, and because Pepto-Bismol was successful the previous year, I began treating her with it again. Because I gave Diane Pepto-Bismol I didn't know when she began to bleed from the injury to her duodenum. In mid-April Diane felt abdominal pain, so I took her to the Cooper Urgent Care, then to the Cooper Hospital ER. Tests showed no sign of a heart attack, and she was sent home with the advice to see her primary care physician. She saw her doctor on April sixteenth; no urgent problems showed then, but her doctor gave her a script for an MRI of her abdomen. Diane had an MRI done at Jefferson Imaging that week.

On April 20th I worked outside in the yard, and I when came in the house I met a critical situation. Diane had a bruise on her chin and she was groggy. She must have fallen. In the kitchen I found a large amount of dark diarrhea on the floor next to the dishwasher. I thought she must have had sudden diarrhea, slipped, and fell there, bumping her head as she fell. Very worried, I cleaned her up and cleaned the floor while she sat in the living room. Lauren came over. We thought Diane should lie down and rest. When we stood her up to walk to the bedroom, she began to tremble and then she fainted next to the front door. We laid her down on the floor. I told Lauren to call 911 and we waited for an ambulance. We followed her to Cooper Hospital in Camden. In the ER Diane had critically low blood pressure and signs of passing blood. She was hemorrhaging internally. They started Diane on a transfusion and admitted her to the hospital.

An ordeal began. Her first surgery attempted to stop the bleeding by applying a clip to the area around the ulcer. That failed. A second technique failed. At last, the surgeon inserted a block into one of the two gastro-duodenal arteries that feeds the area of the bleeding, and the hemorrhage stopped.

Between surgeries Diane was either in the ICU or a step-down unit. Nursing care was a huge problem. For a person with dementia, the standard of care calls for a one-on-one aide to ensure her welfare. Even though I told them explicitly that Diane had dementia, it was not done. I sat next to Diane to watch her, but she was in a semi-private room and another woman was in the second bed. The nurse was adamant that I must leave. Under protest I went to lie down in the closest lounge.

At one AM the nurse woke me up and brought me back to the room. Diane had pulled out all her IVs, spilling blood all over the floor and her bed. She didn't understand why she had needles stuck in her and she wanted to go home. I helped calm her down and sat with her the rest of the night. In the morning, either Lauren or Jennifer came to relieve me so I could go home and take care of the pets. We set up rotating shifts so that one of them could sit with her at night, but they couldn't always do that. Diane pulled her IVs more than once, except when she was in the ICU because then she had constant nursing care. When she was in the step-down unit (a level of care between intensive care and a surgical ward) there were fewer nurses. Finally, the hospital moved Diane to a private room so I could stay with her.

The MRI done just before Diane's hospitalization showed thickening in the anterior duodenum, and the Jefferson radiologist interpreted that as a cancerous growth. Diane was diagnosed with duodenal cancer. Surgery for her condition was ruled out due to her dementia. On May 9, Diane was discharged to home hospice care, not expected to survive. The hospice nurse visited the house, trained me on how to administer medications for pain if needed, and ran through the other information I'd need as Diane's condition declined.

By mid-May I was waiting for a call from Cooper Hospital with results of the pathology report. Was it cancer? Yes or no.

Was it H-pylori? Yes or no. Diane's life seemed to hang on that thread of information. Knowing the results wouldn't affect her treatment or the outcome, but I needed to know what to expect and when. I felt tense, flat, anxious, and held my breath unawares. I had to consciously breathe in and out to break the tension. Nothing seemed important or relevant or worth doing. I was just passing time until the answers came. Then? I couldn't envision the alternatives we faced—another gray wall of fog shrouded the future. Waiting.

This suspended animation overwhelmed all other moods. Knowing that it could be relatively good or awful, and not knowing which one, was drawing all my energy into a place where nothing emerged. An emotional black hole. Like being on hold, holding for that one person whose words stand between you and the rest of your life. I felt the tension as a physical weight on my neck and shoulders, bearing down like the straps of a fifty-pound pack. Each day I tried to exert as much effort as I could to deaden the swirl of sadness, anguish, and fear that lurked just below awareness. At times it boiled up so that I couldn't speak, holding on to my words to keep the sobs from pouring out with them. At those moments all I could feel was the dull ache in my neck and shoulders. Perhaps that thread of hope or denial was what prevented me from feeling any more.

When I thought that Diane was dying I felt the anguish of saying goodbye to her, to all the common threads of our life together, envisioning cleaning out her clothes, her books, the things that meant much to her once, but now meant little, and would then mean nothing. She'd been letting go of her life unknowingly for several years as her memories of the past gradually vanished. Because of her low blood count and oxygen levels her awareness was worse than ever. I wanted to get her blood tested to see if the hemoglobin had come up, but first I needed to learn the results of the biopsies—was it cancer? H-pylori? What was doing this? How long would it take for her to recover—would she recover? These were deeply troubling questions, but as I pondered them I felt nothing—just tired, sore, and numb.

Finally, my daily call to Diane's doctor yielded results for the biopsies done May seventh. The report stated "moderate chronic duodenitis with focal erosion" and stated there were "reactive epithelial changes present with no tumor identified." I looked up reactive epithelial changes and found it meant inflammation, as in ulcers. It is distinct and distinguishable from dysplasia or cancerous changes. There was a lot of inflammation but no indication of cancer. Diane's surgeon said that if after a month or so she didn't have significant progress that could indicate an underlying cancer. He said that her case would be a highly unusual presentation; most cancers present as polyps or adenomas. He recommended a follow-up endoscopy with her Jefferson gastroenterologist. He was puzzled that she was seeing a gastroenterologist until I explained that it was for her longstanding colitis. After almost a year of chronic abdominal pain it was finally clear that her pain wasn't from inflammation or bowel disease but from the injury she had on May 14, 2012. The cancer diagnosis was incorrect. The thickening in the duodenum, resultant ulcer and hemorrhage were due to inflammation and scarring from the fall and injury that occurred the previous year.

Late one night, Diane reached over and touched me in her sleep, the first time she did that since well before she went to the hospital. It was a sign of improvement.

I was haunted by images of black blood—the sight and especially the smell of it. Melena is the medical term. The nurse in the ER said she knew Diane was regurgitating blood by the smell because it is so distinctive. Yes, it is. I know now how it looks, feels, and smells. And I wish I didn't. The memory weighed me down until I felt the pain of it somewhere below my heart. Three weeks passed after the last bleeding episode. Diane's blood pressure remained steady and her stool was clear of blood. For weeks afterward I kept checking the toilet after she went for that pungent odor of digested blood. There was none. Gradually I relaxed that surveillance, but I remained guarded against a sudden onset of bleeding. I was 67 years old, but I felt raw and inexperienced dealing with this health crisis, as if no time had passed since I was living on my own in college, fifty years earlier.

No news is good news. That old saying has two distinct meanings. If no cancer was found it could mean none was present, or it just meant if there was any they didn't find it. They looked in all the places where it might be. Also, there was no H. pylori. No antibiotic treatment was needed. The only treatment was to continue taking the pantoprazole and remain alert for signs of bleeding. At what point should they do another blood test for hemoglobin and red blood count? What else did the blood tests show? Were there any blood chemistry results that would indicate cancer? Every day with no bleeding or pain was another day of progress. In another month Diane would see her gastroenterologist again. By then maybe she would have enough oxygen in her blood she'd have some energy and brain power. Each day she seemed to me infinitesimally stronger, more normal. I hoped that wasn't just wishful thinking and I knew it could be. The anxiety was wrecking me.

On May 30 I wrote that Diane would not last more than a few more years unless they finally found the fabled cure for Alzheimer's disease. It seemed every time a new product to treat the brain plaques was announced it would be another five years until it would be available for use if the new miracle cure passed clinical trials. None of them did. What we needed was a medicine that was so damned effective that they would break the code early and rush it through final approval—and find that it didn't have lethal side-effects. I wrote: "Shadows lengthen and darkness covers all. Today's decisions are filled with reasons to doubt them. Demons lurk in the corners and cannot be scrubbed away. I feel bad and nothing feels good. The day passed and no catastrophes occurred. That's the best I can say about it now."

On a typical day Diane slept all but a few hours and ate nearly nothing. I was discouraged. That afternoon Diane lost her balance; she had positional hypotension. That scared me. I took her blood pressure, and it was 85/55. That was low. I gave her a glass of V8 juice to boost her fluid, salt, and potassium levels. She laid down. An hour later her blood pressure was 20 points higher at 105/65. The lesson: watch her fluid intake in hot weather. It's easy to get dehydrated. That worried me.

I often worried about her during that period. She was frail, lacked energy, couldn't stay awake all day, was confused and her mood stank. In the back of my mind I was thinking about stories of people with dementia who go through illness then fail to recover to the cognitive level they had before. I feared that happening. I didn't know what the future would bring—certainly no cure for dementia in time to help her. Every year some promising lead would come up, go into trials, and nothing was ever again heard about it. I just wanted her to be able to enjoy traveling with the pups and me while she could tolerate that.

Diane was back in the hospital in July, Sunday through Tuesday, with suspected bleeding. The good news was that her stomach and duodenal ulcers were all healed with no signs except some edema. She was discharged a day early so she could get away from the hospital, on condition she get the colonoscopy as an outpatient. That left me to prep her for a colonoscopy. I hate hospitals.

She didn't die. Her condition was misdiagnosed starting when she fell a year earlier. She had significant injury to her spine and duodenum, and some to her pancreas in the adjacent area. The pain in her back and abdomen came from those injuries. After eight to nine months she began to bleed from an ulcer that formed at the site of the wound in her duodenum. It eventually hemorrhaged and caused the crisis in April that nearly killed her. After the surgery to cut off blood pressure to the bleeder she slowly recovered. Blood tests to measure her hemoglobin showed a gradual increase to normal levels by late summer.

By late July Diane had improved greatly. She spent two days that week awake from early morning until five or six PM . Amazing. She still had dementia, but she was better except for the back pain. She finally agreed to try physical therapy. That was supposed to happen the following Monday. Following her usual pattern, she agreed to one session then refused to do another.

The central issue I grappled with: how to be a good caregiver 24×7 and still have a satisfying life of my own. The central axiom was to seek fulfillment in bringing satisfying experiences to Diane. On a good day, for instance, what did we do? Got up. Ate breakfast. Went out to lunch at a Mexican restaurant in Westmont. From there, I easily persuaded Diane to go shopping at Trader Joe's rather than sitting in the car at Wegman's. Good choice. She enjoyed the shopping and even recognized a former neighbor who was also shopping there.

October found me somewhat burned out. Constant attention to Diane, who doesn't remember what I do for her, exhausted me. She took exception to me watching Cal football one night, so I shut the TV off and listened to the game on internet radio.

One night in December I found my pills in disarray when I went to take melatonin and acetaminophen. The pill dispenser was on a different shelf. The acetaminophen was on the counter. Did I do that? Maybe. Maybe not.

Jennifer and Lauren were good sources of advice but that was only occasional help. I had no one to lean on for day to day support. Somehow I had to address that issue. Caregiving is a lonely job—but not like the loneliness I felt growing up, with no one to talk to and no one I believed cared for me. Diane provided some company, Lauren and Jennifer a bit more, and even Facebook friends offered a bit of dialog. It was entertaining and it took my mind out of here and now for a while. As a teenager I had only books for an escape, and the loneliness was at times crushing.

TRAVELS WITH DIANE

Even though people experiencing dementia
become unable to recount what has just happened,
they still go through the experience—even without recall.
The psychological present lasts about three seconds.
We experience the present even when we have dementia.
— *JUDY CORNISH*

Diane's dementia progressed slowly in 2014. One afternoon following her nap, she asked me, "Why are you wearing my wedding ring?"

"It's my ring," I told her, and pointed to her ring on her own finger, identical but smaller.

"You shouldn't be wearing it."

"Why?"

"Because you're not my husband."

"Who am I?"

"You're my father."

"Who is your husband?"

"I don't have one."

That was sobering and scary. A vision of things to come. An hour later the ring was forgotten.

In February I felt alone again. I was alone most of my waking hours by then. Diane would wake up and stay up for an hour or two at a time, then go back to bed for another nap anywhere from a half hour to two hours. Between 7:00 AM and 8:00 PM she usually was awake about six to seven hours. Sometimes when I didn't sleep well, I'd join her on one of those naps, but most of the time I remained awake and alone. That's when I'd go to the store or clean the kitchen or the rest of the house, putter around, work on my website, or read. I sat so much it was giving me back pain.

I didn't always feel loneliness. At times I felt deep sadness and grief, when I would face the situation and the awful future. At other times, those emotions were close to the surface even though I wasn't aware of them. A sentimental scene in a movie would give me an unexpected surge of feeling, and I teared up over small matters. Diane had already let go of most of the things that once mattered a lot to her, things she no longer remembered. They were literally gone from her past. When I thought about that, I felt a deep sense of loss because it included shared memories we both had. Once that part of her was gone, that part of us was gone, too.

I read the posts in an online Facebook group called "Dementia: The Road Ahead." In it different caregivers, mostly women, told many similar stories about the people they loved: the deterioration, the struggles and issues of caring for them, battles they faced with ignorant and selfish relatives, banks, nursing homes, and so on. By then our family was calm and peaceful, we all agreed, and we were blessed to have this agreement and each other's understanding. I deeply regretted not doing more to help Diane stop smoking. It was slowly killing her.

How long should one live? Diane was 74 in 2014. An average American woman might expect to live another ten years. At least Diane was comfortable, not in pain, able to see her daughters and talk to her aunt and sister now and then, and she had me to take care of every need. That was some comfort to me. But I was lonely. I missed her. I missed the companion she used to be, the adventurous and impulsive woman who lighted up my life in unexpected ways.

In May 2014 our camper was all repaired and ready for the road, so we set out on an adventure, a long trip. I convinced Diane to go to Springfield, Illinois to find the house where she lived with her Aunt Charlotte and Uncle Gus when she was ten. We'd gone on a couple of short day trips earlier. This would be a real expedition for us. I spent hours planning the route to avoid thunderstorms in the Midwest that might frighten her. We ended up taking a southern route along the Ohio River and northwest through Indiana to Springfield. We took our dog Plato along and left Frida the cat in a kennel while we traveled. I took photos during the trip but didn't write in my journal. I was the only driver. I spent most of the time setting up or breaking camp, cooking, driving, and other chores. That left no time to take notes. I planned the route to allow plenty of time after driving so we could unwind, sit outside in our camp chairs and enjoy the afternoon, prepare dinner, and turn in early. Diane seemed to be comfortable and enjoying the scenery throughout the trip. I felt my idea of traveling in the camper was a success.

In July we left on a quick trip, just three days and 450 miles. We kept moving. That seemed to work, to keep both of us engaged and feeling normal. We'd done a lot of road trips years ago, when it was all we could afford. At this stage in life it afforded us a traveling smoker's lounge and pet kennel, so we could avoid the stress of finding a hotel that met our needs. I wanted to go on a long trip to Canada in July or August but first, I needed to get Diane more used to the road. I was hopeful that she'd feel at home no matter where we were because we'd be in our "home" all the time. This camper also seemed familiar because the inside resembled a pickup camper we once owned and drove throughout the west coast and Colorado.

I was constantly aware of how limited our time could be and how we needed to use it while Diane's health allowed. My neighbor's story haunted me—he bought a Roadtrek in the 1980s to go on trips with his family and drove it until his wife's health failed. Then it remained parked in the driveway until his health failed too, and he died. He left it to his grandson, having driven just 14,000 miles in all. I made his daughter an offer to buy it, but she turned it down. Later it was sold to another buyer. It would have been cheaper than the one I did buy, but the one I eventually bought suited our needs better.

Whenever I thought about going on a long trip with Diane, I felt fear and doubt: dread of the unknown, of what could possibly go wrong. The flavor of adventure was tainted by anxiety over—what? The thought that Diane would adamantly want to go home or have a disastrous bout of colitis. It wasn't so much her mood as it was my own anxiety that I feared. The fear that I wouldn't be able to calm her down and refocus on enjoying the trip—or was it calm ME down? Xanax helped.

Diane was fatigued and sleeping a lot. I contacted her doctor to suggest cutting out the Namenda (a drug for Alzheimer's) and she agreed. I browsed suggestions on quitting Namenda and some sources said they stopped immediately, but the recommendation was to taper off on the same schedule as the ramp-up. I used an accelerated schedule and closely monitored her cognitive function, sleeping habits, and fatigue. She never showed any sign of a change except less drowsiness.

Another caregiver said, when asked how his wife was tapered off the drug, "We just quit. Didn't taper off at all." I tended to get wrapped up in the technical details of caregiving, maybe to distance myself from how I felt about it. Another caregiver in my group does the same thing—intellectualizes—even more than I did.

All the travel planning and preparation belonged to me as well as all the work of driving, navigating, cooking, cleaning, and anything else. But Diane still functioned as a willing companion, at times surprisingly astute in her comments about the people, places, and things on our trips. I can remember a Fourth of July weekend trip in 1967, looking over a foggy Tuolumne Meadow still covered by snow, and feeling a lonely desire to have a soulmate who would travel by my side and share those vistas with me. Two months later I found her. Forty-seven years later we still had that emotional connection even though she couldn't remember those times, and she wouldn't remember these times either. She lived in the moment in a breathtakingly literal sense. She didn't dread the future or bemoan the past. She seemed to feel no regret or pain at losing her own history and the memory of everything we did. I did. Because neither of us knew how long this could last, I tried to learn from her how to savor and cherish each moment, hour, and day.

Diane's personality gradually diminished, becoming much less of the distinct, emphatic, sometimes eccentric woman she was during most of our life together, but she was lucky that she settled into a mainly calm and pleasant mood. If I watched my own moods and what I communicated to her, she would go along with most of the things she needed. There were some challenges, like personal hygiene and grooming. I chose her clothes each day because she needed help finding things to wear. She didn't remember to look on the chair where she dumped most things after she wore them. I'd go through the pile, fold and put away anything that looked and smelled clean, and slip the rest into the laundry.

On the second day of our planned departure for the next trip, Diane didn't feel well, said she felt dizzy, and wanted to lie down. Her most recent blood tests were fine with no sign of blood in her stool. There was no sign of fever, but she may have been dehydrated. She didn't want to go anywhere. I had everything packed, with food in the ice chest ready to go. Diane had agreed to leave in the morning to go to Nantucket. She had no idea where that was. She said it was a good idea to have breakfast on the road. The next morning, Diane woke up cranky about going to the mountains she was dreaming about, and she was absolutely set against going anywhere.

Diane was too tired to go on a long trip, she said. Jennifer invited us to come over for coffee. Diane agreed to that. I packed all the essentials, including the dog, in the camper in case I could get her to go on the road after that. Meanwhile I was melting down from frustration and boredom, feeling I needed to go somewhere very, very badly and she stood in my way. I felt angry and disillusioned, as if all my preparations, time, and money spent rehabbing the camper for our travels, were wasted and I was a fool to think it could ever work.

When we left Jennifer's after a dip in the pool, I felt better and Diane was settled down. Rather than go straight home I extended the trip a bit, angling off toward Shamong to try to find a root beer stand on Route 206. I used to pass it on my commute to Atlantic City. From a distance I saw the closed, abandoned stand, so I turned toward home. We drove past a farm stand where we used to shop, but it was closed. Next, I stopped at a Mexican food store and grill in a strip mall on the highway. Diane stayed in the van while I walked in to order an enchilada dinner and an extra pork tamale. I brought out a cold Coke to share while we waited for the food. I considered driving to a park to eat but didn't know of one close by, so I started the generator and the air conditioner. We could eat our dinner there in the parking lot. I brought the food out from the store, set up our table in the back and we sprawled out on the cushions beside it to eat. Our meal concluded, I tidied up, shut off the air conditioner and the generator, and we drove home.

After we returned to the house, I asked Diane how she felt about taking little trips around the area to places where we could picnic and she seemed to like that idea. Notice I said she "seemed" to like it, because by then she was unable to express many of her feelings. I thought taking short trips might relax her enough to agree to a longer trip. At least we'd picnic in comfort. That was the scope of my ambition then. In some vague future I still saw us adventuring across the prairie to the Rocky Mountains, but that remained a dream. I was at least able to calm myself. Desire is the source of unhappiness, say the Buddhists.

The main issue I struggled with: had my life become one hundred percent caregiver? I hoped the answer was no, because there were stretches of hours at a time when I could work on other things if I was close and able to attend to Diane as needed. However, concentrating on anything else was tough. I never figured out how to do that—in other words, the answer was . . . yes.

One August afternoon I succeeded in getting Diane to go out. She wanted to go to the root beer stand. I said "Let's take the camper so I can see if I fixed all the rattles. Then we'll go to the root beer stand."

She agreed. Mission creep.

"Let's get some root beer and non-dairy ice cream at the store and make our own root beer floats at the park."

Again, she agreed.

We stopped at Wegmans in Moorestown and bought non-dairy vanilla ice cream (she was lactose intolerant) and diet root beer. We headed for the Strawbridge Lake park. I found a nice spot under a big shade tree next to the parking lot. I helped Diane out of the van, turned to close the door and she walked away. She walked onto a sloping lawn and immediately fell.

"Ohh!" she cried out, and I saw her head hit the ground face-first. It was sickening.

Full of fear and horror, I rushed to her. She fell onto her sunglasses, leaving a mark around her left eye and scraping the bridge of her nose slightly. Her knee was a bit red from bumping the ground. She said nothing hurt. She couldn't stand up by herself (not because of the fall) so I squatted behind her, wrapped my arms around her chest under her arms, and stood her up, lifting her with my legs. I didn't even feel her weight. She came up. I held her while she tried walking. No problem. I had her stand holding the tree while I brought the folding chairs and set them up. Then I eased her into a chair.

I brought the bag of sodas and ice cream. I saw that we need our little folding table, so I fetched that and set it up. We proceeded to have our root beer floats as if nothing happened. She was calm and not in any discomfort. I felt the horror of it for days. I think I lost control of her while I reached for the bag with the ice cream and root beer. I realized that the next time she'd have to stay in the van until I had everything set up and ready for her to come out and sit.

Later that month I took Diane with me to "go for a spin" and stop for some dinner. We drove around a bit and ended up at a Mexican restaurant. I parked and walked inside to order chicken mole enchiladas and a chili relleno. While the food was cooking, I walked back out to the camper and set up the table in the camper. When the food was ready, I brought it out and we ate there in the parking lot in our "private dining room."

It got us out, and we had good food.

Diane was comfortable in quiet surroundings.

I thought we should do this more. Maybe a couple of times a week. We could go almost anywhere and the atmosphere in the restaurant wouldn't matter. I hoped she'd enjoy it and not tire of it. One sour note was that she complained of a sore back. Maybe I needed to get her to lie down and rest while waiting for the food.

One Sunday night near bedtime, I felt disenchanted with life. I went from enthusiasm in the morning to flat fatigue just before bed. In my mind the dream (is that all it was?) of hitting the road with Diane seemed more remote than two years earlier, before I bought the camper, and then medical Hell came to her and Jennifer, who had a gastric hemorrhage a month before Diane in 2013. But with a wedding just days away Jennifer was thriving and happy, and Diane was at least calm, and usually in a good mood. I was tired, obviously, or I wouldn't have been in this down mood, yet I didn't feel drowsy or crave sleep. Another acetaminophen would carry me through until dawn, and I felt grateful that I didn't need anything stronger. I knew I'd feel enthusiastic in the morning when I saw the sunlight again. Then I'd think about the Western mountains, plains, valleys, and canyons. I hoped then I would again feel the hope and excitement they once aroused in me.

In September Jennifer and Mike married in an outdoor ceremony at a winery near their home. Jennifer planned every last detail. Hiring a harpist to play before the ceremony and an accordionist to play during the reception. It seemed like we'd been flown to France. Diane attended and enjoyed the wedding, but we had to leave early as she could only tolerate a large crowd for a short time. Jennifer's many friends attended, sharing her joyous, triumphant celebration of life and hope.

THE LAST ROAD TRIPS

Was the dementia of old age a blessing in disguise?
No more thoughts. No more damage inflicted.
No more memories of damage survived.
— *JANET TURPIN MYERS*

In December 2014, I tried to contact Diane's former sister-in-law Cindi in Florida. I called and left messages, sent her emails, and never got a response. I didn't know if she was in the hospital, out of town, or just didn't feel like answering. The phone rang and her answering machine took messages, but no answers came. I wanted to arrange a visit to her in Florida so Diane could see her. I also wanted (my ulterior motive) to use her as an anchor for a trip south in January so we could get out of the frozen north and venture to the sunny south in our camper. In other words, another trip. I thought I could use the connection to Cindi, whom Diane still vaguely remembered, as an inducement to go on the road. I began to plan the trip.

On January 19, 2015 we departed just after lunch. It was a late start, but it was a win because I got Diane into the camper and on the road. We drove down the Delmarva Peninsula to escape a bad winter storm that tracked west of us on the mainland. On the third day we reached Jacksonville, Florida, arriving about eight o'clock at the quiet suburban street where Cindi lived. I parked and walked to her door. As far as I knew, she wasn't expecting us. I knocked on the door and Cindi answered. I asked if Diane could come in and see her.

"No, you can't come in. I've been fighting a bad cold for two weeks."

I persisted. She changed her story. "My brother is here and we're all sick."

Then she did an about-face. She said she didn't want to see Diane because she just found out from Diane that fifty years earlier when Cindi was dating a boy in Alhambra, Diane told him that he shouldn't get mixed up with Cindi's family because her brother was schizophrenic. I knew this was false. When she last talked to Cindi in the fall, Diane had no memory of her time in Alhambra. Cindi was adamant that she didn't want to see Diane, so we left.

After we left Cindi's we stayed overnight in a nearby campground where I had a space reserved. The next morning we ate breakfast in a chain restaurant, then left town. Diane didn't see Cindi, but the trip was already a success. I wanted to get us out of the house and south to Florida, where the weather was nicer and the sun still shone. We were free to wander at will. We headed southwest toward the Gulf Coast across the flat scrub pinelands of central Florida, through Gainesville and into a little RV park right on the Gulf. The owner squeezed us into a space between two big unoccupied RVs, and we sat outside in the warm air eating dinner as the sun sank into the Gulf of Mexico. I couldn't have planned a better outcome.

Recently I received an email from Cindi's son in Florida. I called him and he informed me of her death just a month after we were there in 2015. I told him about the strange encounter I had with her, and he said she probably was embarrassed to let us into the house because she was a hoarder and her house was in bad shape. While Cindi was asleep a fire broke out, and the house was so packed with hoarded belongings that rescuers couldn't reach her. Poor Cindi died in the fire, a sad ironic twist to her lifelong attachment to material things. Her father died in an accident when she was in her twenties, her brother was schizophrenic and killed himself twenty years earlier, and she suffered from obsessive-compulsive disorder her whole life. She was an unhappy woman, and the possessions that she clung to killed her.

From Florida, we turned north toward the home of some old friends in Atlanta, Georgia. We stopped overnight in a Georgia state park, enjoying pleasant warm air next to a quiet lake, below an afternoon sky streaked with a few cirrus clouds lit by the setting sun. Continuing north the next day, we arrived in Loganville, Georgia by late afternoon. We enjoyed seeing Diane's protégée Renee, who spent many afternoons in Diane's care while her mother worked and attended college. Renee grew up and married, and lived with her husband and three friendly, smiling daughters, sharing the house in a convenient arrangement with her mother, Diane's old friend. Surrounded by so much love and attention, Diane was completely at ease and comfortable. We stayed two nights with them, then left for our return home via Savannah. We meandered through the Georgia countryside, stopping for lunch at a small local barbeque. I took a picture of Diane smiling over her lunch of barbecued pork, slaw, and French fries, looking happy and relaxed. Moments like that convinced me I'd made the right decision to travel with Diane. We camped west of Savannah that night, and we drove through the city on a bright, sunny morning. We turned north and drove along the coast through South Carolina.

A word about winter camping. Before we left to go south, I winterized the camper, draining water out of all the tanks, then putting in non-toxic RV antifreeze to fill all the water lines so they wouldn't burst when the temperature dropped below freezing. We could use the toilet but had to flush with antifreeze. Antifreeze doesn't work as well as plain water for that purpose, and maybe I used too little to clear the drain. When we reached Wilmington, the toilet was clogged. That's a show-stopper. I found an RV dealer with a repair shop to clean it out, and we spent about three hours in their waiting room while they worked. Diane seemed fine waiting. She was so pleasant throughout this trip that I felt really encouraged about prospects for more travel. With our plumbing cleaned we motored on north, staying overnight near Rocky Mount, North Carolina. The next day we drove straight north on I-95, thirteen hours to home.

In April we made another journey, this time to Tennessee. Diane was less enthusiastic, the overcast skies didn't put either of us in a good mood, and the trip was less successful. I hoped once we reached Tennessee, we could continue south and west to visit Jennifer's friend in Austin, Texas. However, once we reached Tennessee, Diane wanted to go home. Maybe Diane wasn't feeling as well as she did in January. We returned home after about a week out.

In July I persuaded Diane to visit our niece Lisa and her family in a Chicago suburb, a two-day drive. I hoped once we reached Chicago, we could travel on to Minneapolis. We reached Lisa and Mark's house in the afternoon and spent about two hours there. We met their kids for the first time, and enjoyed two pleasant hours with them. Lisa's husband Mark was somewhat brash when he was younger, and he and Diane had exchanged heated emails years ago over an issue that's since been forgotten. Diane enjoyed meeting Mark as if it were the first time; for her it was, even though we attended their wedding. I asked Diane if she'd like to go on to Minneapolis and see her aunt Bernice. She said she would. Done.

We loaded up and headed for Minnesota. Diane was fine. It was summertime and sunny. That made a difference. Near Rockford, Illinois we stopped for lunch in late afternoon, and as we sat inside a restaurant with our lunch, a squall blew past with such heavy wind and rain that I couldn't see our camper two rows out in the parking lot. We were lucky we stopped when we did. We drove on in sunny weather after the storm passed.

That night we stayed in Wisconsin with friends we met in Minneapolis in 1970. They were wonderful hosts, and Diane was very happy to see them and talk. Being with warm, friendly people brought out her best behavior. They offered us a bed for the night, and we slept there. After breakfast the next morning, we continued to Minneapolis. We stopped in the city and visited our old friend Darryl, who was Diane's friend since childhood. He was soft-spoken and did not have a lot to say. We last saw him in 1993, when we traveled to Minnesota for a memorial service for Diane's mother. We continued to St. Cloud, Minnesota where Diane's 94-year-old aunt Bernice lived. The last time we saw her was also in 1993. She was a World War Two veteran of the Women's Army Corps. Her health problems already would have killed a less determined woman, but she persevered. She'd survived the Whipple surgery, a grueling operation involving three organs that is believed to be one of the most difficult of all surgeries. Diane's surgeons considered that surgery for her when she was misdiagnosed with duodenal cancer but we decided against it due to her dementia. It would have been unnecessary anyway.

After a short visit with Bernice we returned to the highway, this time heading east toward home. To avoid Chicago on the return drive I routed us along the north shore of Lake Michigan, across the Mackinac Strait then south through the center of Michigan until we connected with Interstate 80. This scenic route continued our pressure-free trip and Diane was content the whole way home (although she had the usual complaint about seeing nothing but trees). The takeaway from our three trips in the year, a reflection on travels with Diane: she was less restless while we were driving, but sitting in the car for hours on end was bad for her edema. I bought some over the counter diuretic pills and that helped relieve some of the swelling, but obviously sitting too long was a problem.

October 11 was Diane's birthday. Jennifer and Mike, Lauren and Kevin, and his son Keegan were due at our house that afternoon for birthday cake. Diane was skeptical. She didn't know who they were and wanted them to stay outside. She relented, and she had a good celebration. I made a video of them singing "Happy Birthday."

Two weeks later, our world collapsed.

Jennifer

I will never forget the moment your heart stopped,
and mine kept beating.
— *Angela Miller*

During the 1990s Jennifer started to feel short of breath when she went on exercise walks. She had to stop often to catch her breath. After feeling dizzy on most of her walks, she consulted her cardiologist, who referred her to a pulmonologist at Jefferson University Hospital in Philadelphia. In the fall of 2000, after diagnostic exams and tests the doctor gave her a stunning diagnosis: idiopathic primary pulmonary hypertension, or PPH. The cause of PPH was unknown, and was generally fatal within five years after presenting symptoms.

A few years earlier Jennifer fell in love with a man who also worked in the Philadelphia film community. They were together for several years and they were engaged to marry, but when she was diagnosed with pulmonary hypertension, he couldn't cope with her illness and he left. Later he tried to get his engagement ring back and threatened to sue her for it. He didn't sue her, and she kept the ring.

Jennifer sought a second opinion, determined to know what she faced. Months later she obtained a correct diagnosis: secondary pulmonary hypertension. "Secondary" because it is caused by another condition, and the cause was known. The radiation treatments for Hodgkin's disease ten years earlier damaged her heart and lungs, resulting in pulmonary hypertension. Radiation therapy was the most effective treatment when she had Hodgkin's. Years later, pulmonary hypertension emerged as a long-term consequence. Her condition was very serious, but it would not be not fatal in five years. She adapted, she learned to live with her condition, and she continued to thrive.

In 2003 I nominated Jennifer for the Philadelphia Women of Distinction Awards, sponsored by the Philadelphia Business Journal. I lobbied her friends and colleagues in the area to vote for her, and she was one of twenty-five women given the award. On December 8, the Journal published a long article about her life and her success despite the health problems she faced. They quoted several people who knew her well.

"She brings an absolute enthusiasm, integrity and knowledge to every project she works on," said Anne Marie Starker, director of sales for Shooters Post & Transfer, a Philadelphia film/video production company. "She has the rare ability to take control of a situation without being overbearing. She can take any situation and make it a good one."

"When she walks into a room, she lights it up." Sharon Stein, a personal and professional friend since the 1990s, said, "She's probably one of my favorite people to work for. She gets the big picture." She had "the ability to roll with any punch that is thrown."

After her success in the Philadelphia media market, in 2008 Jennifer wondered whether to take the plunge, go to Los Angeles, and try to make it in the capitol of the movie business. She believed her years of experience in Philadelphia and New York and her connections in Los Angeles would help her get a toehold. She discussed it on social media and her friends encouraged her to do it. In the spring she announced she was going.

One of the friends who saw the announcement was a man who once had a crush on her when they went to grade school together. Mike Ligthart realized if he didn't connect right away, she'd be gone. He contacted Jennifer and they started dating. In June, when she was ready to leave for the long drive to Southern California in her old Volvo sedan, Mike went with her. They traveled a long, meandering route ending in Los Angeles. Mike flew back to New Jersey and Jennifer stayed for several months. She realized she would rather be with Mike in New Jersey and work in the Philadelphia media market than be alone in Los Angeles. Not long after returning she moved in with Mike. She found joy with Mike, the love of her life. Mike stood by Jennifer to the very last moment.

In 2010 a routine mammogram detected suspicious growths in Jennifer's breast. A biopsy revealed ductal carcinoma in situ (DCIS), an early form of breast cancer. Testing showed that she didn't have the breast cancer genes. Her oncologist attributed the DCIS to radiation damage caused by her lymphoma treatments thirty years earlier. She consulted several specialists to discuss the diagnosis and treatment options, and chose to undergo a double mastectomy with reconstruction in one surgery. In September 2010, Jennifer had a ten and a half hour operation at the University of Pennsylvania Hospital which included reconstruction using her own tissue. She did not want separate surgery later for reconstruction, and she did not want artificial implants. Afterwards, she was exhausted and haggard. She didn't tell very many people in the production community, fearing that her work as a freelance director would dry up out of concern that her health might affect her performance. Despite her determination, she couldn't work normally for several months as she recovered, and her business never reached the same level as before her breast cancer. Normally, breast cancer is treated with radiation, but that was ruled out because of her previous radiation treatments. She was treated with only chemotherapy. She had most of the usual debilitating side-effects from the chemo drugs like tamoxifen that she took over the next five years.

Jennifer's life as a cancer survivor made her especially sympathetic to others with similar experiences. In the 1980s she met Kasey Hall, a young woman who survived brain cancer and established a summer camp for children with cancer and their brothers and sisters. Kasey named it Camp No Worries. With donated facilities, funds, and supplies, the camp was free for the children who attended, and staffed by volunteers for the week-long session every year. Jennifer shot photos at the camp for their website, and eventually produced and directed fundraising videos for the camp. Camp No Worries continues to thrive and offer its sessions to campers every year.

In June 2012, Jennifer went back to Jefferson for another cardiac catheterization. The results showed she had a seventy percent blockage of an artery in her heart, and leakage in one mitral valve. They performed angioplasty and inserted a stent. Later she had stress tests to see how much the faulty heart valve was affecting her. A week later she was back on location at Camp No Worries for another video shoot. Jennifer supported them pro bono for several years making fund-raising photos and videos. One of her videos helped raise a half million dollars for the camp.

January 2013 was a tough month for us and especially for Jennifer and Mike. Because of her heart condition she was taking powerful blood thinning medication. She was also taking a non-steroidal anti-inflammatory (NSAID) like ibuprofen for pain. The combination of those drugs is risky and for her the danger was real. She started to hemorrhage at home and an ambulance rushed her to the closest hospital emergency room. By the time they began care she'd lost half of her blood. We drove to the hospital as fast as we could, arriving about half an hour later, meeting Mike in the ER with her. Jennifer was getting transfusions, but her face was gray from lack of blood. The hospital itself was newly opened and half empty. We waited in a vacant lounge while the doctors attended her. We were scared, not knowing what to expect. After several hours and several units of blood she was stabilized. Surgery to clip off the source of bleeding was successful, and she was on the way to recovery.

In September 2015, Jennifer reached her five-year breast cancer survival milestone and was pronounced free of cancer for the second time in her life. She and Mike embarked on a delayed honeymoon to Italy, driving through Tuscany in a rented car, stopping at small inns and restaurants in the countryside. She posted many photos on Facebook showing a wonderful trip. She knew that when they returned, she faced another major surgery.

Jennifer had been discussing a heart valve replacement with her doctors. Over the summer she consulted with heart surgeons at Jefferson, Cooper, and Penn to find the best recommendations and the best team to perform the surgery. It was a critical procedure and she wanted the best possible outcome. Based on the extensive tests done beforehand, they were planning replacement for two heart valves that were damaged from radiation and scarring, and bypass surgery for blocked arteries. On October 19, she entered the University of Pennsylvania Hospital for the surgery. She sent out selfies in her hospital gown, ready to go under the knife Tuesday morning, October 20.

On October 20, after a much longer surgery than expected Jennifer was moved to recovery in critical condition. Lauren said Jennifer's surgeon looked so exhausted that she had a horrible feeling about Jennifer's prospects. About eighteen hours after the surgery Jennifer's heart stopped and she was put on life support. On Friday, October 23 I was called to the hospital. Jennifer didn't revise her healthcare power of attorney when she married Mike, and I still was named in the POA. At around noon Mike, Lauren, and I agreed to remove her from life support. I told the staff, who turned it off. She was pronounced dead at 12:59 PM. In a nearby lounge, Diane waited with Jennifer's friends, unaware that anything was wrong. I remember feeling numb, absent, and emotionless. I had to return immediately to care for Diane and continue as though nothing happened.

In her life, Jennifer survived critical illnesses and close calls many times after her cancer in 1981: two car wrecks in the year after, when she totaled one car; acute kidney failure from a pathogenic e. Coli infection; pulmonary hypertension; breast cancer; and acute blood loss from a hemorrhaging ulcer. Her radiation treatment for Hodgkin's lymphoma saved her life, but at a cost. At last, the bill came due.

The following month we held a memorial service for Jennifer at the Camden County Boathouse next to the Cooper River. Five hundred people attended—friends she had known since childhood, college classmates, family, and most of all her friends from the Philadelphia film and video community whom she had worked for and with for years, who knew her and loved her because she always treated them fairly and considerately, and she never abandoned a friend.

If you came face to face with death, and death granted you a reprieve, what would you do with your life then? That was Jennifer's choice when she was treated for Hodgkin's lymphoma at seventeen. What she did then affected everyone in our family and many others. At first, she floundered, making mistakes, and risking her life at times as she learned to accept that she had no control over fate. But she matured in the years immediately after her cancer, and she chose to live her life the way she wanted it. She chose to do what she loved with her talents. She enrolled in college five times and washed out twice, but once she sorted things, she graduated and set out on the "path with heart."

She wanted to be a director. Even with a college degree, she had to start out carrying coffee and serving food on set. We knew young women her age who rejected such menial work and looked for other careers. Jenny persevered. In the early years, working a production job, she found herself one of three Jennifers on location. She didn't want to be just another Jennifer, so she reinvented herself. After that she went by her middle name, Palmer. She became Palmer Enfield.

The name had a certain cachet that fit what she was determined to become: the ring of an old-money, Main Line family with lots of connections. That had a smidgen of truth. Jennifer was descended from settlers who built this country, pioneers who moved West for opportunity that was missing in the places they left behind. Like them she never lost sight of her goal, and she never lost her sense of humor, her concern for others, her loving spirit, or that smile.

It wasn't supposed to end like this. Jennifer was a guiding light, a source of strength, a voice of sanity and love in a world of dementia. Why did she leave us? What would I do without her? My world steadily contracted once I began to spend full time caring for Diane. Jennifer was a lifeline to the outside, a voice of sanity and love. She encouraged me, gave me suggestions, invited us to her house and took time away from her work so that I would have some relief, even when she faced deadline pressure. She gave me strength while her own strength was failing. It hurts when I look at old photos of her and see how brightly her spirit shone. She was a beacon of light in a darkening world, beaming hope and love. Seeing those photos is painful, but I can't stop looking at them. I don't want to stop seeing her face, her smile, the way she always lit up for the camera. I never want to forget what she looked like, who she was, what she meant to me and to all of us.

We never told Diane that Jennifer, her firstborn child, the baby Diane said was once her reason for living, was gone. She never knew. Sometimes Diane asked me if Jennifer was coming over for a visit. I told her Jennifer was working on a long project in California for a pharmaceutical client.

After a few years, she stopped asking.

A Settled Life

Caregiving often calls us to lean into love we didn't know possible.
— Tia Walker

As Diane slept on a typical day the living room was quiet but for the constant hiss of the air cleaner, wiping smoke from the air for the sake of my lungs if not hers. Alzheimer's caregiving is a hard job. It continually put my love and character to the test. Each day followed much the same script. Let's go through the steps as they took place in 2016.

About 7:00 or 8:00 AM, I stumble out of bed cramped and sore, usually feeling a lack of sleep (which I will explain later). Walking out of the bedroom I perform a morning ritual that varies slightly day to day but contains the same elements always.

Open the blinds to let in light.

Peel off my nasal strip and toss it in the trash. (I broke my nose in college, leaving it a bit tweaked and needing help to breathe at night.)

Fill my tea mug with water and set it on the stove burner so the cat won't drink out of it, then walk over to the pantry for an Irish teabag. Plop the bag in the cup and heat it for two minutes, 30 seconds.

Go to the downstairs toilet and empty my bladder.

Weigh in on the digital scale, noting slight variations in weight, body fat, water, muscle and bone according the scale's erratic judgment. Reflect on how the weight was affected by yesterday's salty snacks.

Let the dogs out in the back yard for a pee. Bring them back in.

Stir a spoonful of fiber, coffee creamer, and sugar into my tea, and cool it to drinkability with an ice cube. My muscles are loosening up as I move about, stiffness easing and the perennial soreness in my low back fading.

Pour a small glass of orange juice and dump my pills into a small cup, Diane's into another one. The cups are blue ceramic sauce dishes from Red Lobster that Diane gifted herself with, back when she still liked to eat in restaurants. They serve well as pill dispensers.

Swallow my pills and fill a glass with juice for Diane. It will sit on the counter and warm up while she continues to sleep.

Settle into my reclining chair with my cup of tea and perhaps a couple of cookies if my stomach feels empty, and read the overnight email and Facebook posts.

After about an hour get up, dress, and collect the dogs for their walk. This is the high point in their day.

Write today's day, date, and weather forecast on the little whiteboard I keep next to the television where Diane can see it. I started doing this to forestall her endless questions about the date and the weather. It works. Below that I write "TOOK THE DOGS FOR A WALK. BACK SOON. LOVE, R." That's in case she wakes up while I am out with the dogs and wants to know why I am not there. She usually sleeps through it. I erase it when we return.

Make myself breakfast: dry cereal or oatmeal, or whole wheat toast with peanut butter and jam.

Some mornings instead of taking a long walk with the dogs I exercise, doing a round of the Royal Canadian Air Force Five Basic Exercise (5BX) program and a short run (one or two miles) or just a longer run (maybe three miles). It helps to work out the tension that builds up in me from this endless Groundhog Day routine.

That was just the morning . . . Bored yet?

Diane woke up. I was glad to see her. I wondered "Who will I talk to when she is gone?"

Every day I felt sad about Jennifer, who died so suddenly the previous fall that I didn't have a chance to say goodbye, and about Diane, who spent most of her days and nights sleeping, a shell of who she once was. Her life was gone for all practical purposes. My mind wandered over our past life together, and even though it was no more gone at that moment than a year ago, it still pained me to think about it. Still in shock from losing Jennifer, I still wanted to drive to her house and have her greet us as she always did, warmly and lovingly. She embodied love and kindness, enthusiasm, and optimism. After everything she went through from seventeen onwards her amazing spirit kept shining on, lighting up her own life and all those around her. I was just starting to recognize the loss six months after her death as I realized all the ways she helped us.

Diane was usually awake about four to six hours every day. I could map it very exactly using the alerts from motion sensors I installed to help keep track of her movements, but exactness didn't seem important. Per Parkinson's Law, my work expanded to fill the time available. I cycled through weather, Facebook, endlessly negative election analyses, checking email, and a few actual tasks such as laundry or cleaning. Those were all things I could do while still being a few steps away from Diane in case I needed to respond to her quickly.

One typical morning Diane woke up about eight. She stayed up for a few minutes then had diarrhea. I cleaned her up and got her back in bed. At 11:30 she was still asleep. This was like many other days as far as her pattern of waking and sleeping. I spent a lot of time waiting for her to wake up. It felt like a sort of confinement for me. Sometimes I reminded myself that this was a form of service and a manifestation of love and concern. Much of the time I felt emotionally flat, vacant.

On a gloomy day, thoughts about the afterlife would come to mind. No, not life after death. At least, not my death. What would I do after Diane? I thought about places across the country that I've seen before: Minneapolis, Colorado Springs, Garden of the Gods, Santa Fe, Mount Whitney, Malibu, Berkeley, the Oregon coast, Portland, Vancouver, Seattle. Places to go, places to scatter ashes perhaps; an itinerary of sorts. Then I thought about this house—suddenly realizing that I will want to get away from here, at least for some time. When would that happen? I did not know.

Diane was still asleep. I went to wake her up so she could eat.

What a week! Saturday April 23, I ran in a 5K race in Atco near Mike's. It fell on a date six months after Jennifer died. Mike signed up for the race, too. He wasn't an experienced runner, but he left me behind. My pace was off, and I felt sore in the lower abdomen. On Monday, I still felt sore. I thought it was gastritis. I went to urgent care, and after it was diagnosed as diverticulitis, to the emergency room near home. I was away from 10:00 AM until after 5:00 PM . Lauren stayed with Diane but told me that Diane missed me while I was gone! I believe she did and it made her anxious. Lauren gave her some Xanax, which guaranteed she'd be MIA on Tuesday. Thursday I went to the Alzheimer's spouse support group, and Friday to the doctor for a follow-up visit. I believe the effect of my absences built up in her. We ventured out together Friday afternoon, first to the urgent care clinic, where she was diagnosed with conjunctivitis in her right eye. Then we went to Friendly's Restaurant just down the road for lunch. Finally, we went to Trader Joe's to stock up on food items, then home. We were out for a quite a while during the day on Friday. But she couldn't remember that, so in her mind she hadn't been anywhere. Friday night she wanted to go out, and absolutely failed to understand why I didn't feel like it.

We reached the shouting stage, with me shouting things like:

"Don't you understand? I am sick! I am tired and I don't feel like going out! This is serious! I could get sicker and then who would take care of you?"

She met those statements with zero comprehension. I wasted my breath and my energy. After an hour-long standoff she was tired enough to go to bed. She didn't want me to hold her hand to help her get up.

This spilled over into breakfast at the unusual hour of 6:00 AM on Saturday. She was still agitated and wanted me to take her home.

Then.

At 6:00 AM.

In her pajamas.

I waited her out again. She got tired and wanted to lie down. Back to bed for both of us. Slept until 9:00 AM. That happened frequently—up for a few minutes, then back to bed and sleep two to four hours.

I learned that I could wait her out. I think I always had that advantage, but I gave in to her many times over the years because I wasn't sure of myself. When she was at her peak in past years she could overwhelm people because she had a strong personality. But so did I. I was the rocky shore to her crashing waves. At times we made a great tumult together.

Three days during the first week of May were indeed strange. On Tuesday Diane was a bit more restless than usual and wanted to go out. We headed for Silver Diner. I got her into the car with moderate effort (more on this later). We reached the diner and walked inside without issues. We sat at a table close to the door. It was kids' night; kids were running all over the restaurant. A little boy walked past us carrying a balloon animal and stopped to stare at Diane for a moment, enough to engage her attention. She was happy to talk to him and he let her play with his balloon. A young woman walked past dressed as a princess, wearing a cardboard tiara. She was there to entertain the kids. Diane was pleased to meet her. I got a nice photo of the two of them. We left feeling upbeat. I had her sit on a bench outside the door and wait for me to bring the car up, and she sat in the car without falling. We went home in a good mood.

On Wednesday Diane woke up early, ate breakfast, and didn't nap afterwards. In fact, she stayed up most of the day. She napped twice, less than she usually does. She was awake when a supervisor from a caregiving company arrived at 2:30 PM for us to meet with Janice, a prospective caregiver. The meeting went well, Diane liked Janice, and after a half hour they left, with Janice scheduled to return Thursday.

That's when things went south. Diane said she wanted to go home. Diane and I had a long, repetitive discussion about where her parents were (they died in 1992 and 1993 and are buried in Minneapolis). I said they were in Minneapolis and she insisted no, they were just here. This went on for some time. Diane asked where her sister was.

"Did Pat get home?"

"I don't know, she's in Los Angeles," I answered.

"No, she was just here," she said.

And so on. I finally was so frustrated I left the room and worked on finishing a grab handle by the front door.

I was impressed by the slip-on shoes the supervisor wore when for her visit. I wanted a pair for Diane, to make it easier to dress her. I found them online at a nearby department store and decided to go there and buy a pair. We walked out to the car. Diane sat down before she was close enough to the passenger seat to slip in sideways. I had some trouble lifting her into her seat, but we managed. We arrived at the store, found a pair of the shoes, and bought them. I walked Diane back out to the parking lot. When we were next to the car with the passenger door open, Diane sat down long before she was even close to the seat. She ended up squatting on the ground. As I was trying to figure out how to get her up and into her seat, a woman in a car next to us saw what was happening and offered to help. With her help I lifted Diane into the passenger seat, lying sideways on the seat. She sat up and straightened out. That stress set the stage for the next scene.

Back home at around 5 PM, I turned on the news. Diane saw a story about someone who shot the windows out of a building, walked inside, and killed the boss who fired him two weeks before.

Diane was upset. "Now I can't go home. They've shot up all the windows there."

Then she started on whether I had enough money to take her home—home to Minneapolis. She was telling me that she knew we couldn't afford it, because the lady who was here last night or today told her so. No matter how I tried to tell her there was enough money to send her to Minneapolis, she wouldn't believe it. I was wasting my breath, violating a rule of dementia caregiving: don't argue over facts; you can't win. Finally, she put on her shoes (the new slip-on shoes she could put on by herself!) and walked down the ramp to the front door, ready to walk home. Just at that moment Lauren pulled into the driveway. She was going to spend the night here. We all sat down to talk. When I was out of the room for a moment, Diane warned Lauren about me.

"Don't let him come back here," she said, "When is Ron coming home?"

Lauren realized that she was paranoid. We decide to try to give her some Xanax. The usual method of mixing it in a beverage didn't work, because she refused to eat or drink anything. Somehow Lauren convinced her to take a pill, and we waited for it take effect.

Diane still intended to walk home. I offered to drive her, and she agreed. With the usual effort I got her into the car. It takes care to get her positioned before she pulls the trigger to sit. By then I was determined to drive her around, looking for her house until she tired out and wanted to go back. There was one more surprise. We slowly cruised along every street in our neighborhood. She didn't see her house. Finally, after we covered every street I headed back down our street.

Diane looked over at our house and said, "There it is."

I helped Diane into the wheelchair, into the house, up the ramp, and into her chair. She was calming down. At last she told me I could spend the night there. She believed she was in her house. We went to bed.

A weird anomaly about that day: Diane was sitting in the love seat in the living room when something happened to her. Diane told Lauren that her left hand was cramping up and she couldn't move it. Diane also said she had a feeling of great peacefulness and calm. She could smile symmetrically and squeeze my hand with both of hers. She was awake and responsive. Just to be safe, I gave her an 81 mg aspirin tablet. That happened before her manic episode started. Nothing else unusual happened.

You might be inclined after an event like that to seek medical attention to check for a possible stroke or transient ischemic attack. That would be a prudent approach. I knew she would not cooperate to see a doctor, and from previous episodes of TIAs she had years earlier, a doctor would probably find nothing requiring treatment. It was certain that if I managed to get her to an emergency room, we would wait for hours while critical patients were seen ahead of her. I decided to wait and keep an eye on her for more symptoms.

The next day Diane was up and out of bed three times, for a total of less than an hour. That half Xanax tablet the day before, and the energy she burned during her manic episode wiped her out for the whole day. In the morning she woke up, had a sip or two of tea but no pills, then went back to bed. About 2:30 she was up again, went to the toilet, took her meds, ate a grilled cheese sandwich and fruit, then went back to bed. She was up a third time about 7:00 PM and went back to bed in a few minutes.

The day after Mother's Day, Kevin and Lauren came over for dinner at 2:00 PM . Lauren woke up Diane and persuaded her to dress, brush her hair, and put on perfume and makeup. She wore a one-piece lounge robe that hadn't been out of the closet for at least twenty years and looked good on her. Diane got loads of attention from Kevin while Lauren and I set up dinner. There wasn't much cooking to do. By late afternoon, when Kevin and Lauren were leaving to go home, Diane was ready to leave and go "home," too. We trudged out to the car and drove away. I made a five-mile loop through town and home. The weather was clear and sunny, and it was good to be outside. By the time we pulled into the driveway Diane wanted to go inside.

After we were home awhile Diane wanted to go out again. Where? She didn't know. I offered the root beer stand. Fine. We set out to have dinner at the drive-in root beer stand. It went well. We each drank a root beer. Diane ate a cheeseburger and we split an order of mediocre French fries. We came home. It was just getting dark. We made it safely into the living room and watched TV awhile. Finally, around 9:00 PM Diane wanted to get ready for bed. We had a good day: a nice dinner, conversation, and two trips out without stumbling or falling. I had a method of getting her into the car safely. We even sat outside for a while before we left to have dinner at the drive in.

A pattern of sorts emerged. An active day, with visitors, stirred up Diane's anxiety so we'd end up driving around at ten PM looking for her house in the dark. On a day closer to "normal" (in dementia world) Diane would sleep more and not dress until late afternoon. Then we'd go out, do a couple of errands, and return home uneventfully. Some days we had to deal with diarrhea, some days we didn't. That day we did. I'm glad we had a good washing machine and dryer.

The long night began. The stimulation of visitors on Mother's Day, like the sedative effect of Xanax, lasts a long time. We were up four separate times totaling an hour and a half. I finally got Diane back in bed near 5:00 AM. I slept until 9:30 or so. She woke up around 10:30 or 11:00 and ate breakfast, then went back to bed until after 3:00 or 3:30 PM . I fixed her lunch and back she went. At 5:30 PM she was asleep.

So the pattern I saw was:

Social stimulation = sleeplessness

Boredom = sleepiness.

Another incredibly crazy day followed later. Diane was awake half the night before and all day on Thursday, getting progressively more agitated as time went on. She wanted to know where her mother was. Was she coming home? Where was everybody else in the house? Where did they go? Where's Jennifer? Isn't she upstairs?

I tried to take her "home"—twice. But unlike the previous time she recognized we were back where we started. The really striking thing about her state of mind was what I will call her emotional memory. Diane was possibly in a dissociative state, and while we sat in the car she started saying that what we had was over, that it never could have worked out. She denied we had ever been married and didn't recognize Lauren as her daughter. She was almost re-enacting a scene we had years ago before our marriage when she was feeling a deep, tragic sense of failure and wanted to break up. In fact, she made me think she WAS re-living it when she said "It's been hard for me these last four years, with Tom..."

Earlier in the progress of her dementia Diane sometimes revisited her relationship to Tom, insisting that he was still alive. She believed she talked to him, that he was homeless and living in the woods near us or living in a house just on the other side of the shopping center. A couple of times I drove Diane around, looking for the house she insisted she knew how to find. Of course, we never found it because it never existed. When we couldn't find the house, she was frustrated and confused, but she held onto her delusion until eventually she completely forgot about Tom.

This reference, however, seemed more like she was reliving a memory from the time when we recently met, when Diane was fresh from separating from Tom and he was still alive to harass and stalk her. I couldn't get inside her mind to know when and where she was in her thinking, but the tone of her voice was uncannily like the breakup scenes we'd had more than once, many years before. Finally, Diane realized herself that something was wrong, and she agreed to take a pill to calm down. I gave her half a Xanax tablet.

After having that conversation in the driveway, we drove over to Lauren's, where Diane broke up with me again because our relationship would never work out. We finally left close to midnight when she was calmer. When we reached home, she didn't balk at being there. We walked inside and I got her into a nightgown and into bed. I crawled into bed around 12:45 AM. At 1:00 AM Diane woke up and we sat in the living room while she smoked, then went back to bed. She slept until late morning, got up to go to the toilet, then went back to bed. It was a rest day for us.

Another aspect of that situation that may have had a big impact: how I looked. I started to grow a beard just to see what I'd look like and how it would feel. My appearance was changing. I hoped it would remind Diane of how I used to look in the past when I had a beard. I think that backfired. It probably made me look more like a stranger than I did already. That may have added to her anxiety. I shaved it off.

Late that day Diane got up, changed, and ate breakfast at 7:30 PM . She balked at her pills again but did swallow the thyroid tablet. Shortly afterward she was back in bed. I sat quietly outside watching the sunset. The loudest sound in the early evening was the neighbor's air conditioner, across the driveway from our front door. Next loudest, some small kids playing outside, two houses up the street. Then a few birds in nearby trees, and last of all, the low rumble of traffic half a mile away. Another quiet day followed a manic day. I only had to take Diane "home" once. She had Xanax three days in a row, so it must have calmed her down.

After a quiet summer, we had a frustrating day. Diane refused to go in the camper because she didn't like it but couldn't say why. I think it was partly just to spite me because of the time I spent working on it. As Jennifer once said, I needed to spend more time just loving her and sweet talking and being affectionate. Diane said as much.

SIMON SAYS

Whoever you are, I have always depended on the kindness of strangers.
— *TENNESSEE WILLIAMS*

In October, Simon joined us. Simon was British by birth. He didn't own a car. He traveled by bus from Rockland, Maine to Boston, then by train to Philadelphia where I picked him up at the 30th Street Station. He stayed for a couple of weeks as a trial run caring for Diane, then flew to Miami to visit a girlfriend, returning the following month. We wanted to use Simon as a caregiver if the trial was successful. He would care for Diane a set number of hours a week, so I could get on with the things I needed to do. Lauren suggested it. She's known Simon since they met at the Bancroft School summer camp, where Simon worked as a health care aide for disabled residents. His years of experience helping disabled people and his caring and gentle character were strong recommendations for this position. When he returned from Florida Simon began to care for Diane.

On New Year's Eve 2016, I made one resolution on the spot: to be kinder to Diane, who too often found a way to annoy and anger me, and tested my kindness almost every day. Simon had been sharing in Diane's care for about six weeks. His schedule was loose, as we both preferred. I was very schedule-resistant like him. Diane settled into taking her daily medications. It became routine and she nearly stopped asking what it was for, but when she asked, we told her it was just "thyroid pills." She accepted that.

I learned one very important technique from attending the Alzheimer's spouses' support group: lying—or as they called it for people who were squeamish about lying, "therapeutic fibs."

Depending on the stage of their disease, people with dementia often ask questions like "Where is my mother?" They often don't remember how old they are and think they are still young enough to have living parents. If you tell them “She died,” they are going to be upset, no matter how many times it is asked and answered. You learn to lie for the sake of the person with dementia.

My answer was always “She is in Minneapolis.” That was true because Diane’s mother was buried there in 1993. She just wasn’t *living* in Minneapolis. Sometimes Diane disagreed and I’d insist that her mother moved to Minneapolis in 1993.

Diane liked a breakfast of one and a half slices of frozen Cinnamon French Toast with real maple syrup. I suppose we could have tried using regular syrup instead—a lot cheaper, and as long as it was sweet she probably wouldn't have noticed any difference. Eventually I changed to a low-sugar syrup when her sugar intake became a concern. She never noticed.

Nearly every day Diane felt herself in a strange place and wanted to go home.

"When are you taking me home?"

"This is your home," Simon would reply. "You and Ron have lived here for fifteen years."

"This isn't my home. I want to go to my home."

So it went. Sometime in the morning or afternoon she’d want to dress and get ready to go home. Some days I’d take her to lunch at the Silver Diner, but not on a Saturday or Sunday when it was always crowded and confusing for her. I started trying to minimize the meals out since it usually cost around $20 per meal, and with Simon on the payroll I was trying to economize. Sometimes we’d drive out to go "home," and as soon as she asked where we were going it meant she’d forgotten that I was taking her home. Then I’d drive to the store or do some other errand, and eventually head home. If we were lucky, the trip gave her enough stimulation to forget about going home for awhile. The issue of going home from never-never land is full of paradox. Where are her clothes? All at home (here) except for a change kept ... here.

At twenty-five minutes past five on a typical day I’d usually be counting the hours and minutes until Diane went to bed. One day in March, she started wanting to go to bed at four-thirty.

"When is Simon going home?"

"Tomorrow at ten AM."

"Not 'til then?"

(pause)

"When is Simon going home?"

"Tomorrow at ten AM."

"Not 'til then?"

— and so on —

Late afternoon was "what'll_we_do_until_bedtime" time. Maybe you've heard of sun-downing—a phenomenon of people with dementia when they tend to become agitated near the end of the day. My personal experience was that it was the time of day when the caregiver (me) was the most tired and stressed out, and my mood affected Diane's mood. I got most stressed in mid-afternoon, especially if on a given day Diane wanted to go home and going out on a simple drive didn't do it. One day we did that twice, and five minutes after returning the second time she wanted to go home. We went out again, and made a stop at the bank and at Aldi. Then she was fine. My new rule: when taking Diane home, we must make at least one stop.

It seemed clear that Diane's confusion and poor coordination had something to do with the high blood sugar resulting from giving in to her craving for sweets. In one afternoon blood test her non-fasting glucose was above 280. A few days later a fasting blood test at home read 182. After stopping all the cookies and other sweets, and switching to low-sugar pancake syrup, her fasting glucose dropped to 110. Once I stopped allowing her unlimited sweets it also made her more alert and physically stronger. She regained the ability to stand up and walk, a remarkable change, and her swollen ankles returned to normal size. Her left ankle still swelled a little, especially if I forgot to elevate her feet, but the right ankle remained normal. I could slip her shoes on without using the shoehorn, and she didn't complain the shoes were too tight.

At the time, her drug insurance had dropped Xanax from its formulary, so her doctor switched her to Ativan. That may have contributed to her confusion and weakness. I switched her back to Xanax, and when I gave some to her three mornings in a row, she didn't have the same physical side-effects as Ativan. That was Diane's individual reaction. Different members of my support group reported a variety of reactions to the psychoactive drugs for treating people with dementia. I continued using Xanax. She didn't need to use insurance to pay for it, as a prescription for the generic cost only nine dollars without insurance.

I wanted to do something to commemorate Jennifer. I was thinking of a hike up Mount Tammany where she and I and Mike went a few years back. It is a beautiful spot, a good one for scattering some ashes. Maybe Lauren and Kevin would come too, along with Mike. There are other places I wanted to take her as well, but

I didn't know when or if I'd ever get to do that. I tended to think of high mountain tops—Mount Whitney for one. Other places: Garden of the Gods, the redwoods, Olympic National Park, even Evergreen Memorial cemetery where her grandparents are buried. I didn't know then how this idea would grow into a grand plan and an extended odyssey across the continent.

I had a great day of skiing March 16. Two days before, a storm dropped twenty inches of snow on Blue Mountain, so I skied on real snow for the first time that year. What a difference! I could control the skis better, control my speed, and concentrate on form. There were moments of sheer pleasure when everything worked, and I felt like I was dancing on the snow. The weather was perfect—it was windy and cold with a sky full of fluffy clouds and bright sunshine, and shining white fields offset by dark patches of woods across the hills and stretching to the horizon. The scenery matched Stratton or Okemo and gave me an eyeful of natural beauty—winter viewed from a mountain top. I stopped often to take it in and memorize it. It helped me get through the days I was stuck inside with Diane.

Several times I felt pangs of sadness and loss driving to the ski resort when I thought about the ski trips I took with Diane after we met, to Big Bear, Breckenridge, and Brian Head. I let myself feel sad in those moments when I was alone. When I was with Diane I directed my attention and love to her. Taking care of Diane was an all-consuming task and I needed to be completely focused on her. In a way, that comforted me because giving her the care she needed left me no time to lament what we lost. Sounds odd, I suppose. I read somewhere that you can't feel more than one emotion at once. Caring for her in a loving way brought a response from her that felt to me like love, or as much as she could give.

On March 18 Diane was in bed early. Life with Diane was simple, but challenging. There were few routines and few variations. Other caregivers in my dementia support group made diligent efforts to keep their spouses active and engaged. They wanted them to have as close to a normal life as possible. I wasn't as successful as they were at finding activities to interest Diane. I tried quite a few, but she wasn't interested.

Her diet seldom varied. It wasn't the most nutritious balanced diet, either. When feeding Diane the first consideration was always what she would eat. No matter how nourishing the food is, if she refuses to eat it, its nutritional value is zero. I wanted her to take in enough calories and to enjoy what she had as much as possible.

For breakfast she'd usually have French toast—one slice with crusts trimmed off, cut into twelve or sixteen bite-sized pieces; one soy sausage, cut into small pieces; all garnished with low-sugar maple-flavored pancake syrup. I had to switch from real maple syrup when I cut sugar out of her diet. Fortunately, she never noticed the difference. Some days she would eat two of these breakfasts.

Lunch was normally a grilled cheese sandwich—one slice of cheese on white bread with crusts trimmed, fried with mayonnaise instead of butter, and cut into four or six pieces; a small bowl of sliced bananas and canned mandarin oranges, pineapple, or cut up fresh strawberries.

At dinner I'd get creative. Maybe frozen ravioli or other stuffed pasta with tomato sauce or sun-dried tomato pesto, or maybe mac 'n' cheese, and steamed broccoli with olive oil, garlic, salt and pepper. Some days, she had no appetite for dinner.

A speech therapist visited Diane to make an assessment. She was the one who recommended cutting the sandwiches and French toast into small pieces. That made it easier for Diane to swallow food and avoid choking. Choking is a real hazard as dementia progresses. My father died from choking on food when he was in assisted living.

Usually by afternoon Diane wanted to go home and she wanted Simon to leave. She was often bored to death by then. She wouldn't read, play games, or engage in arts or crafts. She watched TV but couldn't follow the stories. Maybe she followed the sound and motion on the screen, or the feelings the actors projected each moment. I don't know.

On a calm day in March, Diane rode with me to the ski shop, where I left my skis for edge sharpening and waxing. I picked them up a week later and then put them downstairs until winter came again. Winter isn't always certain to come next year in the Mid-Atlantic, with global warming messing up the climate. In the afternoon I had to take Diane home again, and I used the trip to pick up a few things from Wegmans as usual.

I took some time to write. Beside me sat the cherry wood urn I made for Jennifer's ashes, a reminder of a responsibility that I fulfilled. It began over 50 years earlier when I met Diane and Jennifer, and took on the job Jennifer's father rejected. I married Diane because I loved her, but Jennifer was part of Diane, and I loved her too. Also, they needed me and I could not walk away honorably.

Diane was lying down at 7:30 PM one evening. She was anxious and endlessly repeated the same questions.

"Where are we?"

"Who's here?"

"When is Simon coming back?"

"Where will he stay?"

— and so on —

I didn't know what our life would be like in a year. I was afraid it would be unchanged. Looking back, I could see how it had changed from last year, but I couldn't see ahead a year. I hadn't taken advantage of having Simon here as I should have. I thought he might only be here another six weeks or so. I needed to pin that down and look for a caregiver to come in after he left. I didn't look forward to it.

Diane had a good day, but she was bugging me about going home. Then she went quietly to bed instead. She seemed to know she really couldn't walk home. This disturbed me. The adventurous woman I met on the mountain went away without me. She left me to take care of her body, but her spirit was gone.

One day in April, as Diane slept in the afternoon, I tried to remember the days following Jennifer's death. We held a memorial service and hundreds of people attended. I stood in a receiving line while people filed past to offer condolences. I spoke to many that I knew, others I only knew by name because Jennifer or Lauren had mentioned them before. Later I said a few words in front of the group. I couldn't recall many details of that day. A year and a half later I still struggled to accept what had happened. During this time I was caring for Diane and couldn't disengage from that role. I still hadn't grieved Jennifer's loss properly. At unexpected moments something—a phrase of music, a sad scene or a happy scene in a movie, often unrelated to her or to my past life—would trigger an upwelling of emotion, sadness and loss, but regardless of the source I always knew it was about Jennifer and Diane.

Diane was stable between May and September, and I wrote nothing in my journal. In July I took a trip to northern Vermont for a week and visited my old friend Gene. Labor Day weekend I drove to North Carolina for a football game. Those excursions helped to renew me and my sense of self. I resolved to go out at least once a month for a social event so I could remember who I once was.

In mid-September Diane fought an upper respiratory infection for over a week. I started her on doxycycline. I suspected it would have no effect because what she had was a virus, but defending her from pneumonia was important. While she was sick she lost significant function. Her walking coordination was worse, so I needed to ferry her to and from the bedroom in the wheelchair. She was less cognizant of her surroundings and slept most of each day. Due to her incontinence, I finally put reusable incontinence pads on top of the sheet to save having to remake the bed and wash out the sheets every day.

Occasionally Diane told me I should get rid of the camper. That was valid from her point of view. Not mine. It was my refuge, my man-cave, my escape pod. I read posts in the Facebook Roadtrek group about the travels of others and day-dreamed about joining them. Meanwhile, I took short trips here and there and kept doing the maintenance to keep it roadworthy, so someday I could jump in and disappear down the highway. I was a different man than two years earlier, before Jennifer died. I choked up every time I saw a story about loss. It didn't matter who. It just welled up in me. It seemed like I had an endless fount of sadness in me.

Simon packed for his flight to England on Monday, September 25. We asked Cheryl, the new caregiver, to come and meet with Simon, and go through his advice for caring for Diane. She postponed coming twice. I rescheduled her for the Saturday before he was due to leave. If she didn't make it, I'd have to find someone else.

She didn't show up. I found someone else.

LAST DAYS

People fear death even more than pain. It's strange that they fear death. Life hurts a lot more than death. At the point of death, the pain is over. Yeah, I guess it is a friend.
— *JIM MORRISON*

In November, Diane's health changed dramatically. Around Thanksgiving she seemed less responsive, less aware, and her appetite dropped. She became less coordinated and needed the wheelchair to move to and from the bedroom. She suffered both urinary and fecal incontinence. Her temperature was normal, with no signs of fever. I was preoccupied with just taking care of her, and I didn't keep good notes at the time. My memory of December is just a blur.

In January, with Simon gone since September, I had two women helping take care of Diane on different days, leaving me with full care three days a week and respite on four days. Heidi, my little rescue dog, stayed close all the time and comforted me. A shaggy little mutt, she lived with a reclusive retired professor down the street, who died from a fall just before Jennifer's surgery. She adopted me just after Jennifer's memorial service, when I was out taking a walk near the professor's house. A member of his family was out walking her, and our paths crossed. Heidi trotted up in front of me and rolled over at my feet, paws up. She chose me. I offered to take her if the family did not want her. The professor's family accepted my offer when they learned she was not completely housebroken. Heidi soon was following me around and sleeping on the bed next to me. She'd crawl under the covers if I let her. When I sat in my chair, most of the time she'd be on my lap. If I got up, she'd follow me. She would only get up to bark at some imagined disturbance outside, or bark at Plato when he was exiled to the porch to stop him begging from Diane.

Plato would sit on his hindquarters like a squirrel, wave his front paws in the air, and whine endlessly for any morsel of food you might happen to be eating. Diane couldn't stand to see him do that, so she'd order me to give him a dog biscuit. The diet of so many biscuits was making him fat.

Winter was upon us in every way. Lauren had an abscessed tooth. The high temperature outside for the day was about sixteen degrees Fahrenheit with high winds, and as I wrote this the wind-chill was one degree below zero Fahrenheit. With a blanket of snow turning the area white, it felt like the winter it was. I felt housebound then, a combination of winter weather and maybe just not having Simon here so I could have free time every day. I really did feel my life was penned in by my duty to care for Diane. That was difficult the last few weeks due to her incontinence. Cleaning up was messy and unpleasant, one of the duties of care-giving no one wants to talk about. I told myself that I got through most of my life without facing any real shit. Now it was my turn. That calmed me a bit but didn't remove my lingering distaste. At least I got out for a few days last summer. I wondered when that would happen again.

Maybe it was the changing light, maybe the weather, but I had a pervasive sense of sadness lurking below the surface and welling up at the least trigger. A sad story about someone else's loss often made me feel like crying. A happy story sometimes did that, too. Anything that stimulated my emotions seemed to open the door to that sad, true sense of loss and mourning. Many times during the day I'd see or remember something about Jennifer and I would miss her. She loved Diane like no one else in the world. I had her photos from Facebook on my phone, thousands of them. I spent some time weeding out the photos of people I didn't know. That was saddening and comforting at the same time. She and Mike were the most common subjects. She was a selfie queen. After those two, Diane was the next most common subject of Jennifer's photos.

I would ask myself "What have I accomplished today?" On any given day, no answer popped up at once. The answer was not exactly nothing. What did I accomplish? I got Diane up and changed her wet underwear and nightgown. I gave Diane tea and breakfast and she ate all of it. I cleared snow off the driveway. I learned I could run the snow blower without putting the key in. Why it started and ran I'll never know. I made it through most days feeling reasonably good.

Cooper Internal Medicine called me back. My message about Diane's declining health reached Diane's primary physician. She said she didn't believe Diane's latest issues were side effects from the antibiotic she was taking. She thought it was appropriate to put Diane in home hospice care.

The criteria for home hospice care are simple: your doctor agrees you have a terminal illness, and you could die in six months or less. I told Lauren about it and we cried together. We knew this would come eventually. But I'd thought about it recently and I speculated that Diane might live as long as her mother did. That might have been another four years. It might be a year or two years. It might be months. We didn't know.

The hospice doctor saw Diane the following Tuesday and confirmed her primary care physician's recommendation. She contacted a local hospice and started the process of admitting Diane to hospice. The nurses came on Thursday, January 11 and assessed her immediate needs. By sundown that day a hospital bed was delivered and set up, and Diane was resting comfortably with oxygen to assist her breathing. In the next two days Lauren and I learned from the nurses and aides how to care for her bed sore and for the inflammation and sore spots that developed on her skin. Hospice provides palliative care to make the patient as comfortable as possible, not to treat or cure the disease. On Friday, a wound care nurse visited. When I asked her how much longer she thought Diane might live, she said "A day or two." It was one week.

I talked to Lauren about making the house a beautiful place, a place of comfort, playing Diane's favorite songs softly to ease her way to the end. Thus an association formed in my mind: music to sing the warrior woman to her death—not an awful, monstrous ending, but a welcome peace at the end of a long life filled with love, struggle, happiness, and disappointment; gains and losses; soaring victories and stunning defeats; searing injustice, grievous wrongs, and victorious battles fought—the end of a completed life.

When it comes your time to die, be not like those whose hearts are filled with the fear of death so that when their time comes they weep and pray for a little more time to live their lives over again in a different way. Sing your death song and die like a hero going home. — Tecumseh

One of the songs playing the afternoon before she died was Joan Baez singing "Forever Young." Diane once watched Lauren sing that song to an audience at the New Jersey State Fair while she was Miss Burlington County. Lauren sang along to the song and Diane took her hand and held it tightly, one of the last times she responded to anyone. By Friday, Diane was clearly failing as we stood by her. She took her last breath at 4:45 in the afternoon. Lauren insisted on washing and applying lotion to her skin and I helped her clean and dress Diane's emaciated body. She was so thin. I called the funeral director who had handled Jennifer's cremation and made arrangements for Diane. Within hours they picked up her body, and she was gone.

I placed four pictures of Diane on the wall for her memorial service:

One from the day after we met in 1967, facing the camera, hiding behind the mask of her giant sunglasses, looking defiant and incredibly beautiful at the same time;

The next, laughing over her shoulder, full of life and joy in San Miguel de Allende in 1989, when we flew on Continental passes first-class to Mexico City and north on a second-class bus, staying in the hotel once favored by the famous Mexican comedian and movie idol Cantinflas;

One that I shot at the Tower of London in 2007, smiling but subdued, a bit dazed by the crowded city, lingering jet lag, and encroaching confusion as her mind began to slip away;

Lastly, a faded, sepia-toned photo of her, still an infant in a frilly baby dress, her hair in curls, a period photo, remote in time and theme from the adult woman in the other pictures.

When I studied that image from Mirror Lake where we met, I choked up. I saw her stunning beauty, more clearly than when I met her, and I wanted to go back in time and relive the life we had but avoid my mistakes, direct it to a happier outcome, and on and on...

I remembered a scene in the movie, Dr. Zhivago, where Lara asked Yuri what it would have been like if they had met earlier, had married and had children together.

He answered, "I think we may go mad if we think about all that."

Classical piano music drifted across the room from the stereo as I retreated from an abyss of regret and longing.

Later, the Philadelphia Women in Film and Television (PWIFT) group held a fundraising gala to announce a grant fund for new women directors, in honor of Jennifer. Jennifer helped found PWIFT with a few close friends in Philadelphia, to help women succeed in the male-dominated film and video business. She conceived it as a networking group to give women filmmakers the kind of leverage men have had through informal networking since the business started a hundred years ago. The organization has thrived thanks to the efforts of the founding members and the women they mentored.

On their web page PWIFT said, "Palmer's voice and vision are all over who and what PWIFT has become. Her absolute belief in the power of women to create and make stories that matter, and her willingness to act on that belief again and again, is what we celebrate today, and is what will always be part of the work PWIFT does in the future. As a filmmaker, entrepreneur, producer, director, photographer, networking genius, mentor, etc., Palmer is known in all corners of our Philly media world as a warrior woman and creative problem-solver extraordinaire. But it's her unlimited generosity, her kindness of spirit, and her deeply-realized loyalty that helped bind us all together."

Later in the year PWIFT awarded the first grant. In 2019 PWIFT hosted a premier in Philadelphia at the Kimmel Center of The Great Flip-off, directed by Dafna Yachin, one of PWIFT's founders along with Jennifer, and her good friend. At the premier Dafna paid tribute to Jennifer, whose spirit and influence live on in that organization.

Jennifer's favorite quotation was written by Steven Callahan, in his book *Adrift - Six Days Lost at Sea: Bearing these things in mind, when I feel most alone and desperate, I take comfort from all those who have suffered greater ordeals and survived, especially those who, despite it all, have even learned to thrive.*

Camp No Worries now has a permanent home in a South Jersey YMCA campground, where camp is still provided for free to children with cancer and their brothers and sisters. Near the office stands a memorial bearing plaques with the names of campers who have succumbed to cancer. Jennifer's name is now among them.

Lauren and I began planning a journey to say farewell to Diane and Jennifer at Mirror Lake in the Sierra Nevada mountains, where I met Diane in 1967. In May I made a playlist to use when we were at Mirror Lake. On the playlist I included the Dolly Parton song "I will always love you" and as I listened to it, I thought about Diane and the last words she wrote to me when I went on a respite getaway to Vermont. She and Lauren and Simon signed a birthday card for me, and in her shaky hand she wrote "Ron, I love you. Thank you forever. I hope you are in good condition. And come home to me soon."

Those were the last words she ever wrote, in July 2017. I also have the first letter she wrote to me, almost 50 years earlier, that closed with "Oh, Ron, be real and be lasting. If I should lose this happiness again, I don't know..."

She did not lose it. I lost her instead.

Tears streamed down my cheeks as I wrote this.

Odyssey

Not I, nor anyone else can travel that road for you.
You must travel it by yourself.
It is not far. It is within reach.
Perhaps you have been on it since you were born, and did not know.
Perhaps it is everywhere - on water and land.
— *Walt Whitman*

Even before the memorial, Lauren and I talked about what to do next. We decided to scatter some of Diane's ashes at Mirror Lake where I met her in 1967. The Mirror Lake campground was packed with campers that Labor Day weekend, but in 1972 the Forest Service closed it permanently due to environmental degradation. Years ago, too many people camped there, long before the back-country rule was "leave no trace." For the last forty-five years traces of human use have been fading, and the former campground has been returning to its natural state. We wanted to dedicate it to her memory. Our ceremony would disturb no one, no one would disturb the site, and there would be no sign that we were ever there.

One does not simply walk into Mirror Lake. You need a permit to hike the Mount Whitney Trail. Each February the Forest Service holds an online lottery to award the permits, so I entered the lottery to get an overnight permit for two people. When you choose a date for a permit, it matters whether the trail will be clear of snow and ice, unless you're an experienced mountaineer. That date could be any time from late May until early July, depending on the winter snowfall. I anxiously studied the Sierra Nevada snowpack reports to guess when the trail would be clear. The winter snowfall in 2018 was below average, but a strong storm in late spring could change that. I felt the earliest date would be around the middle of June or later. Earlier than that, a permit might be unusable because of trail conditions.

Our first setback: we didn't get a permit in the lottery. After the Forest Service awarded lottery permits, they made remaining permits available for online reservations first-come, first-served on April 1. I had to try for a permit then. At 12:01 AM the first day of April, I was online and ready on the Forest Service website. As soon as the web page was updated, I began searching for an available overnight permit for two people, two nights, in June or later. There weren't any we could use. They were already awarded in the lottery.

I had a backup plan. If we could get a one-day permit we could hike from the trail head at Whitney Portal to Mirror Lake in one day, climbing 2,400 feet in four miles. If we started at first light, we could get to Mirror Lake by mid-day, carry out our ceremony, and return to the road before dark, exhausted. I found an open permit for June 14 and reserved it. Our date was set. Our plan could proceed.

I know I focused on planning for the journey so I could avoid dwelling on my own grief. Lauren herself was in an awful state, with her marriage in limbo and still profoundly grieving Jennifer's death two and a half years earlier, made far worse by losing Diane. She threw herself into planning for the trip along with me. She set up a Facebook group "It's All About the Journey" as a blog for the trip. We began to post about our preparations, our route, and what we wanted to accomplish on the way. After several days working out our route across the country, I posted our itinerary online. We wanted it to be a travel blog. We would post the daily events of the trip, and above all we'd write about the mental and emotional journey from our old life to a new one.

We had two reasons for going. First, we would complete a sacred circle by scattering Diane and Jennifer's ashes at the spot where Diane and I met more than 50 years earlier. Second, and equally important, we would embark on a journey of discovery—a pilgrimage to prepare for new lives, in the future we had no choice but to enter. Our old lives were shattered. We would be starting over, this our maiden voyage.

We planned to drive in the camper I bought in 2012 to travel with Diane. Our Roadtrek camper is a nineteen-foot self-contained conversion van, with two narrow beds eighteen inches apart on opposite sides at the back. It has a generator, refrigerator, stove, microwave, hot and cold running water, toilet, shower, furnace, and air conditioner. A curtain slides out to divide the front from the back for privacy when dressing or using the toilet. The water tanks carry thirty-three gallons of fresh water and thirty gallons of wastewater. We would stay in commercial campgrounds, state and national parks and forests, and even on the side of the road in places that allowed it. The two of us must be self-contained too, and get along with each other for six weeks and ten thousand miles.

We would leave May 29, four months and ten days after Diane's death. We loaded our clothes, food, and gear into the camper and drove west from New Jersey on schedule. Our dogs Plato and Heidi came along with us, and went everywhere with us except the trail to Mirror Lake. Plato is a twelve-year-old Bichon Frisé we've had since he was a puppy. He has come along on every camping trip since we rented a camper in 2012. Heidi joined the family too late to tag along with Diane and me on our trips. This would be her first. Our cat Frida stayed at home and Lauren's husband Kevin agreed to care for her.

I dreaded the long, flat, boring drive from our starting point in New Jersey through the Midwest to Boulder, Colorado, especially the miles of Pennsylvania Turnpike. The highlight of our day on the Turnpike was a billboard somewhere in the middle of Pennsylvania, clearly an area with deeply pious residents, advertising "Jesus—Live on Stage." We were mildly curious to see a live Jesus, but we had a schedule to keep. We passed through Pennsylvania and well into Ohio without passing anything else worth remembering. In Iowa on the third day, we abandoned the interstate and pushed south on a quiet two-lane highway across gently rolling terrain. No eighteen-wheelers barreled along that highway, and the road brought us closer to the land and the towns we passed, curving in places and slowing down as we drove through small, quiet villages. An east-west two-lane took us to Omaha, Nebraska, where we met a friend of Lauren's for lunch, then rejoined the interstate west of Omaha.

A day later, on June 1st we left Interstate 80 on a cutoff to U.S. Highway 30, which runs roughly parallel, headed for our first destination. My father, uncles, and grandfather helped build Highway 30 during the Great Depression, working bulldozers and heavy equipment from Iowa all the way to the Oregon coast. My grandfather—my father's stepfather, as his parents divorced when he was three—told me a story about working on the highway when they reached the Columbia River. He said that one night, the camp cook baited a hook the size of a grappling hook with salt pork, attached it to a chain, and threw it into the river. In the morning, the cook used a mule to pull a huge sturgeon out of the water. Maybe. Sturgeon living in the Columbia can grow to more than a thousand pounds. I loved to listen to his stories, like the time the family was homeless during the Depression and sleeping in a churchyard. He said he woke up to see a gun barrel inches from his face that looked as big as a cannon. The man was ready to rob them at gunpoint when someone else said, "I know these folks. Let's get out of here."

As we crossed the Platte River, Lauren saw a man fishing in the river below the bridge. We turned west on U.S. 30, stopping beneath an overpass so Lauren could take pictures of a nearby farm. When we got out of the camper we saw hundreds of swallows' nests built under the edge of the overpass. As she photographed the swallows, a young man approached us from the east on a bicycle pulling a trailer. He stopped and introduced himself. His name was Jacob. He was the man Lauren saw by the river. He noticed us passing and was curious. Originally from Fort Morgan, Colorado, he said two years earlier he had "philosophical differences with modern society." He began his travels, passing through every western state but California. He was headed east but couldn't say why. He reminded me of Christopher McCandless, the young man John Krakauer wrote about in "Into the Wild," but Jacob appeared better equipped and organized. We parted. He pedaled away to the east and we continued west to Sutherland.

The small town of Sutherland sits along the South Platte River in the southwest corner of Nebraska. During the Depression, my grandparents lost the Stockton family farm in Grant, Nebraska. They moved to Sutherland and lived there the rest of their lives. My earliest memories were of their house. My mother, brother, and I lived there while my father attended the University of Nebraska in Lincoln on the G. I. Bill after the war. That modest old house surrounded by tall cottonwood trees and a weathered picket fence felt like my ancestral home to me. Diane and I visited Sutherland a few times, the last on our way to Minneapolis almost fifty years before. The year after that, my grandfather died of the flu while he was recovering from surgery. In Minneapolis at the time with a new baby, I wanted to attend his funeral but I was broke, and couldn't. My grandmother lived there alone, with her granddaughters near, until her death. She lived to be ninety years old. While she lived, my uncle cut down the aging cottonwood trees so they wouldn't blow onto her house during one of the storms that raged across the prairie. I wanted to touch the earth there, where I sat as a small boy digging in the ground of the front yard.

We reached Sutherland by noon. Driving through back streets in Sutherland we passed the Farmers Bank. When I lived with my grandparents in Sutherland the summer of 1963 I worked for my grandfather on his remodeling jobs. I rode with my grandfather in his rattling black pickup to that same bank to collect my pay each week. I saw an old man crossing the street in front of the bank, so I stopped in the middle of the street to talk to him. He was 89 years old, had lived there all his life, and he knew my grandparents. The man, and the bank behind him, seemed suspended in time, like the bar where I used to play snooker and drink a Coke with Grandpa. As soon as I walked in the door I recognized the layout of that bar, unchanged for over fifty years. The old men who sat along the bar could have been there all those years earlier and not looked any different.

That summer I stayed in Sutherland, the owner of the bowling alley bought new automatic pin-setting machines to replace the pin boys who did the job by hand. The Saturday his machinery arrived, he put out a call to the neighbors: anyone who wanted a day's work could bring their tools and help install them. Alongside my father, grandfather, two uncles, and a few men from town, we worked the whole day at $2.50 an hour, twice the minimum wage. I felt deep connections to my family and those men then, just eighteen but accepted as one of them.

After a nondescript lunch at a franchised sandwich shop, we headed for the west side of town. We located the house where had I lived as an infant, a young boy, and again as a young man. The screened-in front porch, where I once played pinochle with Grandpa on warm summer evenings and listened to trucks rolling past on Highway 30, was enclosed by windows. Otherwise, the house was the same outside—except the paint was flaking off. After my grandmother died, the house and land were auctioned off. The current owner once lived farther down the same street, and he also knew my grandparents. I felt a bit sad to see it neglected, but the people I loved who lived there were gone. What was left was just a house that needed paint, and I no longer felt a connection to it. The garage where my uncle Jack taught me how to pee on the wall still stood, its paint peeling and flaking like the house. I liked Jack, but years later I found out he beat my aunt Lois. She was an enormously obese woman, but jocular. Cancer carved her flesh away to a gaunt shadow of herself before she died, a sad and horrible ending to her life.

For years I wondered how the old house and the town would look to me after so many years had passed. Being there in person allowed me to close the book. I don't need to return. I hoped to find my grandparents' graves in the cemetery in Sutherland, but I learned that they were buried in the small town on the prairie where the family farm once was. We took a few photos and then drove west on Highway 30 to visit my grandparents' graves at the Fairview Cemetery in Grant, Nebraska.

At Ogallala we turned south toward Grant. The highway climbed from the South Platte River Valley onto the wheat-growing plains where flat fields stretched from horizon to horizon, set off by a blue sky full of giant clouds that dwarfed the insignificant houses, barns, and silos dotting the featureless tan landscape. The pure sunlight and austere simplicity of the land dispelled my lingering nostalgia about Sutherland. We passed through several small towns to reach Grant, a town of one-story red brick shops along Central Avenue, next to huge grain elevators at the farmers' co-op by the railroad line. My mother was born in Grant and grew up there. Her grandmother, Mary Lee Ballard Stockton, was descended from wealthy Virginia planters. She bore three sons and three daughters in Missouri and became a settler in Nebraska, homesteading a farm south of Grant that later passed into the hands of bankers during the Depression.

My Aunt Lela told my cousin that after my great-grandmother's oldest son died in 1903, a neighbor with a grudge repeatedly called great-grandmother Mary Lee on the telephone, pretending to be her son. Lela said it drove her mother mad. She was admitted to the Nebraska State Hospital for the Insane in 1906. According to her medical records she suffered from sub-acute mania. She never was released from the hospital. In 1934 she had a disabling stroke, and she died there in 1938. Now she lies next to her husband and my grandparents in Fairview Cemetery a quarter mile west of Grant, across the highway from the railroad. My mother kept this secret from us, once mentioning that the kids in her town teased her cruelly, but never telling me why. I pieced the family tree together online during the hours I spent sitting with Diane in the hospital in 2013, eventually finding my great grandmother's name at the state hospital in United States census records. I bade farewell to them all, and we left the cemetery.

We drove west across the prairie toward Boulder, Colorado, passing through Denver during rush hour traffic in the late afternoon. After reaching Boulder, we wandered around the city looking for a place to boondock, and parked in the Boulder Public Library lot where we spent the night. In the early evening we heard some noise from university students relaxing on a Friday night by Boulder Creek, but later it grew quiet. We slept with the windows open, savoring the cool night air.

ACROSS THE DESERT

Though the road's been rocky it sure feels good to me.
— *BOB MARLEY*

After a light breakfast in the library parking lot, we drove up Boulder Creek to Nederland, where we stuffed ourselves with omelets at an outside table. Then we meandered along a scenic highway to Loveland to meet our friend Charlie, who recently moved to Colorado from New Jersey. Charlie date Lauren's for a brief time in the 1990s, but she broke up because he was too tame for her. He remained a family friend. He and I skied together in the Poconos a few times. Charlie worked his way through Rutgers, running his own landscaping business in the summer to pay for his tuition and expenses. He graduated and started a career in IT. His zeal for rock climbing and skiing eventually brought him to Colorado. He found a position at the University of Colorado and stayed. Charlie met us at his friend's house in Loveland, where he helped me replace the corroded ground cable for the coach battery. We repaid him by helping him unload a massive chest of drawers from the back of his car and carry it to the house. That took all four of us. We ate lunch with Charlie and his friend at a quiet Mexican restaurant in Denver. We left, promising to return someday, and drove northwest.

I organized next stage of our journey around scenic stops and side trips. On this leg we would visit parks and monuments; most were places Lauren had never seen before, some I hadn't. Along the way, we planned to meet a couple of friends, but we would be sightseeing most of the time. We were leaving an old life behind and searching for a new one with a new outlook. We would flood our senses with spectacular wilderness beauty and hope for healing as we progressed toward our fixed goal, the trek to Mirror Lake on June 14.

We drove in the entrance to Rocky Mountain National Park and up the Trail Ridge Road, which climbs to 12,183 feet above sea level with stunning views of surrounding snow-capped peaks and wide glacier-carved canyons. The director of the National Park Service predicted during the road's construction, "You will have the whole sweep of the Rockies before you in all directions." Lauren sat in the passenger seat while I drove, trying to maintain calm as she gazed over the edge of the road at thousand-foot drop-offs. We stopped at the Forest Canyon overlook, an observation point in the alpine climate zone well above timberline. Lauren walked to an observation platform two hundred yards from the road, perched above a steep drop and surrounded by distant, blue peaks crested by dwindling cirque glaciers. Filled with wonder at the indescribable scenery, passing snowbanks by the road as tall as our camper, we crossed the Continental Divide and descended to a wide valley by the headwaters of the Colorado River. I found a campsite at Timber Creek Campground and prepared to spend the night.

After dinner we sat outside by our campfire at dusk calmly watching stars appear, smoking a filtered marijuana cigarette that Lauren bought at a shop in Boulder. We took turns lying on our backs atop the picnic table and looking straight up at the Milky Way. Where we live near Philadelphia, the night sky is so polluted by city lights that only a few stars are visible. At nine thousand feet elevation in Colorado, far from any city, the universe revealed layers beyond layers of stars in three dimensions, almost pulling me up into the sky. After a while Lauren felt cold and tired (partly from the Xanax she took to calm down on the drive) and she went to bed in the camper. In a mellow mood, I sat up a while longer watching the fire die down and savoring the hypnotic crackle of the logs. I remembered a camping trip years before with Diane and the girls in California, when I sat by the fire that night as they slept in our tent, simply enjoying being alive as the logs burned to coals. This night in Colorado, I felt a calm assurance that our journey west was taking us on the right path.

In the morning Lauren took her camera and followed a trail from the campground to the Colorado River. She wandered off the trail into a brushy meadow full of chest-high willows and found an elk herd. Intent on her photography she crept closer and closer to the herd until a cow elk charged her. Frightened, Lauren backed away and returned to camp. She and I walked back through the meadow, picking our way across small streams to the riverbank. We passed within a few feet of two moose, and saw several piles of fresh bear scat. This simple walk in cool air under a clear morning sky helped mend our bond to each other and the past, weakened by years of illness and grief.

I wasn't happy to leave Rocky Mountain National Park. We drove west along the Colorado River, leaving behind the greenery and entering the desert. The landscape grew barren and dry. The desert has its own austere beauty, but I wasn't in a mood to enjoy it. We drove on a two-lane highway to Kremmling, jumping-off point for white-water sports downstream on the Colorado, then the GPS took us onto a gravel road that seemingly disappeared into nowhere. After some twenty miles of anxious climbs and descents, the gravel road joined a paved highway and led us to Interstate 70. By evening we reached a campground a few miles south of Moab, Utah.

The next morning we toured Arches National Park, then drove south to Goosenecks State Park. That afternoon, the outside temperature was close to a hundred degrees as we drove. We ran the generator to power the RV air conditioner, so the dogs stayed cool in the back. Near sunset we reached the park and the temperature was still in the nineties. The campground there is a flat gravel clearing next to a fifteen hundred foot drop-off to the San Juan River. It has no facilities except picnic tables and a pit toilet. I left the generator and air conditioner running to cool the dogs, but after a few minutes we heard the carbon monoxide alarm inside the camper. I shut off the generator and turned the ventilator fan on high to push fresh air inside. I didn't know if the generator was overheated from being run so much that day, or fumes were accumulating inside the camper because there was no breeze to blow them away. After the end of the trip I found that the generator exhaust pipe was missing. It would have carried the exhaust fumes away from under the camper.

The late afternoon shade and falling temperatures helped us stay cool without the air conditioner. Once I shut off the generator, we felt the utter silence of the desert. No cars passed on a barely visible highway in the distance. No birds called. No wind blew. No planes flew overhead. All afternoon, one plane passed unheard near the horizon. We ate a cold supper and watched the last light fade to darkness listening — listening hard — to nothing. Miles and miles of nothing.

In the morning we drove a back road through the Valley of the Gods toward the Natural Bridges National Monument, another tourist destination. The highway has a three-mile unpaved stretch called the Moki Dugway, originally built for trucks to carry uranium ore to a processing plant near Mexican Hat. It's been called one of the most dangerous roads in the country. As we drove across flat desert terrain toward the steep face of a far-away mesa, I could see no place for the highway to climb that sheer bluff. We passed a sign that warned us:

3 MILES OF UNIMPROVED ROAD
SHARP CURVES
STEEP GRADES
6 MILES AHEAD

As we approached the mesa I could see a faint track twisting up the cliff. Increasingly worried, I drove on. Another sign appeared:

10% GRADE
5 M.P.H. SWITCHBACKS
NARROW GRAVEL ROAD
1 MILE

When we reached the base of the cliff, we passed the last warning sign:

NOT RECOMMENDED FOR
TRUCKS OVER 10,000 LBS G.V.W.
RVS – BUSES – VEHICLES TOWING

We weighed just over 8,000 pounds and weren't towing anything, so I continued. I knew I'd climbed steeper grades before—but that was on pavement at much lower altitudes. I looked at the grade above us climbing out of sight around the steep cliff and hoped I wasn't going to screw this up. The pavement ended, the road immediately made a hard right turn and we began our ascent up the six switchbacks that cut across the face of the cliff. We didn't meet any cars coming down. That would have been harrowing on stretches of the roadway barely wide enough for two vehicles. After half an hour we finished the one-thousand-foot climb up the Moki Dugway. At over six thousand feet elevation, the air was cooler on the mesa, and a sparse forest of low cedar trees covered the hills around us.

This whole area was once part of the Bears Ears National Monument, from Goosenecks State Park at the south end to Dead Horse Point in the north, and near Blanding on the east to the edge of Glen Canyon National Recreation Area on the west. Bears Ears was in the news recently as the Trump Administration reduced the size of the monument by eighty-five percent to allow oil and natural gas exploitation in areas that were once inside the original boundaries and protected from development. Utah Senator Oren Hatch claimed that he proposed this reduction so that taxes and fees raised from mining companies could help fund schools in Utah. He neglected to mention large contributions from mining interests to Utah politicians' campaigns, including his own.

We drove through the rolling hills and cedar forest, watching small herds of free-range cattle meander along paths near the road or relax in the shade of cedar trees. In late morning we visited Natural Bridges National Monument, then turned east toward Blanding where the highway would take us south to Monument Valley.

I planned for us to stay at the Navajo Tribal Park on the Little Colorado River, but that fell through. The daytime temperature was around one hundred degrees. Without the generator and air conditioner, we couldn't keep the camper from getting too hot for the dogs and too hot to sleep. I booked a space at an RV park in Monument Valley. We arrived by mid-afternoon at the brand-new park, and there was literally nothing to do there but sit and bake in the desert sun. A few small trees were planted around the new park. They might provide shade in another ten or twenty years. I canceled our reservation even though it was too late for a refund, and we headed for Flagstaff, Arizona. I knew it would be cool and comfortable in the mountains at 7,200 feet elevation. We'd be fine, I thought. Fate had other plans for us.

As we approached a junction near Cameron, Arizona, a passing truck threw a large rock from a rear tire straight at me at nearly a hundred miles an hour. "God damn!" I shouted as it smashed almost through the glass, pulverizing a two-inch circle and spraying tiny glass fragments all over the inside of the cab and back into the coach. Shaken by the impact, I pulled over to the side of the road/ Together we cleaned glass out of the inside as best we could, then continued toward Flagstaff. Just then I received a text message from the bank that my credit card had been flagged with a fraud alert. We were in the middle of the Navajo Reservation with no cell service for miles, a compromised credit card, and a smashed windshield. We pulled into Cameron, Arizona and found a weak cell signal. I made a reservation at an RV park in Flagstaff. Then I searched for an auto glass shop in Flagstaff to replace our shattered windshield. None of them were open. I'd have to call in the morning and find a shop to replace the windshield. I called the phone number for the bank and had them cancel the card. They promised to send a new one, which would be useless since it would be mailed to New Jersey and we would be in California. What else could go wrong? Would this keep us from reaching Lone Pine in time to use our permit? Feeling uneasy, I continued driving.

We reached the campground in Flagstaff and spent a comfortable night in cool mountain air, with the desert heat just an unpleasant memory. I started calling auto glass shops at eight o'clock and got an appointment at ten with a shop in Flagstaff. They took us in promptly and we sat in the waiting room— Lauren, Plato, Heidi, and I—while they removed the shattered windshield and replaced it with a new one. Repair complete, we ate lunch at an Indian restaurant in Flagstaff then drove northwest through Ponderosa pine forests and open meadows toward the South Entrance of the Grand Canyon National Park. We arrived late in the afternoon at an RV park where I had reserved a space weeks earlier. The park had no pool, and the facilities were nothing special, but it had a laundry so at least we could get clean clothes. Despite setbacks we were still on schedule to reach Mirror Lake on time to use our permit.

I left the camper to dump the trash and wash some laundry. When my thoughts returned to the camper, for a moment I felt that Diane was there waiting for me to return. Immediately I knew it was Lauren and I felt a sense of loss, as if Diane was there somehow and then left. I realized that even as Diane's health grew worse during her last days of life, I still felt a vital connection to her. I felt her inextinguishable spark of life and awareness until she sank into a coma and slipped forever out of reach. I painfully missed that beautiful woman I met at Mirror Lake who took me with her through love and adventures; who challenged me and fought with me; who loved me and all around her with fierce intensity. Yes, I missed her, and somehow emotionally I continued to feel that she existed despite all knowledge to the contrary. She lived on—lives on—within me.

Early the next morning we left the campground and entered the park, greeted by a ten-point buck elk that grazed calmly on the decorative shrubs at the entry gate, less than six feet from us. We bought coffee and breakfast at the store near Park headquarters, then drove along the rim of the Grand Canyon, slowing as herds of deer and elk wandered across the road in front of us. We parked and walked along the edge of the canyon so Lauren could stand by the abyss and release a primal scream into the empty air, trying to express and rid herself of the mass of grief within her from losing her sister and mother. She said she felt better after that. We stopped at an overlook and walked down to a viewpoint perched at the edge, protected by guardrails, and imagined falling into the canyon from that height. About eleven o'clock we left the park through the east entrance, passing the Navajo Tribal Park where I once thought we might stay. I realized it would have been a mistake when I saw that it was a barren parking lot. We reached Cameron and headed south, retracing our previous route to Flagstaff, this time with no deadly missiles launched at us. We stopped for lunch again at the Indian buffet, then reluctantly rolled onto Interstate 40 West toward Las Vegas.

In 1999 Diane and I passed through Seligman, Arizona late at night, returning from a side trip through Sedona and Jerome. We could not help noticing the Roadkill Café. Earlier in the evening we might have stopped, but it was late, we were tired, and we just wanted to find a motel room that didn't smell like a whole bottle of disinfectant was used to clean bloodstains off the carpet. We drove on until we reached Kingman where we stayed overnight. I never forgot that restaurant, and when Lauren and I neared Seligman we had to see it.

We exited Interstate 40 and headed for the Roadkill Café. We downed pie and coffee, surrounded by stuffed animal heads mounted on all the walls, then returned to Interstate 40 and continued west. We entered Las Vegas late in the afternoon and crossed the city to the house of old friends Susanna and Dwayne from California. They received us with hospitality and conversation, and gave us dinner and beds for the night. In the morning, they offered advice and directions on how to get out of town fast, and after a light breakfast we departed, heading west to the California desert.

The Mojave Desert hasn't changed since the last time I crossed it in 1975. I don't enjoy driving through the desert—a root canal doesn't take as long, and you're asleep during a colonoscopy. I have no fond memories of the Mojave. The air conditioner struggled against the desert heat. We stopped for lunch at the Mad Greek Cafe in Baker, California midway between Vegas and Los Angeles. The World's Tallest Thermometer across the street told us the temperature was 105 degrees. We climbed and descended long grades like those in Colorado and Utah, and after a long drive reached Southern California.

By the time we arrived in Chino Hills, another problem appeared. The transmission was acting strangely, not shifting right, and making odd noises. The engine wasn't running right either, sounding like a diesel when it idled. When we pulled up to our niece Kim's house in Chino Hills, I was worried. Would it keep us from reaching Mirror Lake? Did I make a mistake trying to meet a fixed date three thousand miles from home?

We asked Kim and her mother, Diane's sister Pat, about finding a good mechanic repair it. They recommended a local mechanic. The next morning, a Saturday, we talked to him and agreed to leave the camper on Monday to assess the damage and repair the transmission and other issues. We'd have to scramble to salvage the leg to Mirror Lake. Later that day I reserved an SUV at a car rental agency, hoping it would be big enough to carry us and the gear we needed from the camper. We had a tent and sleeping bags with us from home, in case we got an overnight permit for the Mount Whitney Trail. Now it appeared we'd be using them our whole time in the Sierras. Sunday morning Pat drove me to pick up the SUV.

The rental agency told me that overnight someone smashed the windows of the SUV they were holding for us. Fortunately, they had another vehicle, and they gave us a free upgrade to a larger four-wheel drive SUV. I guess that was some compensation for taking a rock in our windshield in Arizona. It was large enough to carry all our gear and well-suited for the mountain roads. After repeated obstacles in our path, our plan held. Our permit for Mount Whitney wasn't in jeopardy. I had planned to camp three days at high altitude ahead of our trek so we could adjust to the height and avoid altitude sickness. We would arrive at Convict Lake Campground Monday night, one day late but still with time to acclimatize.

High Sierra

The only journey is the one within.
— *Rainer Maria Rilke*

Sunday evening in the fading light of the sunset, we transferred our gear from the camper to the new, white SUV, ready to leave Monday morning after we dropped off the camper. We had the gear we'd need to sleep in a tent and cook on a borrowed stove before and after our one-day hike to Mirror Lake. We had hiking boots, knapsacks to carry supplies and water bottles for the hike, and a pair of walking sticks that I made from driftwood washed up on the beach in the Olympic National Park in October 1973.

Mine is a stout oak staff carved with the name of the park, tipped with a rubber cap at the bottom for better traction, and decorated with metal badges from the places where I've walked: Mount Whitney, Yellowstone, Appalachian Trail, Muir Woods, Devil's Postpile, and others. Its rough, deep brown bark has peeled and flaked away in places, giving it an aged, rustic look. It came with me on every hike since 1973. I used it the last time I climbed Mount Whitney in 1974. It helped me years later on the trail with Jennifer and Mike to the top of Mount Tammany in New Jersey, and again with Lauren to scatter some of Jennifer's ashes at the same cliff top overlooking the Delaware River. Now I use it every time I go for a walk with a friend.

Diane had a slender hickory stick with smooth, tight black bark, a rubber tip, and similar badges, for Yellowstone, Mount Whitney, and other places she once walked but forgot. Up to a few months before she died, Diane occasionally used her stick for balance. Lauren carried Diane's hiking stick up the trail to Mirror Lake.

Monday morning, we drove the camper over to the repair shop and left it with the owner to diagnose and repair the broken transmission, and we left Chino Hills in the SUV. We drove to Arcadia to meet our old friend Rita for lunch. We have known her since Lauren and her daughter Stephanie were in the gifted children's program together in San Gabriel in 1976, and we have kept in touch since we moved to New Jersey. We said goodbye after lunch, stopped to fill up the tank, and rolled onto the I-210 freeway. We passed along the northern edge of the San Fernando Valley toward the Mojave Desert, drove north to the merger with U.S. Highway 395, and continued through the Owens Valley toward Convict Lake. I've driven this route many times, and the miles passed quickly. We were a day behind schedule, but still had time to get used to the altitude before our hike to Mirror Lake. We were in no danger of missing our permit date now.

Lauren and I arrived at the Convict Lake Campground after dark Monday night. We located our space, set up our tent, and lugged our food from the SUV into the red-brown heavy steel bear box at the campsite. The Sierra Nevada wilderness is bear country. The Forest Service provides facilities to keep campers and bears safe. Maybe you've seen videos of bears breaking into cars to get food, heard about them ripping open tents and bending car doors. The instructions at the campground warned us to put all food and everything that smells like food, including toothpaste, lip balm, and such, into the bear box. We followed those instructions meticulously.

Tuesday morning we drove to Mammoth Lakes for supplies, then set out to find a nearby hot spring. Wild Willys Hot Spring was somewhere in a thirty-mile-wide valley between the Sierras and the White Mountains. The GPS reference was vague, and we spent about an hour wandering around to find it. We left the paved highway on an unmarked gravel road that meandered through Bureau of Land Management acres, a wide geothermal basin of low hills and hollows covered by dry yellow grass and short dusty green sagebrush. Mineral water pools and natural hot springs sent plumes of steam up into the cool mountain air. After bounding over ruts and bumps for a mile, we arrived around midday at a gravel parking lot, where a path wound down the hill out of sight. We took Plato and Heidi with us rather than leave them inside the SUV, since without the camper, there was no way to keep them cool inside.

We walked about a quarter mile on an elevated plank walkway to the hot spring. I tied the dogs in a shady spot under the walkway, poured cool water into their bowl, and left them there while we checked out the hot spring a few feet away. Around the spring, patches of rock and gravel and stretches of grayish clay mud were topped with a crunchy white crust of mineral salts. I was already wearing a bathing suit, so I removed my shoes, walked to the pool closest to the end of the boardwalk, and waded into the warm water, lowering myself in to soak up the heat. An Asian couple across the pool told me there was a warmer pool nearby. I walked gingerly in my bare feet across the rough mud and gravel to a shallow pool about ten feet across and two to three feet deep, and eased into the hot water.

It was wonderful: bright clear sunshine and crisp cool high desert air. Low sagebrush, pale gray-green hued in late spring, spread across the dusty land. I took in a hundred-mile-wide view of the surrounding mountains, jagged purple peaks with white snow patches outlined sharp against a brilliant blue-sky backdrop. The morning sun rising into a cloudless sky warmed my exposed skin while fresh air chilled it, and my legs and body soaked in a relaxing warm bath. Lauren walked back to the car and changed into her swimsuit so she could go into the water. We lingered about an hour, relaxing and photographing the spring and the surrounding mountains. We gathered Plato and Heidi and trudged slowly back to the car, our limbs limp and sluggish, too relaxed to hurry.

Right after our marriage, Diane and I bathed in several hot springs. I was naive, optimistic, and full of hope then for a life not yet lived. None of them had the cleansing power of Wild Willys. At this oasis in a wide-open high desert valley, I came to wash away pervasive grief for those I lost, to find relief from sad memories of a lifetime. That broad, sunlit valley of primitive hot springs, with fresh breezes and unfettered view in every direction, soothed our aches from thousands of miles on the road and lifted our burden from the years of Diane's decline. Lauren and I drove back to camp feeling relaxed and purified.

Near sunset we drove back to the basin to take photographs. The time and place were perfect as the sun set behind the Sierras, splashing the top of the peaks with red-orange highlights above purple shadows. We considered going back to the hot springs for a dip at sundown, but from a distance we saw the parking lot was nearly full and more cars were barreling along the entry road. The small pools would be jammed with so many people there. We headed back to camp, satisfied by our photo session.

Wednesday morning we rose before dawn to photograph the sunrise, as golden morning light breasted the ridge of the eastern mountains and touched the top of the Sierras. Because the hot spring basin had such a sweeping view of the Sierra Nevada and the White Mountain ranges, we drove there again. After a quiet, productive photo session, the cool air lured us into the hot springs for the last time. In the early morning only two other people were there. Afterwards, feeling calm and clean again, we drove back to Convict Lake and packed up camp. Then we drove south to Bishop to drop off the dogs. They could not come with us to Mirror Lake, and would stay with a dog sitter for two days.

Tom, the dog sitter, lived in Chalfant Valley, a development of a few dozen houses about ten miles north of Bishop, surrounded by desert in every direction. It looked like a dried-up desert rat kind of town, a place people inhabit to escape from whatever in their past they wanted to forget. I was a bit apprehensive at first, until we met Tom and saw how he approached Plato and Heidi and they responded to him. I felt reassured. We left the dogs with Tom and drove back to Bishop, ate lunch at El Pollo Loco, then drove south to the Lone Pine ranger station to pick up our day use permit.

When we reached Lone Pine, I asked the ranger, "Is there any chance we can get an overnight permit?" The Forest Service reserves a small number of permits for people who apply in person, augmented by cancellations.

He said, "Probably."

Aha! He canceled our day pass and wrote us a two-night permit. No additional charge. We were all set. However, we didn't have all the gear we needed for an overnight trip. We needed another backpack and sleeping pad, and a lightweight propane stove, as well as bear cannisters to carry our food. We found them at a wilderness outfitter in Lone Pine. I pulled a dehydrated meal from a display rack for our dinner on the trail. We loaded our new gear into the SUV and headed for camp. I made a reservation in April for the Lone Pine campground, but we had a good chance of getting a campsite higher up at the Whitney Portal campground. If we could camp there, we'd be on the trail half an hour earlier in the morning. We drove up the steep grade to Whitney Portal, found a vacant campsite, and claimed it. We spent the rest of the afternoon organizing our gear and packing to hike the next morning.

One by one, many elements of our plan fell by the wayside in our odyssey, like household belongings that migrants fleeing the Dust Bowl had discarded beside the road—left behind in our quest for closure, finality, and relief from our burden of grief. Our camper sat disabled in Southern California, waiting for mechanics to repair it for the rest of our journey. Our dogs played safely at a green oasis in the desert, tended by a kindly soul. We were free to start the final leg of our trek into the wilderness.

After driving more than three thousand miles on the highway, Lauren and I would trudge the last four miles on foot to Mirror Lake, having overcome ordeals and obstacles, haunted by past memories, hoping to find peace ten thousand feet above the sea in the heart of the mountains; hoping to come forth from the wilderness with renewed strength to carry our burdens; ready to begin our lives anew.

A gateway of squared beams flanks the entrance to the Mount Whitney Trail. From one crossbeam a scale with a big hook hangs for weighing packs. Mine was forty pounds, more than I expected, and about what I carried when I was there the last time in 1974. Lauren's was about twenty-five. Years ago, I started out from Red's Meadow carrying sixty pounds, but then I was a fifteen-year-old football player. At seventy-two it would be a grueling haul for me. We started up the trail at about eight o'clock on a cloudless, cool morning. The trail conditions were excellent. The trail is closed by snow until July some years, but the snowfall in 2018 was less than average, and the trail was clear of snow and ice past Mirror Lake.

The Mount Whitney Trail zigzags up the steep mountainside through frequent sharp switchbacks. Soon after we left the trail head, we passed through open areas with little shade, and the intense midsummer sun grew hotter every hour. Despite spending the past two days at Convict Lake 7,500 feet above sea level, the trail was still tough when we started to climb. Thanks to our preparations the altitude wasn't a problem, but the physical effort was. Most of the way the trail was dry and unshaded, cooled here and there by sparse shade from yellow pine trees. We passed over wide expanses of bare glacier-polished rock and crossed clear, cold streams that we forded carefully to keep our boots dry. Wet boots can cause blisters, and that can cripple you.

Lauren and I reached a shaded grove above Lone Pine Lake, having climbed seventeen hundred feet in the three miles from Whitney Portal. We stopped for lunch, dropped our packs, and ate big ham and cheese sandwiches and peaches from our packs, transferring the weight from our backs to our stomachs. We rested for a while and wandered from the trail down to the lake, a deep blue, glacier-carved tarn overlooking the canyon we just climbed. We'd reached the high altitude terrain where as a teenager I felt cool and pure, somehow released from the cares and worries that nagged me in hot, smoggy Southern California.

From Lone Pine Lake the trail winds between a barren talus slope and a steep, rocky ridge, traversing more switchbacks under the hot sun, and we struggled uphill again. Backpacking must create a muscle memory, because I felt like I had years ago, sweating and straining against weight and gravity and rough rocky footing for every step up the hill. In late afternoon we crested a ridge and saw a meadow below us. We were nearly at Outpost Camp, where we planned to spend the night. We encountered one more obstacle before reaching the camp. Lone Pine Creek overflows the trail next to a vertical rock wall, covering the trail with half a foot of water for about five yards. We couldn't avoid walking through ankle-deep water. We took off our boots so they wouldn't get soaked. I unlaced my boots and removed them, and walked painfully in bare feet across the rocky stream bottom. I sat down to put my boots back on, realizing after a moment that the spot where I sat was very wet and muddy. When I stood up the back of my white shorts had a large brown stain, looking like I'd pooped my pants. If she could see me, Diane would have laughed. We were nearly there.

We pushed through a brushy thicket of mountain willows that covered most of the meadow, crossed Lone Pine Creek and arrived at Outpost Camp, a wide expanse of rocks and gravel where camping is allowed. We found a good campsite under the shade of a large pine tree. Campers before us had cleared and leveled a space framed by fallen logs that offered some shelter from the wind that often sweeps through the camp at night. We dropped our packs and set up the tent. Once we had our camp set up, we were ready for the final leg. At about four-thirty we set out for Mirror Lake, another half mile up the trail. Our quest approached its end.

In my knapsack I carried Jennifer and Diane's ashes. As we neared the lake I lost the trail, and we wandered through willow thickets by the outlet until I found the trail again. At five o'clock we reached Mirror lake as the sun was lowering toward the peak of Mount Whitney. The former campground looked just as it had when I passed it in 1974, on the way to Trail Camp with Diane's sister Pat, her husband Ron, and their daughter Kim. The space where I camped in 1967 was no longer recognizable. At first I felt discouraged; I wanted to find the exact place where my life with Diane started. It felt important to visualize the scene as it was more than fifty years earlier, to locate it in time and space, and connect with that past event.

At last I recognized the large boulder where Diane camped in the rain before she asked for shelter in my tent. Large rocks and small shrubs filled the space where she once spread her bag. The ground was washed away where I camped, with large rocks where my tent sat. I reached deep into my memory to confirm the location. Next to that tree—there was where I built my campfire; those boulders were above it to the north; that slight drop-off between my campsite and hers—yes, this was the place. We could proceed.

I turned on a music playlist of sweet, sad songs, of favorites Diane loved in the past: Forever Young, Unchained Melody, Imagine, Can't Help Falling In Love, I'll Never Find Another You ... I opened my knapsack and brought out small containers, part of Diane and Jennifer's ashes. We sat quietly for a few minutes. I scattered a small handful of Jennifer's ashes. I recalled the 1974 trip, when she wanted to come with us to Mount Whitney but couldn't because of an infection. Then I scattered Diane's ashes where Diane and I met and fell in love. Lauren scattered the rest of Diane's ashes. I played Taps. We hugged and cried together, saying goodbye to them. Lauren walked over to the lake shore to capture more images of its beauty, as evergreen-scented breezes touched us gently.

Music played softly on my phone as we lingered. The sky did not burst open. The voice of the universe did not sound—or did it? A soft rustle of breezes passing through tall pines; cold, clear water tumbling, churning, splashing, over the rocky cataract, falling from the lake to the meadow below—the voice of the universe? Yes, the voice of nature spoke as it had for eons before the first people walked there. The campground is closed permanently, and something of Diane and Jennifer will rest there undisturbed for generations, perhaps forever, surrounded by the beauty they loved.

In the sweat of thy face shalt thou eat bread, till thou return unto the ground; for out of it wast thou taken: for dust thou art, and unto dust shalt thou return.

We did it.

Our original goal for this journey was a ceremony to scatter Diane's ashes where I met her. That was why we hiked to Mirror

Lake. Something of her would blend into the earth of that wilderness lakeshore. Despite unforeseen difficulties that could have stopped us, we kept on. Our journey had elements of an ordeal; that's important because a quest mustn't come easily. It requires sacrifice and determination. We sweated, strained, and bled to reach that place and that moment. After scattering their ashes I had hoped to feel a release from grief's burden, but I felt the same deep sadness as before. But I'm content to know that Diane will forever be part of a place that had such meaning for us, even if she was not there to see it herself. We walked quietly down the hill to Outpost Camp and prepared our dinner. We were sad but satisfied. We made it to Mirror Lake despite setbacks that could have stopped us. Random events and the forces of nature didn't deter us.

The next morning we woke up early and broke camp. We packed up all our gear, dividing the weight equally between our two packs. For the trip down the mountain, I carried the knapsack because it fit my body better than Lauren's. She carried the rented backpack. We set out from Outpost Camp, finding a better place to remove our boots for the stream crossing without getting wet. Descending the trail quickly, we reached Whitney Portal at about ten o'clock.

At Whitney Portal we removed our food from the bear box and loaded it into the SUV, and headed down to Lone Pine. We returned our rented backpack in town, then drove north to Bishop to retrieve our dogs. We reached Bishop at midday, hoping to swim in the town's public swimming pool to clean the trail dirt off our grimy bodies, but the public swim was canceled by a swim meet. We gave that idea up, ate lunch at El Pollo Loco, shopped for more food, and continued north to pick up the dogs at the sitter's house. Plato and Heidi were ecstatic to see us after spending forever (in dog days) with a stranger. With the dogs safely strapped into the back seat of the SUV we retraced the route to Bishop, turned right, and drove north.

RUSH CREEK

Once you have traveled, the voyage never ends, but is played out over and over again in the quietest chambers. The mind can never break off from the journey.
— *PAT CONROY*

Lauren and I turned to our goals for the next stage of our journey: to work out a plan for the rest of our lives, and to visit friends and family we left forty years earlier when we moved East. Lauren hadn't seen most of them since she was too young to remember. Visiting them would help build new ties to our family. Both of us needed that. Now that Diane and Jennifer were gone, we felt isolated and alone. We would tour the West and open ourselves to new possibilities, maybe even starting anew there.

Silver Lake sits on California Highway 158, the June Lake Loop. June Lake is a perfect little resort town, full of picturesque cabins surrounding a beautiful lake, in an utterly gorgeous mountain valley. It is a wonderful place for a vacation if you can afford to stay there. Four miles beyond June Lake, Silver Lake Campground borders beautiful and less developed Silver Lake.

Silver Lake is fed by the same Rush Creek where I fished with a group of Boy Scouts in 1961. We'd hiked over 10,000-foot Island Pass on a sunny morning in July to fish in Rush Creek. Our two adult leaders had no previous experience in the back country. By lunchtime, the cloudless morning sky had vanished behind overcast, and a fine drizzle began to fall. We hiked back toward the pass, to return to our camp near Thousand Island Lake. As we approached the pass, lightning strikes hammered the higher ground above us. By the time we crossed Island Pass, sloshing through rivulets that filled the ruts in the trail, icy rain pounded us and lightning struck randomly all around. We carried our fishing rods level with the ground, aware that we were the highest points in that flat, open area. We worried less about the lightning than the cold downpour that soaked through our lightweight clothing. By the time we reached our tent on a slope above the meadow, we were shivering. We quickly stripped down and crawled into sleeping bags to warm up. That's how I remember Rush Creek. Camping at Silver Lake forged another link to my past.

When we checked into the Silver Lake Campground, the camp host warned us that coyotes sometimes live in the willow bushes to raise their pups, and occasionally leap out to seize passing dogs for food. I carefully checked the willows surrounding our campsite and found no coyotes. I kept the dogs close to us anyway. The campground also had abundant cover for roaming bears. Not wishing to meet a bear, we moved our food to the bear box. All afternoon, strong winds gusted across the lake and whipped the tall willows around us, forcing me to stake down the tent to keep it from blowing away.

The campground had hot showers, so we each showered and felt clean again after two days on the trail. Late that night I woke up and walked to the bathroom, about fifty feet from our campsite. As I walked, a brilliant array of stars with the Milky Way in the center hung above the mountain tops. I remembered a trip to the Sierras when I was sixteen, lying in a sleeping bag on the ground with no tent blocking my view of the sky, staring at the same stunning view of the heavens. At sixteen I needed no glasses to see the stars clearly.

Our plan was now loosely organized and less detailed. We had no fixed deadlines as we did for Mirror Lake. For the balance of the trip I didn't plan out the route and reserve campsites in advance. We knew in general where we were going and we had a few people and places to see along the way, but each day we'd decide where to stay that night. We hoped to visit friends along the coast, relatives in Oregon and Washington, and a friend of Lauren's on the Pine Ridge Reservation in South Dakota. From there I planned a northern route through Minnesota to see Diane's 96-year-old aunt, visit old friends in Wisconsin, then loop across the northern shore of Lake Michigan, cross into Canada, and return through the New York Finger Lakes. We would work out the exact route and stops as we went.

In the morning Lauren and I loaded our gear into the SUV and left Silver Lake to drive over Tioga Pass into Yosemite, my first visit there in over fifty years. We met no traffic until we reached Yosemite Valley. On that sunny Saturday the park was packed with cars, preventing me from making any of the stops I wanted.

Frustrated, I drove a circle route through the valley so Lauren could see the views, and we left via the Wawona exit, passing a line of cars at least a mile long waiting to get into the park. North of Fresno we left the mountains, emerging from dry pine and oak forests in the western Sierra Nevada into rolling hills covered by parched grasses and scrub brush. Gradually the hills disappeared, and in the afternoon heat we rolled across totally flat fields in the San Joaquin Valley. Through miles and miles of flat dry terrain we saw almost nothing but fruit trees and grape vines. The afternoon summer sun rendered everything ugly there, looking just like I remembered it from summer trips as a teenager. In dimming afternoon light we stopped for coffee at a roadside café sitting in a dry brown field filled with pumpjacks pulling heavy California crude out of nearly depleted stripper wells. The café and its customers resembled an Edward Hopper painting, and the burned, bitter coffee tasted as bad as the restaurant looked. It served as a metaphor for the day's drive.

Strong west winds swept the valley, raising dust clouds and turning the afternoon sun and sky yellow-brown. The hue of the light accentuated the pale yellow dry grass covering the surrounding hills as we climbed the Grapevine toward Southern California. As we entered the mountains a cloud bank spilled over the top of Mount Piños west of us, looking like a sheet of cotton wool on a diorama. We drove on as the daylight faded. We passed the Oak Flat campground somewhere to our west in the Angeles National Forest. When I was twelve, I drank my first cup of coffee there during a Boy Scout camp-out. Boiled open pot style in a big blue white-speckled enamel coffee pot, served with milk and sugar, it admitted me to the grown-up world of coffee drinking. In my memory it was among the best coffee I ever tasted.

Darkness fell before we reached Los Angeles. I drove through the Southern California freeway network in the night toward Kim's, tired and barely following the instructions from Google Maps. I missed a turn and got lost, but because freeways cross the city in every direction I got back on course to Chino Hills. We arrived mid-evening Saturday, tired and ready to rest, wanting to continue our trip as soon as the mechanic finished repairing the transmission. We didn't know when that would be. I extended the SUV rental for a week. We hung out at Kim's doing various errands, walking the sand at Laguna Beach, and killing time.

At four-thirty PM Thursday, our mechanic called from his shop. The camper was ready. We picked it up, ready for the road with a rebuilt transmission. I transferred our gear from the rented

SUV back to the camper and cleaned out the SUV for return the next day. Kim had welcomed us to her house even as she fought cancer and struggled with the effects of her chemotherapy treatments. I left a thank-you card on the coffee maker as we left so she would find it later.

In late morning, after farewells we returned the SUV and headed north again.

Pacific Coast Highway

You take people, you put them on a journey,
you give them peril, you find out who they really are.
— *Joss Whedo*

We wanted to hug the coast, but a landslide on California Highway One blocked the coastal route north of San Simeon, forcing us to backtrack to U. S. Highway 101, then drive north to a secondary road that returns to the coast. In mid-afternoon we entered Fort Hunter Liggett Military Reservation and turned toward the coast on another notorious road: the Nacimiento-Fergusson road, the only paved rad between San Simeon and Monterey connecting the Pacific Coast Highway to the inland. Its twenty-four miles vary between one and two lanes wide in places, with no center line, no guard rails, many steep climbs and descents, and a lot of traffic going in both directions because of the landslide. The road climbs to nearly three thousand feet at the summit of the Santa Lucia Range then descends to the Pacific Coast Highway in a series of dozens of hairpin turns... who's counting?

Many of the oncoming drivers lacked mountain driving skills. I honked my horn at every blind turn so an oncoming car would know we were there. On one turn, a car coming from the opposite direction rounded the corner almost in the middle of the road. I jammed on the brakes and the other driver swerved, narrowly avoiding a collision. We topped the ridge and the ocean came into view far, far below us. By the time we reached the Coast Highway, Lauren and I agreed that the Nacimiento-Fergusson Road ranked above the Moki Dugway on the scale of scary roads we drove. It would not be the last one.

None of the RV parks along the Big Sur road had any vacancies. We continued north through Big Sur, stopping at a turnout in Julia Pfeiffer State Park to walk a short path for a view of

McWay Falls, one of Lauren's must-see items. Diane and I once took a weekend camping getaway in 1975, driving a borrowed car with twenty dollars to spend. We sat at the Nepenthe restaurant sipping coffee at an outdoor table overlooking the ocean, while soft music from speakers drifted in the air. That was all we could afford then. I wanted to stop for a cup of coffee there, but in the fading afternoon light Lauren and I continued past Nepenthe, wanting to exit the narrow Big Sur road before dark.

At the end of the highway in Carmel, we reached a cell phone signal. I booked a space in a Salinas campground and we made our way there. The next morning, after a side trip for photos at Monterey Bay, we turned toward our friend Kathryn's apartment in Walnut Creek. Kathryn was Jennifer's best friend when we lived in Medford Lakes, and they remained best friends when their lives diverged. Kathryn overcame struggles with marriage, divorce, and raising her son to college age. Throughout her adult life she continued to advance her education, earning a doctorate in leadership and change, and became a leader in organizational development for a national health organization. Kathryn attended Jennifer's joyous wedding celebration, and was present for her funeral. Recently she endured the most heart-rending duty of laying her son to rest after his untimely death.

The outside temperature rose as we drove inland toward Walnut Creek. When we reached Kathryn's apartment complex late Saturday afternoon, the temperature topped a hundred degrees outside. Stepping outside the camper felt like walking into a sauna. We schlepped our bags from the camper and settled into her apartment for an overnight stay with food, wine, and conversation. Sunday morning Kathryn rode with us to Berkeley for a walk on the University of California campus where I went to college in the Sixties. We wandered around the campus, then browsed shops along Telegraph Avenue next to the campus entrance, stopping for hot dogs at Top Dog, a student favorite for cheap eats.

Walking back to our camper after lunch, I realized I left the dog bowls at Kathryn's. Rather than put Kathryn on the BART to return to Walnut Creek as we'd planned, we drove her back home, retrieved the dog bowls, and headed to the Golden Gate National Recreation Area. Lauren wanted to hike down to the Marin Headlands and photograph the Golden Gate Bridge from the west at sunset, but the Sunday afternoon crowd took all the parking spaces, so we couldn't even stop to look at the view. I called an RV park in Petaluma with a pool, playgrounds, and a petting zoo, and reserved a space for the night. We drove on.

Both the Petaluma campground and the one in Salinas had a combination lock on the restroom door. I haven't seen bathroom locks anywhere else. I wondered if it was intended to keep outsiders from using the facilities, in an area with a high concentration of homeless people. After dinner and laundry Lauren and I bunked down for the night. We left early in the morning without stopping at the petting zoo.

After our stop at Kathryn's, we developed our itinerary on the fly, wandering back and forth between the coast and Highway 101, touching the coast at Bodega Bay and leaving it again to drive inland along the Russian River. We were in full tourist mode then, ready to experience the wonder of the redwoods and the rugged coast of Northern California and Oregon. We planned our next stop to see friends in Corvallis, and until then we had only the scenery on our schedule. We rolled north on 101, then took a turnoff to pass through redwood groves and reach the coast at the tiny hippie enclave of Mendocino. We camped in the Hendy Grove State Park redwoods, surrounded by a mix of massive, incredibly tall redwoods and Douglas Fir trees. On our tour through the redwoods in 1968 Diane and I stopped to pick wild blackberries, and she baked them in a cobbler. The blackberries weren't ripe in June of 2018 and our camper has no oven, so we didn't have that treat.

Diane and I never camped in the Hendy Grove redwoods, but it seemed fitting to scatter a tiny bit of her ashes there. I left traces of Diane all over the West, some in places we visited together and some she never saw in her life. Standing close to a giant redwood tree, I reached out my hand and held it against the bark, trying to feel the life flowing from ancient times into the future, as if I could join with that behemoth to diminish my loss.

Earlier in the day I told Lauren I was asking myself, "Now where was I before my life was changed forever?" What was my life like, before Diane's health and mind were taken by illness and dementia, and I gave up my independence to care for her full-time? Who was I then, where was I then, and who am I now? I took this trip to find out. I hoped to find an answer after I got away from familiar surroundings, revisited places that once had meaning to me, saw people who once knew me, and saw places that I once knew.

The next morning we wandered inside the park and walked through the Hendy Grove of redwoods that gave the park its name—a stand of old-growth giant redwoods, some more than 1,000 years old and over 300 feet tall. Words can't convey how I felt, surrounded by those trees of staggering size and age. In 1972 Diane and I camped at the Redwood National Park north of Eureka. We still had some pot that we brought from Minnesota when we moved west. After we both smoked enough to get high, her experience and mine went on separate paths. I stood and stared long at the ancient weathered bark of a giant redwood tree, and felt a profound awareness of the awesome span of its time on earth, years beyond comprehension. Meanwhile Diane was growing more and more anxious that one of those giants might fall over and crush us.

I told her "Redwoods don't just fall over. They're knocked down, like, by wind gusts in a storm."

That calmed her. Later, as we were leaving the park, I asked a ranger about it.

He said, "The last tree that went down just fell over for no reason on a clear, calm August day."

HOMELAND

Breathes there a man with soul so dead,
Who never to himself hath said,
"This is my own, my native land?"
— *SIR WALTER SCOTT*

When I was eight years old, I traveled with my brother from Sylmar, California to Vancouver, Washington to stay with my grandparents in the summer. My brother Roger was eleven. We boarded a Greyhound bus in San Fernando and rode all the way to Portland, Oregon with no adult but the bus driver to keep an eye on us. At Grandpa's house we slept in the attic, played among his cows and sheep, dug tunnels into the hay that filled the barn, ate Marionberries and raspberries off the vines in Grandma's garden, and explored the woods by the back pasture.

Under the deep shade of spruce and fir trees we poked at frothy spit bug nests clinging to the pungent leaves and stalks of Queen Anne's Lace. Across an unpaved gravel road from their house open fields and dense woods beckoned. We watched in fascination while a paving crew laid down asphalt on the road for the first time and smoothed its surface with a big yellow steamroller, and we chewed on pieces of tar cast aside in the process. All of that is gone now. The house was razed and replaced by a parking lot, the evergreen trees cut down, and Interstate 205 shuttles commuters to and from Portland where Grandpa's cows once grazed. The open fields across the street now make up the cemetery where all of them are buried. Yet the memory of that farm will live in my mind until I die, called out by cool, fresh air at a certain temperature and afternoon sunlight at just the right angle and color.

Four decades later, on a trip with Diane to Prince Edward Island in Canada, we found ourselves in countryside that vividly evoked my memories of Vancouver, as if the island was suspended in time since 1953. The warm, fading afternoon sunlight, tall dark evergreens, bleached straw in the fields and wide green pastures between farms on that rural island all joined to perfect the illusion in 1995. Lauren and I drove near Coos Bay, Oregon as the late afternoon sun filtered through two-hundred-foot-tall evergreen trees. The light, location, and ambiance all aligned in my mind, bringing me a deep sense of peace and ease. I knew that place. I belonged there. Somehow, I felt that I was home.

We reached Yachats just before sunset and treated ourselves to a seafood dinner seated at a Formica table, one of about half a dozen in the small restaurant overlooking the harbor. Then we split a Marionberry cobbler made from the delicious hybrid blackberries grown only in the Northwest. Stuffed from our meal, we walked sluggishly to the camper and drove two miles south to the Cook's Chasm overlook. We parked by the road and spent the night dreaming of waves endlessly crashing and thrashing on the rocks in the dark a hundred feet below us.

We left behind the spectacular scenery of the southern Oregon coast and traveled through flatter, tamer terrain to Newport. Then we turned inland to cross the coastal mountain range again, reaching the Willamette Valley near Corvallis after a few hours. We were scheduled to arrive that afternoon at my friend Kris' house, but we were too early to just drop in and monopolize his day, so I looked for a diversion. The camper had a cabinet door that kept swinging open, so I looked for a hardware store to buy a new latch for it. Lauren navigated us to a store in northeast Corvallis. When the GPS told us we were at the location, we were in front of a Wilco Farm Store.

I told her, “It doesn’t look like a Home Depot.”

She insisted that it must be, “Look, it has an Ace Hardware sign on the building.”

Maybe this was what Home Depot looked like in Oregon. We weren’t in New Jersey anymore. I walked inside. I looked around but didn't see much hardware and asked a clerk where to find the cabinet hardware.

"Oh, we don't carry that. You'd have to go to a place like Home Depot."

“Where is that?”

"It's just on the other side of Applebees." He gave me directions.

I walked out in a huff and drove as directed behind a row of other stores to the parking lot of the hidden Home Depot. Inside I bought several latches, walked back out, and installed one on the errant door. We started driving again and the cabinet door opened. I fixed it with a strip of duct tape. That worked until we got back to New Jersey and I adjusted the latch so it would stay shut.

I first met Kris in high school. He survived an auto accident in junior high school when riding in a bus with a youth group. His father was one of the adult leaders. The bus stalled, and as the group tried to push it out of the road a drunk driver plowed into the rear of the bus. It crushed Kris's leg, and killed his father. Kris lost one of his legs and was hospitalized for months. He spent more months in a wheelchair, enduring rehab and physical therapy. Kris swore that he would walk again, and he learned to walk with a prosthetic leg. He graduated from college and became a math teacher in Corvallis, eventually joining the faculty at Oregon State University. During his teaching career he was selected from a group of outstanding math teachers to tour the country, with a team teaching improved methods to other math teachers.

Now retired and living in Corvallis, Kris continues to tutor students. He uses some of his energy to train his shepherd dog on an agility course, maintain his immaculately landscaped grounds and orchard, and continue improvements on an elaborate model train set that fills a room in his garage. In the fall of 2017 Kris trained for a marathon in Portland, and finished. We had a long conversation over a barbecue dinner. Kris encouraged us to move to Oregon where we we'd be welcome, and I could ski with him at his favorite Oregon ski area. We enjoyed the afternoon with Kris and his wife, learning about his life and accomplishments.

We rose early the next morning to leave. Kris and his wife were going kayaking and wanted to get on the water early to escape the heat of the day. She was willing to stay behind to host us, but we made sure we'd be ready to go when they were. Early Saturday morning we rolled out and headed for Portland. With his characteristic attention to detail, Kris had drawn us a map to reach Interstate 5 from his house.

Once on the Interstate we continued north and across the Columbia River to Vancouver, passing through where my grandfather's pasture once was. We exited the freeway and continued to the cemetery where my parents, grandparents, and some aunts, uncles, and cousins are buried. I gave Lauren a tour of their graves, and we scattered some of Diane and Jennifer's ashes at my parents' grave. Then we walked across the street from the cemetery to the properties where my grandparents, parents, and my aunt and uncle once lived. My grandparents' house, where I spent the summer at age eight, is gone. Even the trees around it are gone. The area where the house and garden once stood surrounded by tall trees and shrubs is covered by a parking lot. We stayed in that house in the summer of 1972 when Lauren was two, and again a year later for my grandmother's funeral in 1973. She doesn't remember it. When I returned to Vancouver for my parents' memorial service in 2011, the house was still standing. Now only old photos of it remain; another piece of my life is gone. The road where my brother and I watched a paving crew lay blacktop over the narrow gravel two-lane now carries heavy traffic four lanes wide. We crossed the street into the cemetery, boarded the camper, and drove to a restaurant for a Marionberry pie to go.

Lauren was eager to visit her cousin Cheryl, who lives with her husband Doug in northeast Portland. Lauren was thirteen the last time they met. We crossed the Columbia River and found our way to her house. Cheryl gave us a tour of an iconic Portland landmark, the Kennedy School Hotel, developed from a sprawling old elementary school into a hotel, spa, and theater in highly imaginative Portland fashion. The guest rooms were once classrooms, and the designers left elements like blackboards and classroom cabinets in the rooms where hotel guests now can relive school days. You can use your imagination. The boiler room is now a microbrewery, and the auditorium is a public theater.

We returned to the spa after 6 PM, once children were chased out, to soak and wash away more road grime. We left relaxed and cheerful. Later Doug gave us a tour of the restored Hollywood Theatre that he manages for the non-profit foundation that owns it. Built in 1926 in the heyday of silent films and sinking into disrepair, it might have been demolished and perhaps replaced by an enclosed shopping mini-mall, but not in Portland. The original large theater was divided into three smaller ones, and after being refurbished now screens first-run features as well as independent and off-beat productions.

Sunday morning we breakfasted on coffee, granola, and yogurt in the kitchen and talked with Cheryl and Doug. We left Plato and Heidi to play with their little border collie, bundled into their car and they showed us around Portland. Returning to their house we said our goodbyes, hugged our hugs and parted from another renewed family tie, reluctantly venturing away from the beautiful coast toward the vast dry interior of Washington, Idaho, and on east to the Continental Divide.

We made our way along the Oregon side of the Columbia River to Cascade Locks, where we stopped to buy smoked salmon, an Oregon delicacy, at a local fish market. The smoked salmon lasted us through several days of snacks with crackers and cheese. We crossed the Bridge of the Gods over the vast Columbia River to Washington and continued east. On the Washington side, the highway climbed away from the river and crossed rolling hills populated by wheat fields, wineries, windmills, and a few people. Near sunset we reached Kennewick, Washington and the house on a golf course where my 87-year-old aunt Jackie Minton lives and plays golf regularly. She's healthy and whip smart. Lauren met her for the first time in her memory, though as an infant she had seen Jackie many times. She is the last living member of her generation in our family.

"What a great conversationalist!" Lauren recalls.

Jackie's late husband, my uncle Art, was a local officer in the Oil, Chemical, and Atomic Workers' Union. Art was shorter than all the other men in the family, but seemed like a giant to me as a boy. Grandma Minton once told me Art didn't grow for two years when he was a baby during the Depression, when they sometimes went without food. Art owned a big Harley Davidson and rode precision formations with a sheriff's auxiliary club in parades and fairs. On one visit to Washington, he gave me a ride on the back of his motorcycle.

After dinner, Jackie told Lauren how members of our family bought up buildings damaged in a flood that had been used for temporary war housing, disassembled them and moved the material from its original location to the Minton farm, and reassembled it there to live in. Her house didn't have its own well, so she had to carry water from the pump house in cans every day. That was the same property Lauren and I walked through on Saturday, right across from the cemetery in Vancouver. In the morning we ate breakfast at a family-style restaurant with Jackie and her daughter, my cousin Kay. After breakfast we returned to Jackie's house, packed up and headed east.

EASTWARD

A journey is like marriage.
The certain way to be wrong is to think you control it.
— JOHN STEINBECK

I didn't look forward to this leg of the trip any more than our first few days heading west. We were leaving behind friends, family, and familiar places out of my past, bound for an empty house full of painful memories. We planned to stop at a few tourist spots en route, but didn't feel connected to any of them. Our remaining visits included Lauren's friend Christinia, a tribal elder in the Oglala Lakota Sioux tribe at Pine Ridge, Diane's 96-year-old aunt in Minnesota, and old friends Dennis and Liz in Wisconsin. After that, the end-of-holiday blues would really take hold as we dashed home. How long would it take us? How would we feel when we walked in the door again?

We set out from Kennewick, headed northeast across sparsely populated high plains with dry land wheat farms. My grandpa Truitt, orphaned at age 13, became a farm hand for his uncle Owen, not far from the highway we were driving. I met Owen in 1959 when he was ninety years old, and his advice to me was "Don't drink Coca-Cola." We passed irrigated orchards, and vineyards, eventually reaching Interstate 90. We planned to camp somewhere in Idaho that night. The next landmark on our original itinerary was Devil's Tower in Wyoming. I looked ahead on our route and found a rest area on the Interstate where we could stop for the night. We reached it after dark and spent the night. Driving the Interstate during summer construction season wore me out, navigating one-lane construction zones with impatient truckers riding my bumper for miles. The outlook for the rest of the trip threatened to be monotonous and dreary.

The next morning, hoping for a better traveling experience along a two-lane highway instead of a crowded Interstate, we left

Interstate 90 on U.S. Highway 12. Near Helena, Montana we crossed the Continental Divide and entered a region of broad, open valleys between distant mountain ranges. As we rolled toward eastern Montana and the landscape leveled out, I began to miss the rugged mountain terrain. The idea of nothing but prairie ahead depressed me. We changed our plans and headed south toward Red Lodge, Montana at the foot of the Beartooth Range. I tried to book a space at a Red Lodge RV park, but it was booked up for a Fourth of July celebration in town. We found a fishing camp next to a stream a few miles from Red Lodge, and spent a quiet night there. We saw only one other camper there, and she was a hundred yards away.

After coffee and cereal in the morning, we passed through Red Lodge to the Beartooth Highway. We planned to drive over Beartooth Pass and on to Cody, Wyoming. The Beartooth Highway climbs up rugged mountainsides with steep drops, switchbacks, and awesome views. We were back in mountain mode again, crawling around hairpin turns and peering nervously over guardrails with nothing but air beyond. We crossed into Wyoming and reached Beartooth Pass, surrounded by snow. We stopped to take a few pictures and watch a couple skiing on the remaining snow field at the pass. A spectacular array of jagged, white-capped peaks stretched across the horizon to our West. The view matched the best we'd seen in Colorado and California, making the climb worthwhile and helping us to forget, as we meandered southwest, that our destination lay in the East. We descended from the pass to a junction with the Chief Joseph Scenic Byway and turned south toward Cody, Wyoming.

After more climbs and descents, we reached Cody about midday and turned onto U.S. Highway 14 Alternate crossing dry, barren plains east of the Beartooth Range. We passed through Lovell and headed toward a climb into the Bighorn Mountains. By then I was used to warning signs about steep grades and dangerous roads. This highway had them. They weren't kidding. The road has three runaway truck ramps on the downhill side of the road. I never saw a highway anywhere else with more than one. I pushed the gas pedal to the floor, and the camper chugged up the steep grade, barely managing twenty miles an hour in first gear. I eyed the temperature gauge nervously as it crept toward the red zone. A couple of times I stopped for Lauren to take pictures, and kept the engine running to cool the engine down. We reached the crest of the Big Horn Mountains at over nine thousand feet and the road leveled off, passing through wide alpine meadows and occasional snowbanks. In early evening we found a quiet and clean Forest Service camp. I pumped water from a well with a hand pump to refill our drinking water. It was a bit sandy, but good. The next day we descended from the high plateau with no problems.

When we reached Sheridan, we stopped at the farmers' co-op to fill the gas and propane tanks. Summertime in Wyoming meant most men we saw wore cowboy hats. I've seen enough Western movies not to be surprised. They all had straw hats except for one ragged tourist. We stopped in at a Western wear store in Sheridan and picked up a pair of straw hats to complete our outfits, and bought food at a supermarket. Resupply complete, we drove onto Interstate 90 East toward Devil's Tower National Monument. I planned to see Devil's Tower because Jennifer and Mike stopped there on their way west ten years earlier. As we approached Devil's Tower, we spotted a line of vehicles a mile long waiting to get into the park. We squinted out the window at Devils Tower in the distance, agreed we saw enough that it wasn't worth the wait to get any closer, and headed for a campground in Spearfish, South Dakota. It had two things we needed: a laundry and a pool. We spent an unremarkable evening there, clean and cool. Three nights into our return leg, I felt a bit depressed, expecting that the end of our trip lay ahead with little more to interest us.

As we drove along the Interstate the next morning, the "CHECK ENGINE" light flashed on the instrument panel. The speedometer abruptly dropped to zero, the cruise control turned off, and the transmission shifted out of overdrive. I pulled off at an exit a few hundred yards ahead and parked in a lot next to a truck stop to assess the situation. What was broken? Could it be repaired, and what would that cost, in time and money? I thought of calling for a tow, but realized I didn't know where they could tow us for repairs. I started looking for a Dodge dealer in the area. Luckily, the nearest dealer was only twelve miles away in Rapid City. I called them and talked to the service manager. After I described the symptoms he said that we could drive there safely. We gassed up and drove to Rapid City. The dealer checked the transmission and judged it needed a new speedometer gear. That part was not available locally, so they ordered one from the far end of the state, had it shipped overnight, and installed it the next morning. The speedometer still didn't work. The camper was safe to drive but didn't have a working speedometer. Worried about the camper's reliability, we bypassed a stop at Mount Rushmore (another one of Diane's memories) and headed straight to the Pine Ridge Reservation to meet Lauren's friend Christinia Eala, a Lakota tribal elder. Lauren met Christinia several years ago through a mutual friend on Facebook. They bonded immediately. Christinia has been an activist for much of her adult life. In 2015 she asked Lauren to come volunteer to work with her organization building sustainable housing on the Pine Ridge Reservation. Lauren couldn't travel to South Dakota then, just after Jennifer died. Later Lauren discussed joining Christinia's camp of water protectors in their protests at Standing Rock against the Dakota Access Pipeline project. Again, Lauren was unable to travel. This trip would be her first meeting with Christinia.

PINE RIDGE

It is not enough to have a vision. In order to have its power, you must enact your vision on earth for all to see. Only then do you have the power.
– BLACK ELK

What do you know about Pine Ridge? The name evokes historical clashes—like the Wounded Knee Massacre in 1890 when Federal troops killed more than 150 Lakota Sioux people, half of them women and children. More recently in 1975 a gunfight between American Indian Movement activists and Federal agents left two FBI agents dead and an activist convicted of murder, sentenced to life in prison in a controversial trial, for a crime many say he did not commit. Most likely, people who have heard of Pine Ridge at all remember events like those.

Other facts about Pine Ridge are less well known. It is the eighth largest and the poorest Indian reservation in the United States, and has the lowest life expectancy. Many of the residents do not have running water or electricity. Electric service often comes from generators, fueled by expensive gasoline from stations miles away. Healthcare facilities are abysmally inadequate. Rampant public health problems include mental health issues, substance abuse, diabetes, and malnutrition. Eighty-five to ninety percent of the population on the reservation is unemployed. To call the entire reservation a food desert understates the case.

Driving south from Rapid City, we left the Black Hills behind and rolled across wide treeless prairie. That early July day the afternoon sun baked the dry grassy soil. We saw highway, fences, and prairie in all directions. To me the land was empty, but I am not a native of it. To understand that land, I would need to stay on it for some time—days, or weeks, perhaps—to watch the sunrise and hear the sounds of the birds, animals, and insects, and feel the sun, wind, and rain on my skin. We did not have time to do that.

We passed few houses or buildings other than a large, new Indian casino just inside the reservation boundary. The few dwellings I saw advertised poverty even at a distance from the highway—ramshackle houses in disrepair surrounded by junked cars, decrepit outbuildings, broken fences, and heaps of unidentifiable scrap. A few miles past the casino, we turned onto a small road that arrowed south toward Nebraska. Our destination was a homestead at Slim Buttes, somewhere down the road just past the end of the pavement. Unsure of our directions, I missed it once, turned around, went back, and entered the driveway. As we approached the house, several large dogs bounded toward us, barking to raise the alarm. Christinia came out and greeted us warmly. She especially wanted to meet Lauren after being friends on Facebook for years. She gave us a complete tour of the land, and the structures built to accommodate over two hundred volunteers who would arrive later that summer. She showed us around the facilities they would use in August for the Indigenous Wisdom and Permaculture Skills Convergence event.

Christinia founded *Tiyospaye Winyan Maka*, a non-profit organization empowering women to provide sustenance, healing, and opportunity for their children and grandchildren. Partnered with the Oglala Lakota Cultural & Economic Revitalization Initiative, Colorado State University, and Engineers Without Borders, they work to promote sustainable housing, renewable energy, and nutritional and educational sovereignty for indigenous families. Just before our arrival they started construction of the Indigenous Wisdom Center, designed the previous year. This multipurpose community center will include a classroom, bedrooms, a greenhouse, and a laundry. It will be built with local and recycled materials, and use sun and wind power. We walked through the ground floor excavation and saw how used tires gained new life as the building blocks for the foundation. Christiana's project aims to use the same methods to build smaller buildings such as a walipini (which serves as a green house to extend the growing season), or a root cellar for food storage, in a self-help program to improve the lives of people all over the reservation. For every bit of work done there were five challenges to overcome.

What impressed her most, Lauren said, "At that moment it was that the difficulties involved, which seem insurmountable, were being taken on. Change is palpable. Most amazingly it is the grandmothers who are organizing and motivating."

That evening we cooked pasta and sauce with sausages and broccoli and shared it with our hosts. We sat talking for hours after eating, sitting outside under starlight and cooled by a slight breeze. When our hosts left for the evening, Lauren and I slept in the camper, not wanting to impose on them. Because of the mechanical problems with the camper, we reluctantly cut our visit short to try and reach home before anything else failed. After she wanted to travel to Pine Ridge for years, Lauren was downcast to leave so soon.

The next morning our hosts invited us to share fresh eggs for breakfast from their flock of chickens. Christinia planned to take her car for repairs at her nephew's house on the Rosebud Indian reservation that adjoins Pine Ridge. We offered to drive with her to see that she arrived safely, in case she had any problem with the car. We made one stop along the way in the town of Pine Ridge, where Christinia met a friend and activist at the town's only gas station and convenience store, to discuss his campaign to reform tribal politics. I mentioned that alcoholism and drug abuse are common problems on the reservation, and we witnessed that firsthand. After the meeting, we stopped briefly in town to meet a friend of Christinia's, a descendant of Black Elk. Then we departed for a hundred mile drive to the Rosebud reservation, where we arrived in late afternoon. We met Christinia's nephew and his wife. Despite their warm hospitality I felt somewhat ill-at-ease. That's my normal reaction to strangers. I sat on an overstuffed sofa draped with an afghan and his wife served us tea. He entertained us singing country western songs, accompanying himself on the guitar. The afternoon slipped away. Lauren and I excused ourselves, saying we needed to get on the road. I did not want to stay until they felt compelled to offer us dinner, end up staying the night, and get off to a late start in the morning. As the sun descended over the green prairie grass, we drove north to Interstate 90. After dark we stopped at a rest area for the night.

We spent most of the next four days impassively driving the interstate highways. Our journey was wrapped up. We focused on returning home, except for two side trips: a stop in Mitchell, South Dakota to get some cash at a credit union and to tour the Corn Palace—only because Jennifer and Mike stopped there on their trip west in 2008. In Ohio we turned off the Interstate and drove two-lane roads to the farm where my great-great grandfather was born, grew up, and left to fight in the Civil War for the 80th Ohio Infantry. The farm has been under cultivation continuously since my third great-grandfather homesteaded it. In 1837 President Martin Van Buren signed the deed granting 100 acres to Peter Infield, and the land belonged to the family only until 1860, when he and his wife and three other family members died within a few years, probably in one of the epidemics common to the time. Now it belongs to an Amish family who live in the farmhouse Peter Infield built before 1860. From the farm we continued to the cemetery in New Bedford where he and his wife Christina are buried. Then we continued southeast across Ohio to Interstate 70, and east toward home.

A Memorial

The reality is that you will grieve forever. You will not 'get over' the loss of a loved one; you will learn to live with it. You will heal and you will rebuild yourself around the loss you have suffered. You will be whole again but you will never be the same. Nor should you be the same nor would you want to.
— Elizabeth Kubler-Ross and David Kessler

In March 2018, we held a memorial service for Diane following her death, attended by her friends and relatives from all over the country. It was an impressive turnout for a nonconformist who once thought no one but her daughters would be there. We mourned the passing of a striking, beautiful woman, wife, mother, and friend, and we celebrated what her life meant to each one of us. Lauren and I, and some of Diane's longtime friends gave the eulogies that follow.

Ron

At an elevation of ten thousand feet on the Mount Whitney Trail in the High Sierras, I met a blonde with sky-blue eyes who looked straight at me with disarming innocence.

She hiked up the trail on a wild idea that she needed to do something different with her life, because it was not going well. Her companion for the trip wanted to go further up toward the summit, but she was wet and cold, and so she turned back to the shelter of the Mirror Lake campground. Alone, with a damp sleeping bag and a stove she couldn't use, she saw my fire and walked a few steps to approach me, unhesitating and guileless.

"Do you mind if I heat my cocoa on your fire?" she asked.

I was hooked instantly. We spent that night together in the shelter of my tent, and for the next fifty years we were never apart for more than a few days.

Years later, her daring spirit had largely departed, leaving her diminished soul in my care, and I cared for her to the very end. Every day I would resolve to treat her with compassion, tenderness, and love, and tried my best to live up to that. But she would often find a way to push my patience past the limit; sometimes I would shout at her; sometimes I would storm out of the room, or retreat into silence. And once in awhile, she would talk with me as if nothing had changed since we met, and for some moments we would feel normal.

At night, when I lifted her gently into bed, I would remember how I felt toward her, and she toward me, before dementia stole her mind. I would try to communicate my feelings to her as I laid her down to sleep. Then I would have some time to myself, to reflect and think about the future.

The future finally came.

Again and again, I am pulled back into memories of the past. When I met Diane, she was afraid to tell me that she had a three-year-old daughter, that she was still married to her husband who suffered from schizophrenia, and that she was a high school dropout. I was young, a recent college graduate working in my first real job, and I was six years younger than Diane. Prudence would have guided me quickly away from a single mother with no prospects, still attached to an estranged, deranged husband. But I wasn't prudent then.

The attraction between us, two singularly unorthodox people, meeting in a most unlikely place, overrode any caution a prudent person might have felt. I cashed in a life insurance policy and gave her the money she needed to hire a lawyer and annul her marriage. She was afraid to do that, afraid that he might kill himself as a result, and that held her back before.

Her little girl Jennifer Jay Palmer, bright and outgoing at that age, strawberry blonde hair in a Dutch boy haircut, won me over quickly. It was never just Diane, but always both of them, that I fell in love with. Jennifer's astrological sign was Cancer and her grandmother, who believed in astrology, warned Diane to beware of cancer because Jennifer's astrological sign made her vulnerable. I thought that was nonsense.

At seventeen, Jennifer did get cancer, with lifelong consequences. But after a few very difficult years she found her dream and went on to become a successful and acclaimed director. Just before we held this memorial, Philadelphia Women in Film and Television, the group Jennifer helped to found and grow, honored her when they dedicated a grant in her name for young women directors.

In the last two weeks of June, 1968, Diane graduated from high school, her marriage was annulled due to her husband's mental illness, and we were married. We moved to Colorado, to put some distance between us and Diane's former husband. During our first ten years we moved around a few more times, trying to find the right place to settle: Minnesota, Washington, California, and finally New Jersey, where we stayed until now.

Diane made friends wherever she lived, people who responded to her direct way of talking about everything. She made a few enemies, too, for the same reason. But I don't think anyone was ever indifferent. She gave birth to two beautiful daughters, who grew up believing her when she told them that they could follow their dreams and do whatever they dreamed of doing.

Our years in New Jersey were full of highlights and beautiful memories: trips to Aruba, Greece, Mexico, Alaska, Maine, Canada, and the Caribbean; Diane's graduation from Burlington County College; Jennifer's graduation from Goucher College; Lauren's winning the Miss Burlington County pageant; Jennifer's phenomenal 48-hour Film Project videos; Lauren's brief modeling career...

Diane was devastated when her parents fell ill; first her father died in 1992, then her mother exactly one year later in 1993. Diane had a serious flare-up of autoimmune disease that remained a problem for the rest of her life, but it never kept her from living full tilt.

Lauren, our younger daughter, struggled through the years after Jennifer's first cancer, but she eventually grew to become her sister's staunchest supporter during the worst years of Jennifer's life, and organized Jennifer's memorial service when the aftereffects of her cancer finally overtook her in 2015.

Diane and Jennifer both nearly died from internal bleeding in 2013. After weeks in the hospital, both survived, but it was a turning point in Diane's dementia. Despite her declining health, during the next two years we made several long road trips across the country: to Springfield, Illinois, where we found the house she lived in at the age of ten with her aunt Charlotte and uncle Gus; to Minnesota, where we saw her childhood friend Dale, and visited Diane's 94-year-old aunt Bernice; to Florida and Georgia, where we visited Renee and her family, our friends from Medford Lakes;

and Tennessee, where we visited Erik, an old family friend who lived off the grid in the hills beyond Oak Ridge. Diane didn't remember any of those trips for long, but she enjoyed traveling and seeing people, even when she couldn't remember who they were.

As her dementia progressed, our life together grew smaller and smaller. Long trips across country became short trips to the grocery store, day after day. Daily life followed a repetitive pattern with little variation: the same food, the same activities, the same rooms in the house every day. Diane no longer recognized her own house. Sometimes she did not recognize me. She depended on me for every need, but insisted she wanted to go home so she could be on her own, in her own house.

Some days, she could not walk from the bed to her chair in the living room, so I helped her into a wheelchair. Her bodily functions deteriorated. Her care became more difficult. Infections occurred with greater frequency. In January 2018, her doctor recommended home hospice care. We contacted the hospice organization on a Tuesday. They evaluated her on a Thursday and accepted her that same afternoon. Lauren and I had prepared the living room so a hospital bed could be placed there. By 5:30 PM, the bed was in place with Diane resting in it. By then, she was drifting in and out of consciousness. Soon she stopped eating. A few days later, she stopped drinking. On the eighth day in hospice care, Diane stopped breathing, and her heart was still. We bathed her body for the last time, and gave her over to the funeral home for cremation.

Diane's life has ended. A simple truth. But Diane's story is not over. Her story continues in the memories and the love of those who knew her. It goes on in those whom she nurtured and mentored, and friends who learned from Diane's example. Her story lives, even in people who never met her, but who received gifts of love, compassion, and knowledge from her daughters, as they tried to live their lives the way she taught them. Diane's story lives in everyone who was touched by the love and attention she gave throughout her life to everyone around her.

Kathryn

Today a most powerful force has left this planet. Diane Enfield died. Diane was one of my chosen mothers. She was the mother of my BFF/soul sister, Palmer Enfield and her little sister Lauren Boyce, and wife of Ron Enfield.

Diane was brash, beautiful, confident, courageous, wicked smart, strong, resilient, and exuberant. Diane knew how to live! She was an amazing role model, inspiring me in my twenties to step more fully into myself. I met her just after I had broken a wedding engagement at the age of 21 and was feeling lost and uncertain. She got me right on track. Diane had no tolerance for meek or unassuming. Be big and bold or go home!

My best memories with Diane:

– Intellectual, political, philosophical conversations as we sipped Kona coffee (or wine after 5:00) and chain-smoked cigarettes

–Playing Canasta by the pool sipping margaritas

–Skinny dipping! When Diane learned that I'd never skinny dipped, well, that was it. We all were commanded to strip and dive into the pool. And, of course, we did – she was the queen –we all obeyed.

–Driving to the beach (Long Beach Island) in the winter, listening to Joni Mitchell on the way, and just letting the wind whip our hair ... then eating White Castle burgers on the drive home – because when Diane learned that I'd never had them she was ardent about making sure I had that experience.

–My first March on Washington – We drove down from NJ to the New Carollton Metro and participated in a pro-choice march. She was full of stories about Vietnam protests and women's lib – this woman knew how to speak out and certainly found her voice.

–This one *particularly* amazing dinner after the family came back from a trip to Santa Fe – that chocolate mole! OMG!!! – and great discussions about travel and other cultures as we sat next to the world map in the dining room.

I love you Diane. I'm so grateful you were in my life. Your beautiful spirit will always be with me. You are one of a kind.

Renee

I am a stay at home mom of three girls. Most of what I do as my job I learned from Diane.

Diane was my mom's best friend, and seeing my deep need not to be alone after school when my mom had to work, she took me under her wing.

I would go to her house after school every day. I would get help with my homework, and interesting conversation, and we did chores around the house.

Diane and I grew very close as a result. She taught me everything about running a home and never made me feel stupid or like I was in the way. She never acted like my being there was any kind of burden. It was the kind of woman she was. She saw my need and stepped up to fill it.

I have many fond memories with her and her family, but giving me the idea that being a stay at home mom was important, and a valid thing to want, is probably my best memory of Diane.

Rich

I met Diane one day late in the year 1990, along with I and Lauren. I still remember that day- it was sunny and comfortable, August in Medford, New Jersey, at the Good residence. I would meet Jen shortly thereafter.

I remember the fragrance that Diane wore... (it was Fendi, as I recall, and she would wear that for years after.) I loved that scent, and in the next two years I would grow to love her and her family, whose way of life was so new to my understanding.

I like to think that we realized our differences and similarities simultaneously—we shared respect, mutual love of art and music and books and learning, curiosity of life, celebration of the moment.

Through 1991 and most of 1992, we burned the candle low several days each week with visits and meals and talks, "coffee hours" in the mid-afternoon, discussion, dialogue, arguments—about who we were, what we were doing, why we were doing it, what we felt about it, what it meant to us.

I will always remember the sound of her voice and her laugh, and the little moments of learning and discovery. These memories are an undying flame. Thinking of her always makes me smile.

Kevin

As some of you may know, I met Diane on my very first date with Lauren in 2010. When I picked Lauren up here at this very house, her mother greeted me warmly at the door and remarked that I was handsome. Immediately, I thought, I could really like this woman!

During our date, Lauren threw me a curve ball. She suggested—well, just told me, really—that we were stopping by Jennifer and Mike's house since we were conveniently just a mile or two away. Her mother and father would be there too.

What was I going to say on this first date? No?

It was a trial by fire, and I was anxious, to say the least. But they put me at ease quickly. They were so educated and worldly, sophisticated and eloquent in conversation. They were well-traveled and clearly did not have the mundane conversations that most would have. They—and particularly Diane—asked me so much about myself: Where was I from? Had I been out of the country? What was my heritage? What did my parents do? When they found out I was married before, Diane asked why I got divorced. When I told Diane I worked in marketing, she asked if I made good money. When I said, "Yes, I do OK," she then asked, " Well, how much?" These were not your normal "meet the mother for the first time" questions. You see, I'm a writer first and foremost, and I would find out that Diane was too. She wasn't interrogating me; rather, calling on my background in journalism, I caught on quickly that she really wanted to understand her subject. And on that day, it was me.

We volleyed back and forth, like Woodward and Bernstein sitting around trying to get to know each other. I used to think that I was pretty slick with my interviewing skills. I liked to drive the conversation where I wanted it to go for the sake of a good article. It seems I had suddenly been out matched. Diane was writing her own version of me, and I was drawn to her frankness. And she was fearless when it came to what she would ask you. And she'd demand an answer. If you tried to volley back and creatively skirt her question, she would call you out. She knew the game and, when she finally gave me a knowing smile, I knew that she loved it all as much as I did. Ultimately, she really enjoyed talking to and finding out about people.

At some point, Diane insisted that I light her cigarette. I did and she smiled. It was a beautiful early spring day—Easter Sunday, in fact. I always felt it was ironic to meet the Enfields on one of the holiest days of the year, as I was surrounded by atheists. I mentioned to Diane that the weather was really nice. She replied, "Do you know why people talk about the weather?" And when I inquisitively took the bait and said no, she replied, "Because they don't have anything better to talk about." With her abrupt candor, which came without a hint of irony, I knew right then that it was true: l really was going to like this woman. I never mentioned the weather to Diane again.

As I got to know her more and more, we formed a bond that I struggle to explain. Maybe I don't have to. It wasn't forced or manufactured. We had a natural connection to one another that I will cherish forever. There was no one like Diane, except for maybe Lauren. As time went by, I was no longer fazed by her directness. I came to love it as much as I loved her. If you're lucky in life you might cross paths with a person or two that you're seemingly tethered to with no explanation. No words need to be spoken. No acknowledgment needs to be made that it exists. It just is. Diane and I shared that connection. We shared a link of emotional and intellectual strength that came from common life experiences. The world had thrown a lot at us, and every now and again we'd share a nod of mutual understanding during open, honest and direct conversations. There was no small talk. We were survivors. Before her health took the turn that it did, almost every conversation we had was bottomless and meaningful—and completely unpredictable. Maybe that's what J loved best about her: Total unbridled honesty and unpredictability.

I suppose, for me that sums up Diane best: Unrestrained honesty, strength and unpredictability. She was so much more than that, for sure, but the inspiration I have drawn from knowing Diane Enfield is to strive to be authentic, no matter whom you might offend. Be unique, inquisitive and never stop trying to learn from the people around you, even if they are strangers. Never be so hardened by the world that you wouldn't invite those same strangers into your home to have something to eat or take a shower if they were in need. Let your strength through adversity define your character. Share what you have learned with those also willing to share. Never stop learning. You can always be better. Be honest to a fault if you are speaking perfect truths. And, every once in a while, break out into a spontaneous whipped cream fight in your house. Because you can.

If she were here today and heard me say all of this, she'd ask, " Well, what do you mean by all of that?" And Lauren would try to throw me a bone and begin to say, "He's just trying to tell you he loves you, Mommy." And Diane would tell her, "Shut up. He can answer for himself." Today, more than ever, I would be so happy to do so. I was very fortunate to have her in my life, and I will love her and miss her to the end of mine.

Lauren

When I read my sister's eulogy, no one understood a fucking word l said. So, to not appear to be entirely insane, I am going to make this eulogy for my mother a bit more brief, and hopefully wax a bit less poetic and philosophical.

Yeah, so I am going to start this by adorning what my father apparently thinks was my crowning achievement:

(Puts on the crown she won as Miss Burlington County long ago)

Thanks to my very brief modeling career, I can stand here having fulfilled my parents' goals for me. (laugh) But really, my mother wanted the world for us, she absolutely believed that one day I could be President.

I think everyone here would agree even that would be a better solution to where we are now. But, my sister always knew what she wanted to be and became all she and my mother wanted.

Me?

If you listen to my father, I got to be pretty. I do have my teeth fixed now, thanks to my father, which would have been a really big deal to my mom because her own teeth were a perpetual crease in her self-esteem. I understand her now in ways I simply couldn't bear to hear when I was younger, less aware. He is correct in saying that my sister and I grew up to believe that we should walk in her footsteps.

Until her dementia set in, appearances were critical to my mother. The deficits in her own upbringing made her hypervigilant. She cared very deeply about what other people thought of her, and by extension, of our little family of four, now reduced to two.

I've often said that one could eat off the floor of the home I was raised in.

The way she said it, during the 50 year arrangement between my father and her, he would make the living, and she would make the life worth living. She did that until she no longer could.

So about appearances...

Dad and I have a closet full of navy blue because my mother felt that indicated class. At one point, she insisted on holding a "manners dinner" for my friends. She taught them how to set and use proper utensils, and how to behave at a formal dinner. I own three copies of Miss Manners, by two different authors, all Christmas gifts, because every kid loves books and underwear for

Christmas. Perhaps she was trying to tell me something I could still benefit from today.

My father said that in her dementia their life gradually grew smaller and smaller. But for me, in many ways my life with my mother grew larger during this time. She forgot all the reasons she was angry with me. She forgave me my failures. While I too struggle with memory issues, I have not forgotten these things.

My relationship with my mother was not an easy one. We were tense with each other for most of my life. I am so very much like her, and that terrified her. Because she knew what that meant. She tried to warn me, but rebellious as I am, I would not listen. However,

Like my mother I am mercurial, I am empathetic. I am creative, judgmental, and outspoken.

Also Like my mother, I have created from these truths many deep friends and many enemies.

Most of my time with my mother was lived as a warning.

But in her dementia, I was able to apologize, and she had nothing but forgiveness, grace and adoration for me. Probably more true than the early days of angst. In so doing, I became a better person. I learned how to live with some integrity.

Many days she forgot who we were in relationship to each other, but always I was Jenny, her mother, her sister, or sometimes even me. The point is that she knew who she loved.

She knew me by my eyes.

She would sometimes wake from a nap and say "Hey there, blue eyes!" It was a way I was able to connect with her, I would tell her that I got these eyes from her. She would then proceed to expound on why blue eyes made us special, and more intelligent than the rest of humanity.

Not at all racist.

And then there were days when she demanded the deed for the house, or wanted to go home, and told me I was not her daughter, she had no children. Or we would land on an endless loop where she requested to see the new president on the face of Mount Rushmore. Not Trump, though—she was convinced he had slapped her ass while she introduced him to the crowds on TV. Sometimes we were all fat, red-faced and ugly.

But I do recall a time before that fear which permeated her later years.

Before Jenny got sick.

Before she lost her own parents.

Before she lost herself, and eventually us.

I remember water fights she started with my cousins, and even carried through the house, I remember she and her friend Julie digging up the trees in the backyard so that we could have a pool. I remember us catching butterflies, and closely examining the calls of various birds.

Loons. My mother loved loons because of their call, because of her early years growing up in Minnesota, because they mated for life.

She taught me to sew, and to smoke. I remember her teaching me all about puddle stomping, and dancing in the rain. Insisting that everyone we knew went skinny dipping at night in some dark lake. I remember her inviting all the neighborhood kids over to have farting contests. Or the day some boy called me a slut, and she literally took him out behind a shed and made it clear that would never happen again, or else.

I remember an easy smile. A calm and happy Diane. There were days when we would clean the house listening to Simon and Garfunkel, with incense burning and everyone would break out in dance.

My mother liked to dance. and she was good at it.

She loved autumn. She loved light in a way that taught me to see.

She loved good coffee. She loved enlightening young minds,— My mother ALWAYS took a very keen interest in my friends and Jenny's friends. The details of their lives really mattered to her, and she would continue to discuss them and how to help solve any problem they had, long after they left. Quite a few of you are here now for that very reason.

My friends were my mother's friends, and may they always be so.

My sweet friend Kyle still speaks to me of her memories where my mother held dinners with the world map behind us, where we would pick a spot—say, Ouagadougou in Burkina Faso, Africa— and discuss the food, the culture, the topography and geology of the country.

While she lacked a normal sense of humor, she invited the hoodlums we lived near for dinner and would tell them Jalapenos were Mexican pickles.

She taught young women to be feminists, to speak their minds, to know their worth, to be brave.

I recall a day when she got multiple speeding tickets for driving the bright red MGB my father gifted her, back and forth on

Lenape Trail, blaring the song "I will survive." Three tickets in one day, I recall.

But survive she did.

She was a survivor in the truest sense.

Neglected by her own dysfunctional parents, my mother resolved she would do better. And while she may have over-steered at times, she did much better in parenting. My sister and I are HER crowing achievements.

Some of you may not know my mother spent time in a home for neglected and wayward girls in the northern portion of Minnesota. During that time, she was put in solitary confinement because she tried to escape with some other residents. She never recovered from that, not really.

She was placed there, because she stole a pair of shoes for a Native American friend whose shoes had holes in the bottoms. She was always doing things like that—saving the less fortunate, inviting the homeless to come eat and bathe in our house, caring for our housekeeper until her last days dying of breast cancer with no insurance and no family of her own. She was adamant about teaching others how to survive.

We always had a cache of water and survival supplies stored in the basement for whatever disaster she feared.

She read very book about serial killers she could find—so that we were all prepared for THAT eventuality.

My friend Kellie recalls my mother instructing our group of young female friends on how to avoid "coat hanger abortions" at the particularly traumatizing age of 13.

She really never held back.

And now that I am older and wiser, I am glad.

I recall her teaching me how to stop boys from unwanted advances. She did this by literally demonstrating to me what would happen while dancing, and making me say "STOP!"

I wish I had listened closer.

When I was in the girl scouts, most mothers would teach us to knit, or bake. My mother took us hiking through the pine barrens and taught us how to track animals and create castings of their footprints.

From her I have inherited my looks, my passion for gourmet food, my cultural awareness, my resistance, my determination, my love for painting, my capacity to write well, my interest in reading (Great Gatsby!) She once owned the entire eleven-volume History of the World by Will and Ariel Durant. She was a voracious reader, with a voracious mind.

She gave me my adoration of opera, my sense of classic style, a vocabulary of colors like raw umber, African violet, burnt sienna, and alizarin crimson. She is in part responsible for my concern for the environment, my ability to learn, my knowledge of how to survive in quicksand, a downed airplane, an avalanche, a nuclear war, a famine, and even a heartbreak.

What no one taught me—what I now must draw upon to learn alone—is how to survive the death of those dearest to me.

This I will endeavor to do because if she can survive, then we all can, and must. Until which time the inevitable occurs.

My father also just said, "The future finally came."

Just as suddenly, the future is now the past.

As pretty as I am, if all I am able to accomplish in this new life is to breathe, then I have done what my mother wanted me to do. What my sister wanted me to do.

In closing, My mother claimed she was an atheist throughout most of her life. When my sister died and my mother's Alzheimer's progressed, I began to speak to her about what she believed, as it had all changed meaning to me. She told me that she believed strongly in God. She didn't think there was a heaven, or an afterlife, but that God was an unmistakable reality. Even in her dementia she was at times well-spoken and clear in her thoughts.

While I have not been able to arrive at that conclusion on my own, I am uplifted by the fact that she was, that she believed there was something larger than this lifetime, limited as it is.

It may surprise you for me to say that I hope the God my mother believed in is one who will return her to her favorite daughter. Perhaps believing in such a god is what makes the difference. My family and the friends I count as family are my amazing grace.

Thank you for being here.

APPENDIX: CAREGIVER RESOURCES

If you are thrust into the position of caregiver for a loved one, as many of us are, you will need information and support to help you in that role. I was fortunate to have computer skills so that I could take advantage of the multitude of online resources that are available. Many older caregivers don't have computers and the skills needed to use them as I did. I don't claim that this is a comprehensive guide. There is too much information to begin listing it all here. If I are just starting out on this journey, you can contact the Alzheimer's Association and they will help you find what you need, both information and support groups of others who share your concerns. You don't have to be alone.

The Alzheimer's Association

225 N. Michigan Ave. Floor 17 Chicago, IL 60601
Worldwide, 50 million people are living with Alzheimer's and other dementias. Alzheimer's disease is a degenerative brain disease and the most common form of dementia.
24/7 Helpline
800.272.3900
(https://www.alz.org/)

Alzheimer's & Dementia Caregiving
Caregivers for Alzheimer's and dementia face special challenges. Caring for a person with Alzheimer's or dementia often involves a team of people. Whether you provide daily caregiving, participate in decision making, or simply care about a person with the disease — they have resources to help.
(https://www.alz.org/help-support/caregiving)

Other Information

The 36-Hour Day

The 36-Hour Day: A Family Guide to Caring for People Who Have Alzheimer Disease, Other Dementias, and Memory Loss

Johns Hopkins University Press, sixth edition
Nancy L. Mace, MA, and Peter V. Rabins, MD, MPH

This book is filled with information and practical advice for caregivers for every stage of dementia. It is organized by stages, so that you can refer to the sections that apply to the person you are caring for, according to their condition.

Slow Dancing With a Stranger

Slow Dancing With a Stranger: Lost and Found in the Age of Alzheimer's

Meryl Comer, 2014, Harper One

I included this reference because it explains what caregivers often face, but have trouble explaining to others who have not experienced it themselves. Meryl Comer wrote an intimate story about caring for her husband with early-onset Alzheimer's disease. It tells of her husband's decline into dementia, the difficulty of getting a diagnosis, and her life as a caregiver. It is heartbreaking and informative. In her difficult struggle to understand and adapt to her husband's dementia, her experiences often paralleled those of other caregivers in my support group.

About the Authors

Ron Enfield grew up in Southern California in the 1950s, earning a scholarship to attend the University of California at Berkeley. As a photographer for *The Daily Californian* he shot photos of the Free Speech Movement during that turbulent time. Disillusioned with the university and looking for a more creative path, he transferred to UCLA to study film making at the School of Theater, Film, and Television, where he graduated with a Bachelor's degree in 1966.

After graduation, Ron veered away from film into computing, starting as a computer programmer at the world's first software house and moving on to related positions in the tech industry. A newly-minted but shy college grad, he quit the dating scene and took up things he loved growing up, hiking and backpacking in the High Sierras. One weekend drive through Yosemite, he decided to climb Mount Whitney. He had been on the same trail years before, but never made it to the top. The idea challenged him. That's how he ended up camping at Mirror Lake, where he met Diane.

Before retiring to care full time for Diane, Ron earned a Master's degree in Computer Science from Fairleigh Dickinson University, and spent more than thirty years writing and editing award-winning technical documents for publication by AT&T Bell Labs, MITRE, Oracle, and others. His articles about software engineering and technical writing have been published in MIT *Technology Review* and *Proceedings of the 13th Annual International Conference on Systems Documentation*. This is his first book for commercial publication.

Diane Christopher spent her childhood years in Minneapolis, Minnesota until her mother contracted tuberculosis and was compelled to spend years in a sanitorium for TB patients. Her family fell apart due to her mother's illness, and Diane drifted into the juvenile justice system, spending two years in the Minnesota Home School for Girls after a finding of parental neglect. Following her release, Diane's chaotic life led her into a series of disastrous choices until, at 24, she realized she had to become responsible for the sake of her new baby daughter. After meeting Ron Enfield, she finished high school and earned a college degree, and in midlife began a years-long project to reflect and write on her life, and understand what had happened to her. Her life story is presented here in her words as she wrote them.

Acknowledgements

Many people contributed their efforts and support to make this work possible. The most important among them was my late wife, Diane, who spent decades digging into her past, reconstructing her history, and writing it all down. Diane wrote journals and stories about her life before and after we met, and they provided the source material for the story of her life.

Beverley Hughes did an amazing job in editing the entries from Diane's journals. As I performed the copy edit for the final draft, I was more and more impressed with the choices she made from the deluge of material I sent her. She brought Diane's character to life by the way she selected Diane's words for inclusion, working tirelessly to adapt Diane's writing into this narrative and provide a window into the inner workings of Diane's mind.

Special thanks go to Kathryn Wilder, Renee Hraga, Rich Schmidt, Kevin Boyce, and Lauren Enfield Boyce for their eulogies at Diane's memorial, which conveyed her spirit so well that I included them here verbatim.

Several members of the South Jersey Writers' Group made thoughtful critiques of drafts of this book, in particular Jack Kasabian, who played a key role in organizing regular critique sessions.

Made in the USA
Middletown, DE
21 May 2021

40156520R00179